Richard Richard

By

Hughes Mearns

Richard Richard
by Hughes Mearns

Copyright © 2023

All Rights reserved.

ISBN: 978-93-59958-87-3
Published by

DOUBLE 9 BOOKS

2/13-B, Ansari Road
Daryaganj, New Delhi – 110002
info@double9books.com
www.double9books.com
Tel. 011-40042856

ABOUT THE AUTHOR

Hughes Mearns, whose real name was William Hughes Mearns and who lived from 1875 to 1965, was an American teacher and author. Mearns taught at the Philadelphia School of Pedagogy from 1905 to 1920. He had degrees from both Harvard and the University of Pennsylvania. People now know Mearns as the author of "Antigonish" (also called "The Little Man Who Wasn't There"). But his ideas about getting kids, especially those ages 3 to 8, to use their natural imagination were new at the time. It has been stated about him that, "He typed notes of their conversations; he learned how to make them forget there was an adult around; never asked them questions and never showed surprise no matter what they did or said." Creative Youth (1925) and Creative Power (1929) were two important books that Mearns wrote. Gabriel Gudding, an essayist, says that those books "lit a fuse" under the teaching of creative writing and had an impact on a whole group of scholars. He was also in charge of the Lincoln School Teachers College at Columbia University for a while, beginning in 1920. He also supported the work of John Dewey in modern education.

CONTENTS

CHAPTER I
STONY BROKE

Ever since the "first breakfast," groups of passengers had been trooping down the gang-plank, hurrying with guide-book and satchel to "do" Naples, Vesuvius, Pompeii, etc., before the steamer should sail again in the evening. An angular chap in proper steamer *négligé* lounged contentedly on the starboard rail and watched them go. By eight o'clock he seemed to have the starboard rail to himself.

At that hour he was leaning heavily forward, presumably watching the ant-like stevedores loading and unloading the steamer, but he was quite aware of another lone passenger, slowly moving towards him. He had seen her come on at Genoa—anyone would have noticed the clean-cut, tailor-made figure—and on the journey from Genoa to Naples he had noted her once or twice striding the deck alone; but he did not know even so much as her name. He did not know her, but, as she came up to him and lingered at the starboard rail, he knew instinctively that he would borrow money from her.

She stopped beside him for a moment and observed the Italian workers. He did not once look up.

"Do you know how long we stay in Naples?" she asked.

‗ Shipboard etiquette ignores introductions.

"We sail at nine to-night, the Captain says." He turned his head slightly and smiled as if he had really known her. She lounged over the rail and helped him watch the workers. From the dock below this pair looked like familiar companions.

"Gracious!" she exclaimed suddenly. "What time is it now?"

"Eight a.m." He seem amused in a superior way.

"All day in this hot dirty place!" she exclaimed again.

"It *is* warm," he admitted, "but not unpleasantly so. Dirty? Ye-es, on the wharf; but look back of you." He hardly moved from his lounging posture. "Behold! The Bay of Naples. 'See Naples and die'; that phrase is sure to be in your guide-book. There's a lot of other poetry about it, too: 'The blue Bay of Naples, cerulean blue——'"

"But it isn't blue," she objected. "It's dirty grey and,"—she looked directly below for an instant—"and it's oily—greasy, too."

"Oh, yes, it is blue," he contradicted firmly; "deep cerulean blue, the blue of sapphire shading off to mother-of-pearl." As he talked he half turned towards her. He was tall—she was not; his face was bronzed, and furrowed with lines—hers was not; so without offence he could assume a schoolmasterly air of genial superiority.

"Quite blue—from the top of that hill."

He pointed above the tiers of grey-tiled roofs to a pleasant prospect of trees. "The blue is there, but you must climb for it. You can't expect the most glorious panorama in the world to present itself to you without some effort on your part."

"What's the name of that hill?" she asked aimlessly.

"I don't know. There's a charming inn there, I suspect."

"You suspect? Don't you know?"

"No."

"Haven't you been there yourself?"

"No."

"Then how do you know about the 'glorious panorama'?"

"You get a similar sensation from the hill over there," he flourished a hand; "a much smaller hill. So I drew the proper inference."

"Have you ever been on *that* hill?" she flourished a hand in imitation of the man.

"No."

"Well!"

"Well," he smiled. "The view is there just the same—and the blue, too. If you don't believe me, go up and see. I'm willing to stake my judgment to the extent of——"

He stopped so abruptly and smiled so mysteriously that she was attracted to say:

"To the extent of how much? You wouldn't risk a dollar on your 'glorious view'! Now, would you?"

He speculated for a moment. "No," he admitted finally. "I wouldn't risk a dollar on any of my views."

"Ah!" she triumphed.

"A fog might come up," he explained lamely.

"There!" said she. "Naples is over-advertised by sick poets. Look about you. It's incredibly ugly—and smelly."

"What's wrong about the smells?" he inquired mildly.

She laughed. "Garlic, mostly," she took a delicate sniff, "and paint."

"Garlic, I admit," he sniffed in turn, "and paint, and even tar; but they are merely the dominant notes. The overtones give this spot distinction. I'm a connoisseur on smells. It's a lost art."

"Thank goodness!"

"Not at all. We have lost the knowledge of odours; therefore a great part of life is lost. Do you notice now the smell of resin?"

"No."

"They're unloading resin in sacks from that schooner with the black sails. Think hard for a moment and you'll get it. It is a delicious scent quite unlike anything else."

"No," she tried, "I don't get it. But I smell oil, horribly."

"That's from the tanker," he pointed. "It should strike your national pride. It's U.S.A.—Standard Oil."

"Standard Oil?" she inquired eagerly and shaded her eyes to spell out the name on the side. "So it is! U-m-m!" she sniffed, "that smells good. I own Standard Oil Stock. U-m! Not much, of course—but—u-m!—enough."

Yes, he would borrow; but now he knew he would not pay back; perhaps not. He let her chatter on while he listened gravely or added a word or question to set her going again. In a short while he knew the main points of her life and some of the details; and she believed—so perfect is the illusion of a one-sided conversation—that he had given as much in exchange. To the woman they seemed infinitely acquainted after the first half-hour. She was very young, one could be sure; she had the frankness, the unsuspicious frankness of twenty-five; which, nevertheless, is very artful and quite conscious of itself. The man did not misjudge her; he knew he was not dealing with a child, but with a thoroughly independent and responsible young person.

And he knew also that he was stony broke.

The half-hours sped as they talked. Two bells followed closely by a single stroke clanged suddenly from the fore part of the ship.

She made a brisk attempt to look at a watch.

"No use," she put the watch back. "I have Paris time. Three bells is, let me see—'eight' is eight and 'one' is half-past eight——"

"It is half-past nine," he helped, as if it did not matter how the day sped.

"Gracious!" she exclaimed. "Have we wasted an hour and a half just talking?"

"So it seems."

"I won't stay here all day. I've just got to get on land. Why, man, I've never seen Naples or Pompeii or—any of those places," waving a hand about. "If I had my dog here I'd go it alone. I've been in worse places. Why, I believe there's nobody on the ship but us!"

She looked around. It seemed so.

Smudgy-faced members of the crew appeared here and there, the sort that the passengers ordinarily never see on voyage; cooks, vegetable carriers and knife boys called across barriers to one another; and off in the distance an officer could be observed coatless and heavily suspendered.

"Why aren't you going on shore?" she asked suddenly.

"I?" he parried. "Not interested."

"Not interested in Naples and Pompeii?" she inquired incredulously. "Oh, you've been there before, I see."

"No; I've never been there. I—uh—just prefer to—uh—stay here.... I like to be alone."

"Thank you!" cheerily.

She looked at him expectantly.

He took some time before he said serenely, "I can't say it."

"What?" But she knew what.

"The obvious complimentary thing. A woman does that with amazing skill," he mused. "She directs a conversation into a position where the man must make her a pretty speech. Oh, it's all right; but it interferes shockingly."

"Interferes with what?" This time she did not know what.

"With any rational conversation," he explained calmly. "I don't mind your company. In fact, I have enjoyed it. But I do like to be alone. I've spent most of my life alone. On this trip abroad I've fought my right to be my own travelling-companion. These are just facts, like the boat's sailing to-night at nine; but a man can't tell them to a pretty woman ("Thank you," she slipped in) without her pretending to take them personally. So she says 'thank you!'—only in jest, I know—and then I must say some foolish flattery, but the conversation is—well, it cannot go on with the same directness with which a man talks to a man.... You see I'm not complaining. This is just another fact. I'm really interested in it.... Men are forced to treat women like pretty children. Why do women stand it?"

"They don't always like it," she wrinkled her forehead and puzzled over the matter, "but men are such 'jolliers,' you know."

"Fancy a man flattering another man!" he went on. The idea interested him. He seemed to be forgetting the woman beside him; certainly he had completely forgotten the thought born of her first approach, that she was just the sort of person to have plenty of money—somebody else's, a father's or a husband's—and to offer it, too. Of course he had not intended to ask for anything. He knew enough to know that she would lend. He had been in that precise predicament before. Money had always come to him. You see, if he had looked the part of poor-man, beggar-man, thief, the world would have turned coldly away; but he was built on mighty prosperous lines. One felt, at the first glance, that here was an athletic aristocrat. He was just that in reality; but he was mortgaged to the last hedge-row.

So the thought of taking her predestined offer of money slipped from him. He was not a scheming mind. The gods took care of such things. Let them! The important matter just now was the consideration of the droll picture of two males saying sweet things apropos of each other's eyes and noses.

He chuckled. "Fancy trying to have a discussion with a man on the subject, say, of a possible life after death, and have him lean over, stare at the top of your head, and with a tremendous assumption of interest exclaim, 'Jove, man, I do like the way you brushed your hair this morning! With the sun striking the brown edges it is absolutely stunning!'"

They discussed flattery and women. The man slowly forgot his reserve, while the woman, with subtle native flattery, listened. Four bells rang out sharply from forward, repeated far off in the engine-room below. Ten o'clock.

"Well!" the lady exclaimed. "Perhaps I should prefer to see Naples and Pompeii alone, but I haven't the nerve. I'm willing to knock around in Paris or London, but when it comes to Italy I'm scared. The men look at me, especially the toughs, in a way that makes my flesh creep. Goodness knows *I* wish men would forget I'm a woman, but they don't seem to want to.... See here ... why can't we take the trip together? Oh, I'd let you be practically alone," she answered his quick uplook. "You'd just be there as a protection.... Will you?"

He turned his head and regarded her quizzically, like an amused elder brother. He was older. His clean-shaven face had a medley of lines in it which showed superior years.

"I should be delighted," he remarked. His intonation carried precisely the information that his phrase was absolutely polite and absolutely non-committal.

"Oh, rot!" she laughed, but she showed impatience. "Don't be so foolish and conventional. You do want to see the place. You said you did. And I want to go, too. It's nothing extraordinary. It's just the same as if I asked you to play shuffle-board. Honest, you do want to go; don't you?"

"Yes," he half-drawled, but made no effort to move from a convenient sprawl over the rail.

"Then let's," she begged. "This place is making me ill.... Oh, very well," she took his silence for obstinacy. "I'll stay.... No, I won't. I'll be hanged if I do. The heat is too much and the smells are worse. I'll risk it. I'll go it alone.... *Why* won't you go with me?"

He searched in his pockets carefully and finally presented a flat leather wallet.

"You force me to admit my very embarrassing position." As he fumbled with the strap on the wallet she understood. The word "embarrassing" was in itself illuminating.

"Oh!" she gasped, shocked at her own stupidity. What an idiot! She had been gabbling to this man when all the while he had been warning her to keep off!

By this time he had opened the wallet and had drawn from its case a single five-dollar bill.

"*That* is why," he remarked. "I am down to five dollars, which I must not touch until I land in New York. That five dollars is my sole anchor to windward. Fortunately meals and sleeping-apartment are paid for on board; but my ticket says nothing about side-trips. Therefore I should not dare step on that gang-plank. I consider myself lucky—mighty lucky—to arrive on board so safe financially as this. Forgive me for the confession; but you must admit that you forced it. Awfully sorry, too; for, now that you understand, I don't mind telling you that this is the hottest, dirtiest, ill-smellingest spot imaginable. Would I like to go to the top of that hill and look my fill and breathe!" He straightened up suddenly. "*Lord!*"

"Then let's go!" she cried. "Let's! I've got money; heaps of it." She dived into a bag she carried with her. "Look here!" she flashed a packet of various coloured bank-notes. In an inner compartment she showed him a mixture of sovereigns and gold louis. "The purser will give me Italian money. He said he would this morning. Wait! I'll get a hat."

She sped across the deck and around the corner before he could protest. To her stateroom she went first and added a veil about her hat, selected a parasol and donned long thin gloves. Then to the purser's.

"What time do we sail to-night?" she asked as the official made the change of money.

"To-night?" he echoed. "We stay here until to-morrow morning. We sail at six to-morrow. There is a notice posted."

"Thank you," she said, and sped to the bulletin-board. In three languages the purser was verified. In a moment more she was back on the promenade-deck.

"Here!" she gave him a small purse. "You'll have to do the spending. Come on! It'll be a great lark. We still have time. There's a *voiture* or whatever they call it. He's looking up. He'll take us somewhere. Come on! Oh, it's all right! It's on me. My treat. Come on! Don't be foolish.... Now, what's the matter?"

He had accepted the purse; but otherwise he had not moved.

"Wait a bit," he spoke with quiet authority. "I can't do this as your treat."

"Let me hire you as a guide, then," she ventured.

"No," he laughed; "I——"

"Well, let's Dutch it, then. We'll divide expenses—you pay me in New York."

"I won't have anything in New York but five dollars."

"Pay it back whenever you get it."

"All right," he agreed quietly. "But— —"

"But what?"

"That may be a long while."

"I don't care. I want to see Naples."

"I'm not over-careful about paying debts. I'm likely to repudiate," he warned. "My memory is almost useless."

"Well, leave it to me in your will and—hurry!"

Five bells tolled off smartly. The lady strode forward and tugged at his arm. He laughed quietly and followed.

"Really," he told her as they slid down the steep plank, "I'm awfully keen for this trip."

"Oh, yes, you are—not," she looked him over with a meaning glance. "But I don't care. I couldn't stay on that boat all day. There's that *cocher*. Quick, get him before he drives away. I love those old dinky carriages, don't you? Hey!" she called and waved a parasol. "*Ici!* Come over here! We want to get in!"

The Italian understood perfectly. And where would madame and m'sieu wish to go? To the Italian all well-dressed foreigners are French.

"To the top of that hill first," the madame commanded. M'sieu remarked, "We must not get too far away. We sail at nine to-night; and clocks are not very dependable in these parts."

"Yes, we must be careful about the time," she agreed, but offered no word of the more recent information she had received from the purser. "We can have one good glorious dinner somewhere and be back easily by half-past eight," she told him.

They had turned a corner of the creaking winding road which gave suddenly a little glimpse of the Bay.

"Look!" she exclaimed. They turned their heads. "It is beginning to be blue already! U-m!" she sniffed. "Did you get that delicious scent? What is it? Lilac?... And look over there! Still bluer."

"Cerulean blue, every yard of it guaranteed," he remarked lazily; but there was no doubt he was taking it in as eagerly as she. To the lady this was one of many possible trips abroad. To the man it was a sight of Italy, almost withheld like the Promised Land from Moses of old, now made a reality; the promise fulfilled of seven years' mean living.

"By Jove!" he exclaimed on one rise of ground; the assumption of indifference was hard to keep up. "By Jove!" he stared and breathed in the perfumed air. "This is paradise! And Italians come to America to clean the streets and sell fruit! How can they leave it? How ever can they leave it?"

The "dinky" carriage plodded slowly up the hill. The grey tile-topped roofs began to huddle together below them. Old Vesuvius grew to look less like a flat ash-heap. Far off in the background ranges of higher hills began to push solemnly skyward. And the Bay of Naples slowly expanded, and softened, and yielded up its velvet blue.

"Isn't it great?" the lady said, gazing afar.

"Great!" the man replied. "Wonderful!"

So absorbed were they in their personal sensations of delight that it was not until they had arrived at the top and were moving on the level towards a "hotel with a view," that the thoughts of luncheon coupled themselves somehow with the thought of names.

From a dangling bag the lady had produced a "steamer-list."

"Don't tell me yet," she warned. "This is tremendously exciting. I am wondering if you could be, let me see—'Abbott'—no," she looked him over carefully—"you never would be an 'Abbott.' 'Bacon,' 'Baker,' 'Boileau,' 'Crespi'—you might be that, especially when you spoke Italian to the driver. 'Dr.'—you're not a doctor, are you?" She showed some dismay.

"Guess on!" he played the game firmly.

"Well, there's one thing you're not," she pointed to the "list."

He leaned forward to read the name. The wagonette was stopping with a lurch at the spacious beflowered front of a hotel.

"'Sir Richard Helvyn,'" she laughed.

"Why not?" he inquired mildly.

"Don't scare me," she laughed inquiringly. "Are you?"

The happy driver was waiting at the open door, whip in hand, smiling knowingly. A bride and groom, perhaps. The tip would betray them. Beside him a flunkey or two were ready to escort the pair into the hotel. A wizened beggar-woman raised silent-speaking eyes and extended a hand. The m'sieu opened a thin deep purse, obviously a lady's—and extracted therefrom a gold coin and a smaller one of silver.

"That will be exactly right," he nodded to the driver, who, after one glance, was now certain—they were veritable bride and groom.

Deftly, almost without looking, he dropped the silver coin into the palm of the beggar. It was done with skill; and it said, "Begone, my good woman; the sight of you arouses my pity, but do not, pray, take it to mean a soft heart; and whatever you do, breathe not my generosity to your pestilential fellows."

The woman understood, smiled gratefully, and slipped away.

The smoothness of the two transactions was not lost on the "bride." There had been no noisy, staccato expostulations from the driver, nor any sickening whines from the beggar; the business was handled with the dispatch of accustomed skill. Could he be Sir What's-his-name, after all? What a lark!

CHAPTER II
EVEN

The antiquated horse had taken all the time until noon to reach the summit, so the inn-keeper had rushed instantly to provide the lady and gentleman with a private dining-room. It had a trellised portico overlooking the Bay. Here they sat and gazed. They forgot, for the moment, the interrupted conversation over "names"; even the broad suggestion of "bride and groom" that beamed from the faces of the driver, the hotel porters, mine host himself in the doorway and, afar off, mine hostess. The panorama of Naples took rank above everything else.

"No wonder the poets tried so hard to tell us about this," she spoke finally.

"But I do wonder," he returned. "How could they be such egotists? No writing can do justice to that," he pointed towards the deeper blue; "one might as well try to score it for kettle-drums. It can't be translated. All landscape poetry is a failure, a failure from the start. It can't be conveyed to others."

"Perhaps," she mused, "the poet was not interested in others. Perhaps he wished merely to celebrate himself."

He turned towards her suddenly.

"You touch me hard there," he said. "Do you know whom you're quoting?"

"Yes. Whitman."

"Do you know Whitman—really know him?"

"How blunt you are," but she showed no resentment. "Yes, I really know Whitman. Also, I hereby give notice that I am much less frivolous than I look."

"I'm a little daft on Whitman," he apologized.

"So am I."

"You don't think he is immoral?" he asked incredulously.

"I think he is super-moral."

"You do know him, then," he admitted, half-aloud.

"Any more cross-examination?"

"How did you come to take to Whitman?" This was the first time he had seemed to suggest any interest in her personally. She noted the change in him, but gave no sign.

"The Woman's Club," she answered.

"Where?"

"Penn Yan."

"*What?*"

"Penn Yan."

"China?"

"No, Penn Yan, a town of 4,000 inhabitants in New York. I live there."

"Ah!" he exclaimed mysteriously.

"Dear me! Haven't you heard of Penn Yan?"

"No."

"Not heard of the Walker Bin Company?"

"No."

"Nor the Birkett Mills?"

"No."

"Nor the 'Benham House'?"

"No."

"Nor Quackenbush's chain of two drug stores?"

"No."

"Oh, dear!" she affected delightful concern.

"Surely you have heard of Lake Keuka, and the Keuka grape vineyards?" She leaned forward with mischief in her eyes.

"No."

"Have you ever eaten a grape, my dear Sir Knight?"

"Possibly."

"A good, great, luscious blue grape?"

"Possibly."

"Only possibly?"

"Well," he hesitated, "y-es. Yes; I am sure to have eaten one. Now that I put my mind to it, I recall that it was especially large and sweet and——"

She leaned back, contented.

"Well, *that* was a Keuka Lake grape."

He was studying her, as one would a specimen of the thing you collect.

"Is Penn—Penn Ying——"

"Penn Yan, please."

"Is Penn Yan your summer home or——"

"It is my all-the-year home. I was born there. This is my first adventure from the family hearth."

Rebecca of Sunnybrook Farm might have made that speech.

"Ah!" he remarked. "Ah! That explains much."

"Go on," she smiled. "Spring it. What's the answer? What is the 'much' my living in Penn Yan explains?"

"You are charmingly of the village; for which I am grateful. Otherwise, we should not have been on this delightfully unconventional trip."

"Oh, you must see Penn Yan," she chirped, "especially on Saturday night. Our Main Street is paved," she added archly, "and we have an electric line and sweetly subdued arc-lights. But of course I don't live in the throbbing town—that would be too exciting. We live far off down the Lake, in Jerusalem township. You see, Sir—Sir——" she hesitated, plucked out her steamer-list and went on, "—Sir Richard, we are really not even villagers; we are, I fear, hopelessly rural."

Her satiric tone was not lost on "Sir Richard." He would have been stupid else.

"Rural? Not a doubt of it!" he admitted. "You lend me money on sight and take me for a title and no questions asked. What makes you think I am Sir Richard?"

"I don't think so now; and I'm awfully sorry. Your enunciation is sort of English—you know—clear, broad vowels, lots of sharp 't's,' no 'r's' to speak of; but you haven't once said, 'Quite so,' or 'Really!' or 'Silly ass!'"

"I am half English. I went to school in England."

"Ah!" she mimicked. "That explains much—ah!—much! And was it a school in the country?"

"Yes!" he explained eagerly. "Quite in the country. It was an omnibus and two trains away from London."

"Ah!" She "ah-ed" very significantly, and added, "Much! Ah, much—much."

"We're even," he owned.

"Only even?" she opened her eyes very wide.

He was about to surrender completely when the host in the doorway announced luncheon.

It was a cosy, intimate dining-room; small table set for two; uniformed butler standing rigid off to the side; maid, also in uniform, moving swiftly in and out a door and serving deftly—exactly the suggestion of a dinner *en famille*.

"That is the head of the table, dear," said the lady.

The man was so startled, especially when he glanced back to the placid, innocent face of the lady, that he neglected to take any place at all.

"Can't you see that this is a domestic scene?" she explained; "regular man-and-wife stage-set. They expect it of us.... Beautiful, expensive scenery," she murmured, "spoiled by a wretched actor."

Then she nodded her head towards the uniformed attendant, and began again.

"That is the head of the table, I think, *dear*."

He grinned and made for the seat.

"That is the head; is it not, *my dear*?" she persisted.

"It is," he agreed.

She declined to sit.

"It is—what, *my dear*?"

"It is the head of the table."

"The head of the table, *my——*"

She cocked her head and waited to catch the completed phrase.

"Dear!" he finished, not without embarrassment.

"You miss your cues dreadfully," she went on briskly. "Tell the gendarme to pass the rolls, Richard dear."

"Madame will have the rolls," "Richard" managed in Italian. "I don't think the gendarme comprehends English, so your little domestic playette is wasted, my—uh—darling."

"Thenk you, m'lud," the gendarme remarked in good cockney as he deftly removed the rolls and started towards madame.

"You're English?" m'lud ejaculated.

"Me, m'lud? Yes, thenk you, m'lud."

"The devil!"

"Yes, thenk you, m'lud. And would m'lady prefer the toasted muffins?"

M'lady preferred nothing so much as the open enjoyment of m'lud's discomfiture. There was a certain boldness and a certain shyness about m'lud, typical of England. At present the awkward self-consciousness was to the fore. It was consuming him, although he was intelligent enough to know exactly his trouble and its remedy. Therefore he laughed, owned up to the embarrassment and summoned his will to fight it down.

"Even Half-English is still very English," she told him, after she had explained carefully that his face had flushed and that the tips of his ears were quite red—all more or less comforting. In the give and take of raillery that followed he almost recovered.

"The worst thing I have to contend with is this engulfing shyness of mine," he explained finally. "And the worst symptom of shyness, perhaps you know, is anger and sullenness. It knocks the speech out of me. That makes me hot and angry. Then I'm apt to insult my neighbour, and then it's all off.... But I'm all right now."

"Yes," she helped herself to a hot muffin; "you've gone through all the phases, except that you *began* by insulting your neighbour."

"How, pray?"

He was quite unconscious of any guilt. She saw that, so she preferred not to give her hand away by explaining; yet, somehow, his half-joking reference to her "charming village qualities" rankled. Her forebears had been York State farmers, then vineyard workers and finally prosperous share-holders in the industry of raising and marketing of grapes and grape products. Although the present generation of children had gone to boarding-school and to college, had travelled and were accustomed to shop in New York city, yet the fine touch of the open country had never left them. That was their abiding charm, if they only knew it; it gave them a heartiness and a frankness and an independence of bearing and speech that marked them with distinction. Occasionally, however, in some social grouping of metropolitan dwellers they had been brought to feel a lack and were on the alert to turn even gentle compliment into ironic criticism. The young man with his patronizing air should be punished.

"Never mind," she turned away his sincere questionings. "If you aren't aware of the insult, we'll forget it and call it bad manners. Bad manners are nobody's fault." The English servant was approaching with the meat course, so she added a gracious and distinct "dearie."

"Ugh!" he grunted. "I detest that word. I'd rather be called 'birdie.'"

The luncheon was a ceremonious affair. "It is part of the scenery," the lady had remarked, "so why hurry it just to gaze on other scenery?" Coffee was served in the tiny balcony, by which time the Bay had put on other and gayer apparel; so the view had to be examined afresh. All of which took time. It was three o'clock before the bills were called for.

Several times during the delicious loafing on the balcony m'lady had examined her steamer-list and had stared at the man as if to find his name written on his forehead. He noted her interest, but claimed none for his own. "Look, my dear," she would say, "at lazy old Vesuvius; isn't he a villainous old giant, dirty, evil and full of cunning. I bet he is planning another blow-off." And he would reply without any "dear" at all, not seeming to need that handle of a name to lift his comments.

"Why do you wish to go to America?" she asked, this being the nearest she ever came to breaking into the mystery of their personal lives.

"It is my home," he answered in some surprise.

"I thought you were English?"

"Oh!" he remembered. "I am an American, even if I am half English. My mother was English, but father was so colossally American that it swamped the English strain."

"That's rather unusual, isn't it?" she inquired. "It is more often that American women marry Englishmen."

"Not at all; they're more heavily advertised, that's all. English women are very often attracted by men of the type of my father. There are many marriages of that sort. And the English father is mighty happy over it, I can tell you, for he gets off without the hint of a dowry. No decent American would listen to the suggestion of a dot, you know."

There the subject dropped, and for a time all subjects. In lazy silence they looked on the view and thought their own thoughts.

Once he remarked, "I'm curious to know what that English butler is doing in an Italian inn. He can't be happy outside of the West End. I wager he is hiding from the police. He looks it."

And she replied, "Have you no curiosity about me?"

"Much," he smiled. The word "much" had come to have local significance.

"You don't ask whether I am a baroness or a saleslady, or Miss or Mrs."

"I don't want to know."

"Growing shy again?"

"Eh?"

"Or is it just urban rudeness?"

"Oh!" he laughed as he comprehended. "No. No. Not at all. I don't want to know until I have to. I prefer the mystery, that is all. If you wish I'll tell you who I am, but I hope you won't wish, at least just at present. We'll be together two weeks on that boat. They say ten days, but I know them. It'll be a fortnight. It'll all come out there. Let's enjoy this thoroughly unusual companionship. It really is ideal— —" he went on enthusiastically.

"Thank you," she interrupted, though he hardly noticed.

"—The sort of thing that ought to happen on this earth every day. Human beings are utter strangers to one another. It takes a shipwreck or a national calamity to force them to acknowledge the existence of the neighbour they prate so much about loving. Let's continue our primitive relationship. Call me Richard if you wish. It's a good name. And I'll call you," he picked up the steamer-list and read a name, as he thought at random, but a light underscoring had unconsciously caught his eye.

The owner of that name had done what everyone naturally does with a steamer-list or a programme or a column of "those present," glanced quickly at her own name to discover if it had been printed correctly. It is most annoying to have a "Mrs." where a "Miss" should be. Then her nervous finger-nail had underscored aimlessly, until the name fairly popped out of the list.

"'Miss Geraldine Wells,'" he read. "There! I'll call you 'Jerry.' Is it a go?"

Miss Geraldine Wells almost leaped in astonishment. But his innocent face assured her. She looked aloft critically, as if to judge if the name were worthy. The butler arrived with a tray of change.

"Is it a go?" he asked again.

"Yes, dear."

"Please! Please!" he shook his head firmly. "Please don't do that."

The butler was handed his tip and was waved away.

"Your ear-tips are beginning again," she told him in the tone she might have used to announce a spoon in his coffee cup.

Meanwhile the butler was bowing and muttering half-coherent "Thenk-you-m'lud's." His eye had taken on a fine frenzy.

"That funny remark has cost you— —" Richard calculated aloud, "twenty lire is $3.86, and your share is $1.93. It cost you just $1.93 in American money. You got my mind so upset that I gave that idiot a 20-lira gold-piece too much. He'll probably murder us now for our money, or what is worse, scream the news to the neighbourhood. We'll have to pay high to get out of this. By rights you ought to take the whole cost."

He rang the bell. The butler appeared.

"I made a mistake just now in giving you that 20-lira coin. Oh, it's all right! I'm not going to take it back. I'll be a good sport and pay for my blunder; but I was careless, that's all. The point is— —"

The English serving man was rigid with fright. Fees of any sort had been rare that season, and his wages were negligible.

"The point is," the half-Englishman spoke confidentially, "I don't want the whole establishment to think I am a millionaire and stand in line to blackmail me when I go out. Do you understand?"

The butler began to show signs of life.

"Puffectly, m'lud. I will take you hout myself, by the rear terraces, m'lud, and nobuddy shall presume, m'lud."

And by the rear terraces they escaped, where the old coachman and the "dinky" carriage were duly waiting. A gold coin had done the work for him, too. He had considered himself hired by the day. Rich brides and grooms rarely came into his power.

"And where will M'sieu and Madame go now? Pompeii, Vesuvius?" He named a list that would have been the death of his cadaverous animal.

"Pompeii, of course," agreed Miss Geraldine Wells.

"Do you think we have time?"

"Plenty." She was stepping into the lurching vehiculum. The driver was rattling forth soothing and enticing Italian, which no one heeded.

"But I don't know anything about trains," he persisted.

"Neither do I."

"We don't want to miss our steamer."

"Don't we?" She was comfortably seated.

"I don't."

"Why not?"

"Great Scott, woman — —"

"Jerry," she corrected.

" —I was lucky to make that boat at Genoa. Had to ride fourth class from Munich. I can't afford to miss it now."

"I can," she tempted. He stared at her.

"Let's," she begged softly.

He appeared to be reflecting. In reality his mind was standing still. The driver was in his box looking at them with an ineffable sentimental smile. The rich honeymooners would decide. He would wait. A month's salary in a bad season was his already.

"Get in, Richard," she moved her skirts to make room on the diminutive seat. "Be a good boy and come along. I have money enough. We'll take the next steamer. They sail every Wednesday, don't they?"

He got in and the equipage swung off. On the way down the hill they debated and forgot the view.

Pompeii was so many miles off there, he made it clear. The present vehicle would get there some time, if the horse and the wagon and the driver held together, but not in time for the sailing of steamers. He would not listen to her suggestion to hang the sailings of steamers and be a good sporting Sir Richard and stay over for the next boat, but drove doggedly on to convince her that in the few hours that were left, their only resource was a drive through the streets of Naples, an hour or two at the Museo Borbonico, and an early dinner at some hotel within hail of the ship.

Upon the subject of the Museo he grew suddenly eloquent. It contained one of the most significant collections of Roman remains in the world. The best of Pompeii and Herculaneum was in reality in Naples in the Museo. He seemed to know all about it, indeed, as if he were himself a collector.

"Help! Help!" she called softly, and held his arm. She had interrupted a list of the things that made the Museo unique as an omnium gatherum of Roman curios. "You talk like a personally conducted tour. We'll go to that Museo right off. Tell the curio up front to drive there when we get to the town. But, really, my dear Richard, your interest in things stirs me. It is the first flash of life you have displayed; and you saved that up for a museum! I'd be afraid to see you get really worked up over an Egyptian mummy or something really dead-for-keeps. We'll just have to stay over and let you loose in that dear old Museo of yours."

He remained silent for a jolting minute or two.

"One of my reasons for coming to Naples," he said quite simply, "was to see the Museo Borbonico."

For a moment she pondered in turn.

"Then why didn't we go there this morning?"

"This is your excursion, not mine."

"But we're going shares on expenses, aren't we?"

"I hope so. I warned you that I don't always pay my debts. You wanted the hill and the view—so did I; so did I, believe me; it was glorious—but I felt under obligations to consider your wishes before my own. And—well, I did not suspect at our first meeting—forgive me!—that you would be— uh—up to doing Pompeiian mosaics and Roman bronzes. You are the sort who keep the best of their mind concealed at first. You——"

He stopped.

"Go on."

"Do you mind if I pick you apart like this? It is an absorbing interest of mine."

"I rather like it. It's like having your fortune told. Go on."

"You chatter at first, rather—well, too fluently, perhaps; and in words and phrases of a language you learned at about sixteen. Now I should say that you were at least ten years older than that——"

"Nine."

"Exactly; nine. Well, the girlish extravagant language comes cropping out first, until you get stimulated into thinking grown-up thoughts. Then your very vocabulary changes. Your remark that Whitman is super-moral, for instance, is a summing-up of the man. No youngster could have gotten that so neatly without——"

"Stuff!" she laughed. "I cribbed that for my Woman's Club essay. How *do* you suppose those club essays are gotten up!"

"Of course you would affect modesty naturally; although it's a mistake. When you've done a good thing you should own up. But all that's neither here nor there. If you hadn't come along I'd made up my mind to slip off the boat after luncheon—I couldn't afford to risk buying a meal; I'm so extravagant—and do the Museo in time for the boat dinner at six. There! I've been very frank. And, really, I don't mind if we cut the Museo out of the programme altogether. I have no very deep desires for anything in this world. I'm a terrific loafer."

"Tell Louis Napoleon up there on the box to drive to that Museo; I'm keen for it," she commanded.

It was half-past four when they drove up to the door of the museum. A clear sign announced that the institution would close at seven o'clock. And at fifteen minutes after seven o'clock, when they were finally driven from the place, they had hardly advanced beyond the first few rooms of that wonderful collection. It was almost eight o'clock before they found a suitable place to dine.

"Isn't it a pity," she said as they waited for the soup, "to leave without seeing those other rooms!"

"Horrible!"

He stared at the full dining-room without seeing anyone. "Horrible," he repeated, but immediately plucked up a cheerful spirit. "It is something saved for next time."

"When will that be?"

"I was seven years saving up for this trip—you see, I can't do a thing like this on a cheap scale—I mean I haven't the ability. Suppose we say 1919—that's a nice-sounding year."

"Really?"

She was very sympathetic.

"Really," he mocked her seriousness.

"And if we stayed over we could take a week to it."

The dinner moved slowly. They were within a five-minutes' drive of the steamer and the faithful Louis Napoleon was outside on guard, but Richard kept his watch before him. Meanwhile the lady aimed to prove how easy it would be to miss the boat, have the ticket-money refunded, and do the proper thing by the Museo.

The idea grew in his own mind as the minutes ticked nearer to the fateful nine o'clock.

"You could stay in one of those Woman's League *pensions*," he mused, "while I lived at a nearby hotel."

She baited him with alluring arguments, exactly in keeping, he might have thought, with those village qualities which, he had observed, were part of her charm. Undoubtedly, he noted her seeming artlessness.

At eight and three-quarters he rose briskly, walked to the curb, and openly paid and dismissed the faithful coachman.

Nine rang from a dock-tower or two as he jubilantly received coffee from the large silver-service at which Miss Geraldine Wells presided.

"Jerry!" he cried joyfully. "It's done. The Rubicon is crossed and the Atlantic is not! We'll hunt up one of those Woman's League places right after dinner."

"No," she corrected; "not immediately. My conscience is York State and peculiar. You'll have to drive me down to the boat-landing, so that I can say truthfully that I went there, but it was too late."

"That *is* rural!" he laughed. "My conscience is strictly urban, like a steel bridge; it's built to stand an awful strain."

Jollity came out upon him. He grew witty, quick of tongue, even appreciative of the woman before him. He called her "Jerry" as if he liked the name; he did not resent her occasional "my dear." His vacation had been suddenly lengthened; he was like a child in his unaffected glee; while the lady grew demurer and demurer, to use the language of "Wonderland."

The rural conscience of Miss Geraldine Wells was insistent. It demanded precedence over hunts for Woman's League *pensions*; and it would not walk, it would go in a cab. What if the distance is short and cabs cost money? Isn't a satisfied conscience above rubies?

Not that Mr. Richard objected to the most freakish demands of Miss Geraldine's York State conscience; on the contrary, he was most interested in it; it was one more curious phenomenon of the most curious of all phenomena, namely Life itself. He dealt with it—on the rumbling ride along the docks—both seriously and humorously. In fact, he was in the midst of a rather good joke on the moral iniquity of consciences in general when the vehicle stopped abruptly near the front end of a familiar black hulk on which a string of striking white letters proclaimed, "S.S. *Victoria*."

"Play's over," a laughing voice whispered in his ear. "Wake up, child, and come on home."

But he did not wake up. He stared stupidly and tried to get his bearings.

"She sails to-morrow at six, Sir Richard," the lady explained, again demurely; "not to-night at nine as you so foolishly believed."

"You knew?" he inquired thoughtfully.

She laughed; a little uncomfortably, for he was trying the operation of looking through her.

"Then you had no intention of staying over?"

He asked the question very mildly. It was quite clear that he felt not a shade of anger at the elaborate jest, but anyone could see that he was mightily disappointed.

"Staying over?" she arched her brows. "Why, Sir Richard! What a question! I am not *altogether* rural!"

Then he woke up, paid the driver, and plodded with her up the steep gang-plank.

Sir Richard was himself again; that is, silent and benumbed. He stood solemnly beside her and stared at the announcement on the bulletin-board that the *Victoria* would sail "to-morrow morning at six." Then after a mere smiling nod for a good-night he wandered down the corridor to his stateroom.

Miss Jerry Wells found a lonely steamer-chair on the upper deck, tucked herself in with the help of a clumsy deck-steward and tried to feel guiltless. The lady from the country had had her revenge, but she did not feel very happy over it.

CHAPTER III
"SAW YUH!"

Miss Wells had other reasons for feeling guilty. Travelling about a foreign city with a man whose name she did not know, suggesting to him the dare-devil possibility of a week's sight-seeing together, decoying him into a genuinely excitable interest in the scheme—he *had* been hard to work up to the due pitch; and she had some pride in her art there—and then snubbing him with the reality, these were not the main causes of her uneasiness as she loafed in the steamer-chair and listened very intently to the sound of the voices as each new group of returning tourists struggled up the gang-plank.

Of course she had never a thought of really slipping off with this mild semi-English "Richard." She would not have dared. It gave her a shiver of joy and a shock of fright to think of the thing: the blessed freedom, the strong sense of being protected and catered to without any sickening atmosphere of male—there is no word for it, but she knew exactly what always disgusted her finally in the best of men companions. A smirk of the eye, a pretence at absorbing interest in the lady's welfare, a terrific deference to her whims and a plashing of small talk aimed exactly to meet the requirements of the small female mind; all that plus a fluttering about which is so significantly—male.

The worst of it was, she thought as she waited, the environment of that sort of thing had had its frightful effect upon her. She had developed a feminine helplessness exactly in proportion as the masculine helpers had pressed about her. To-day she had felt her lack keenly. Her voice was high and over-confident. Her talk flashed. She held to no topic, but darted here and there. All this had been applauded for years. Men had shown frank amusement at her sallies. They had flattered her into a sense of security.... And they felt no such thing. It was the male joke to treat women like children, give in to them at every unimportant point, offer them absolutely no resistance, so thereby they should never grow. Men insult each other, argue, deny, speak the truth, give the lie, and so thrive. What man would give a woman the chance of growth that lies in insult!

This Richard chap had told her quietly and frankly that she had not let her mind develop, although he assured her that it was struggling to express its native maturity.

"Your mind is really grown up," he had remarked, after she had uttered a supposedly stinging bit of cleverness, the sort that made other men laugh and pretend fear. "Why don't you hold your speech back sometimes—that rattling, quick-fire, spoiled child's speech of yours? Alternate days of silence would give your real self a chance; but you shout it down; you talk it into helplessness. One of these days, if you don't look out, it will give up, and then you will be like thousands of other women—horribly like."

In revenge she spoke not a word for a full half-hour as they watched the view from the balcony on the hill. But he—good, unoffending soul!—had matched her with a sample of his own silence. And throughout the interminable half-hour he had seemed to be unaware of aught save the peace and serenity of the moment, while she was torn with violent desire to break forth. Before the time was up, her anger had cooled, she noted; the hot, smart phrases appeared in review and one by one were discarded as cheap; slowly the deep calm of her latest self came near the surface; and when she spoke finally it was not a pent-up burst of words, but a quiet, sensible observation that surprised even herself.

And then he had talked to her, the first time, it seemed, as human adult to human adult. The defences of sex were down and she enjoyed a new sensation. Here was a man who conversed with her mind and not with her eyes and her hair. It is difficult for a girl with extraordinary good looks to get credit for sense. Eyes and hair do intrude. They get on the spectator's mind. He feels that he must pay constant tribute to them. Few suspected that to this striking young woman the daily and hourly reference to her physical charm had grown to be annoying. It was a relief to discover a man who seemed to ignore it all.

The cause of her worry was not due to her pleasant little adventure in Naples. By itself that was a charming experience, but she knew it would not remain long as an isolated fact. If she had been alone on this homeward journey all would have been well, but she was in the charge of a thoroughly efficient mother. At any moment Mrs. Wells and her son, Walter, might arrive with the small party that had banded together to take advantage of the day in Naples.

Geraldine had pleaded fatigue and sea-sickness to get rid of that "party," especially of the university instructor who had been piloting them about Europe on a commission; but she had been frank to her mother. The well-oiled voice of the university instructor, his faithfulness, his carefully-studied facts had done their full evil. The mother liked that sort of thing, or, rather, she could use it and ignore it; but she quite understood her daughter's increasing repugnance to the personally conducted tour and especially to the personal conductor. "Oh, very well, my dear," she had smiled an easy agreement, "stay on board if you can stand it. You have done your duty nobly so far. We'll give you a furlough. But it is likely to be my last trip for many years, and I'm the sort of trotter that must nose into every gallery. Mr. Freneau gets on my nerves, too, sometimes. I quite understand. Do just as you please."

But Geraldine knew her mother well enough to be certain that she would not be at all pleased with the sort of "trotting" her daughter had done. With any other man one could patch up an agreement of what to say and what not to say. Without actually fibbing one can conceal a powerful lot of objectionable truth. "Richard" would not fib. She could fancy his mild, detached stare at the suggestion of an illicit collusion to deceive the mater.

Geraldine had almost dozed off in her chair when she heard Mrs. Wells' strong voice at the top of the gang-plank. The softer tones of Mr. Freneau were not distinguishable.

"Hel-lo!" Geraldine called, or rather sang, a sol-me family signal.

The indefatigable mother—she was a woman of imposing size, but agile—pushed along among the darkened chairs.

"Well, my girl," she greeted cheerily, "how is the head? Better?"

If it had not been so dark the mother's appreciating smile could have been observed.

"Head?" Geraldine was only half out of her nap. It took the sweet smile of university instructor Freneau shining behind a bracket-lamp to recall the voluble excuses given that morning to account for Miss Wells' stay at home.

"Surely," the mother poked her jocosely, "you don't expect us to believe you were shamming just to get rid of us—eh, Mr. Freneau?"

"Oh!" Geraldine remembered. "*Much* better, thank you, mother. Breakfast seemed to fix me up. I've been feeling fine all day."

Mrs. Wells dropped into a chair beside her daughter. Mr. Freneau, hovering near, was dismissed with many expressions of appreciation for his day's work. The son, Walter, an excessively thin, bent-over, boy-man, sprawled in a chair. He seemed to be sleeping. Presently the mother tapped him gently on the knee and suggested that he go below and get some rest.

"All right, mother," the boy spoke up suddenly. In spite of his springy rise to his feet and his attempt at an assured air, one could see at a glance that this son was weak. His deep-set eyes roved restlessly, his body swayed gently or became noticeably rigid, as if a natural balance was an effort.

The mother watched him as he swayed along the deck. He disappeared down a stairway with an extraordinary clatter, as if he had fallen over the first few steps.

"How has Walter been to-day?" Geraldine asked. There was no solicitude in her voice.

"I don't like his looks lately," Mrs. Wells replied thoughtfully. "I think he is summoning up courage to rebel, but I am too strong for him. My will has the upper hand and that must be his will for a long time to come. It was a mistake ever to send him to that 'cure.' Firm kindness and the constant suggestion of a right attitude towards life is what he needs. This trip has proved it. Except for that outbreak in London we have had weeks of peace. He is stronger, he eats better and he is contented."

"He seems to be terribly afraid of you."

"I want him to be. But I don't think it's fear, my dear. My stronger will has got hold of him, that is all. He obeys— —"

"Like a whipped puppy."

"Exactly. That's a good comparison, Geraldine. He needs right habits the same as a good dog. They must fear until the bad habit is driven out and the good habit becomes natural. You don't think I treat him badly, do you?"

"Oh, no. You are wonderful. You get results which those people up at the 'cure' said they got by knocking him down. I am only saying that he looks defeated, beaten. Perhaps it is better that way. I am sure it is more comfortable for us."

"Decidedly!"

The two women thought of the horrible years when this boy was growing from a tippler to a hardened drinker. He had become an incurable alcoholic almost before they realized that something must be done, something besides scoldings and cutting off his spending money and driving him out of the house to sleep at the neighbours' or in the barn or, worse, in the puddle at the end of the front lawn. Some men drink heavily all their lives without reaching the condition of this lad. He was twenty-two years old, but he had the slight build of a sickly young boy.

"Did you find the steamer uncomfortably hot?" the mother asked. The other topic was too distressing.

"No; I—I felt so much better that I took a little stroll into the city."

"Not alone, I hope? I don't mind London, or certain parts of Paris, but you know how I feel about Italy, especially at the docks. You did not go alone?"

"Mother! Of course not!"

"The steamer seemed deserted when we left. Who went with you?"

"A friend of the Captain—he's a very unusual——"

"He?"

"Yes, a friend of the Captain. The Captain told him——"

"I don't like the captain of this boat. I hope his friends are less evil looking. What's the name of this friend of the Captain?"

Why can't we have some sense of the future? All day she had lived in the passing hour, and yet a single thought ahead would have assured her that she would have to meet this subtle, inevitable cross-examination in the evening. Mrs. Wells never meant to be unkind or domineering, but she was everlastingly on guard. She permitted the largest kind of liberty, but she always "wanted to know." Concealment, subterfuge, these were her enemies. It would have been so easy for Geraldine to have discovered the man's name. Of course the mystery was charming; but at the dinner, say, it would have been a simple matter to lean forward and say, "This incognito is delightful, my dear Richard, but I have a most exacting, scrutinizing mother who will demand precisely who you are. Now let's call the game off and tell each other our real names." She remembered now, that part of her own game had been to conceal the existence of mother, to play the part of independent young person. Otherwise how could she have fooled him with that audacious suggestion to stay over until the next steamer? And, by the way, how did she ever get nerve enough to do that! The thing did not seem bold in daylight; but here on this gloomy deck with an alert and expectant mother waiting for particulars it suddenly appeared brazen.

"His name——" Geraldine yawned carefully and at length to gain time. "A peculiar name"—yawn—"If I had my steamer-list here I—ooh! I'm so sleepy. It was"—yawn—"Richard"—yawn.

"Richard?" The mother turned the name over. "That's peculiar, for a surname, at any rate."

"Yes,"—Geraldine recovered. "We know a Mr. Dick and a Mr. Richards, but Mr. Richard is singular."

"Is that a grammatical joke, my dear?" the mother asked.

"I"—yawn—"excuse me!—I don't see any joke, mother. Really, I must toddle off to bed."

"Richards, of course, would be plural," the persistent mother followed. Her mind was never at rest. "Do you mean that this Mr. Richard — without — the — 's' was really singular or just grammatically singular?"

"Uh?" Geraldine turned a marvellous imitation of a sleepy face. "I'm afraid I don't see it, mother. Forgive me for being so" — yawn — "dull. *Good-night!* I'm off to Shut-eye town. Good-night!"

But the mother was not so easily shaken off. Mrs. Wells was never fatigued. She required only five to six hours' sleep. At her home on the hills above Lake Keuka she would play bridge until one o'clock and be up at six to superintend the daily distribution of work in the dairy.

"Mr. Freneau began to get on my nerves too, to-day, Geraldine," she pursued her way into her daughter's stateroom and disregarded yawns and sleepy disrobings. "He is so patient," she laughed, "and knows his lessons so well. Of course he is absolutely indispensable for trains, baggage, bills, 'free days' and so on, and, as a rule, he is absolutely authoritative. He digests all the books so impartially. But to-day I began to feel the way you do always, repellent. I disputed with him horribly. He was always right, but that made no difference. I suppose it's the end of the trip. One does get filled up even with ideas and facts. I couldn't listen to-day. His information flowed over me. He saw it, too. I fear I made him uncomfortable. After all, I suppose he's just as sick of us. Fancy anybody giving up his time so devotedly. Did you get to the National Museum?"

"No." Geraldine was putting herself deliberately to bed. Her mother had a species of clairvoyance that inevitably sifted the thoughts out of one. The topic must be kept off the Captain's friend Mr. Richard until some sort of conspiracy could be arranged. Scruples or no scruples this man would have to do the right thing and stand by a lady.

A list of the other stated attractions of Naples were shot at the reclining figure.

No, these had not been visited.

"Then where on earth did you go?"

"The Museo Borbon — something or other. We — uh — —" A perfect imitation of a young woman falling asleep in the middle of a sentence.

"Museo Borbonico? Why, my child, that's the old name for the National Museum. I *have* remembered some of the things Mr. Freneau tried to put into my head to-day. Did you see the bronzes, and the head of Cicero, made probably from life?"

No answer from the berth.

"Are you asleep, Geraldine?"

"Uh-huh."

"H-m," suspiciously. "Talking in your sleep, eh? Well, I'll not bore you further. That's what's making you fat, so much sleep." She looked about the room. "You must stop eating chocolates, too. I believe they are a sort of narcotic, if the truth were known. I notice that fat, sleepy girls are pigs on chocolates. Well, good-night. You can tell me about your trip to-morrow. I'll take a peep at Walter before I retire to see if the absent treatment is working as usual. I have a feeling that if he had not gone straight to bed I should sense it somehow. Good-night."

There was no response from Geraldine, so Mrs. Wells put out the light, fixed the catch on the lock and slipped quietly into the corridor.

Walter's room was on the other side of the boat. Geraldine gave her mother time to get to the end of the corridor before she arose, snapped on the light and donned shoes and a kimono and twisted her plaited hair into a shape fit for public view. Then she sat on the edge of the berth and pondered. To-morrow early she would — —

What was that? A fumbling of the catch of her door and a hesitant knock. She knew that uneven touch. She drew the door partly open. In the hall-way, shrinking far back, was Walter, grinning, breathing long, deep breaths through his open mouth.

"What is it, Walter?" Geraldine asked. She was firm with her question, as she knew she must be. A touch of the pity she felt for him would have come through her tone, he would have grasped at it and all would be undone. "Mother said you were to go right to bed, you know."

The word mother shook him. He leaned forward and looked up and down the corridor. Reassured, he grinned again and nodded his head knowingly.

"Saw yuh!" he managed to gasp.

Geraldine understood without further words. Somewhere on that trip with "Richard" Walter had spied them. She knew, too, that the mother had not, and that Walter was keeping the secret for purposes of his own.

"Saw yuh!" he repeated, and wagged his head, a grinning idiot.

"Where?"

"Museum. Saw yuh goin' in. We were goin' out." Abruptly the boy grew mysterious. His lower jaw shot up into the upper, his eyes popped and the nostrils heaved with his heavy breathing. He wagged a finger. "*I* fixed 'em. I pointed up street. I pointed and said, 'Looka that.' An' then you and him, you went in."

A startling smile illumined his face. His mouth sprang open again. He leaned against the farther wall and asked her as plainly as pantomime could, "Now, wasn't that clever of me? And what do you suppose I'm going to get out of it?"

"Yes, Walter, Mr. Richard and I were in the Museum this afternoon. I told mother all about it. Now, don't you think you'd better run along? It's late."

He pondered on this unexpected turn of things.

"Mr. Richard," he repeated.

"Yes, Mr. Richard."

"You told mother?" he inquired politely.

"Yes, Walter. Now run along, please."

"An' I don't get my little whack out o' this?"

"I'm afraid there's nothing to whack, Walter."

"Aw-ri'," he stumbled off. "Aw-ri'." And farther down the corridor he summoned up a deep voice, the one he used to have, in a thunderous "Aw-ri'!"

Mrs. Wells had been too wide awake to stay in her room. It was only midnight. Walter could be looked after later. She arranged herself in a more comfortable attire, donned an easier pair of shoes and wandered to the upper deck.

She had very many comforting thoughts as she reclined and reviewed her European tour. Except for a single outbreak at the beginning of the trip Walter had been docile and willing. Her control of his mind, she congratulated herself, was as simple as running an electric runabout. She had always had a hypnotic influence over her family, but never before had she known its full power. Whatever she had set her mind to she had achieved, and, she was glad to assure herself, the reclaiming of her son was another victory.

To her intense astonishment her reverie was broken by the appearance of Geraldine in slippers and a kimono. To be sure the kimono was an elaborate thing that might have passed as a gown, and the hair had been wound around and around until it could pass for being "up"; and the ship was not lighted as it would be on the sea. But why should she be prowling about—prowling was just the word—and so wide awake after such a painful evidence of somnolency? Could she be looking for her mother?—No. It was a gentleman she nudged and awoke. Mrs. Wells heard the apology and saw Geraldine move on and glance into the face of another man who had found the deck more comfortable than below stairs. Geraldine passed quickly by and merged into a dark group of men forward.

What sort of goings-on was this? Could Geraldine be walking in her sleep? Mrs. Wells half arose as if to follow, but decided that that was not in her rôle. She would not spy; she would wait.

Meanwhile Geraldine had moved quietly from one end of the boat to the other in the hope of finding "Richard." Ordinarily some sort of explanation could satisfy the mother. There had been nothing extraordinary in her little adventure; but the entrance of Walter spelled trouble. He had a dramatic fashion of causing trouble in unexpected ways. The mother's calm justice would be disturbed and injustice might easily follow.

Geraldine reached the smoking-room, peered in at the assembled card-players, but just a half-minute too late. If her eyes could have distinguished a quarter length of the deck, she would have observed the tall figure of Richard moving towards bed.

So reluctantly she gave up and went below, promising herself an early promenade and a careful look-out.

Loud voices in her corridor gave her a chill of apprehension. Before her door she found her mother and Walter. The boy was disgustingly drunk; and he was ugly.

"Won't be bossed any more!" he announced with a string of dirty oaths. "I'm through!" he shouted, "through with naggin' and bein' pushed into this and into that."

With the help of a steward they managed finally to get him to bed in Geraldine's room, Geraldine sharing with her mother an adjoining compartment. Even with the aid of the ship's doctor and an able-bodied steward the two women put in an awful night.

CHAPTER IV
ORRIS ROOT AND CARBOLIC ACID

Where had the boy obtained money? And how had he got it? Geraldine and Mrs. Wells knew his former methods. The ordinary relaxed figure of the boy suggested a mind without a scheme, but on the trail of money he could summon wonderful powers of cunning. Like a paranoiac under examination who is quite aware of every symptom that might betray him, and conceals them, Walter could temporarily throw off the look of the idiot, the hanging jaw, the lurch. And his begging stories were strikingly plausible.

Money had to be kept from him, of course, and also any article of value—ring or watch. To give him so much as a shilling would mean neat brandy and the beginning of a debauch. That explains the presence of so much money in the possession of Geraldine. She was helping to guard it from Walter.

In London Walter had got a five-pound note from the Bishop of Clewes. Mrs. Wells was taking advantage of a letter of introduction for the sole purpose, as she admitted to Geraldine, of comparing reality with Trollope's *Barchester Towers*. Having listened to a conversation aimed to draw a contribution to the Relic Society's monument fund, Walter had deftly taken the Bishop aside to announce that Mrs. Wells wished to present five pounds to the secretary of the society on her way to the station; that it was not wise to let her interest cool until she went through all the red-tape of banks in London; and that the safest thing to do was to permit Walter to take the money, preferably in gold, from the Bishop. Of course no trouble of banks, etc., would keep Mrs. Wells from paying the Bishop within the week.

The plot worked well in many ways. It gave the Bishop a certain sense of actually contributing himself, it forced Mrs. Wells to forward a P.O. order to the Relic Society, and it gave Walter his chance for a riotous rebellion.

Then the mother took command. Somehow, whether it was hypnotic or not, Walter was unable again to summon courage to beg, although he had many opportunities. On the point of beginning a tale fear, chattering fear, would seize his very voice and throttle the story into extinction. For months he had lived his daily animal round without once giving the suspicion of an attempt to break away. Mother and daughter had begun to feel secure.

And now it had happened again. Somewhere on that steamer a passenger had been gulled into giving money to a well-dressed tramp. Walter was no more than that. Geraldine pondered over each name on the steamer-list and came to a conclusion. Walter never approached strangers. He hadn't the courage to pose on his own recommendation; his game was invariably to strike the most recent acquaintance of one of the family. There were many good reasons for this procedure, one of which was the fact that everyone else had been warned. On the list before her there were only five names of possible persons whom Walter could know, and all of these—except one— had been strictly enjoined from helping a wrecked boy to further ruin. That one, "Mr. Richard," she felt sure had been the mark of Walter's latest story. There was something comical in the thought that to give money to Walter Mr. Richard had been compelled to part with his sole five-dollar bill.

Mrs. Wells and Geraldine had been two days below decks before Walter's ugliness wore off into weak illness. They had taken turns watching him and were spent for sleep; so, naturally, they gave their first hours of relief to bed. The steamer had passed Gibraltar before either woman emerged to the upper deck. With a steward on guard in the corridor—handsomely tipped in advance and with the promise of a definite daily wage—they came up one late afternoon in time to join the deck promenade before dinner.

"Ah!" Mr. Richard popped suddenly out of a steamer-chair. "I've been looking for you— —" He was about to say "Jerry," when he caught both the frightened look on Geraldine's face and the imposing figure of the mother. Then he swiftly changed to "Miss— —" but paused before the "Wells," for to him that was as much a pseudonym as "Richard."

"I want you to know my mother," Geraldine put in. "This is the gentleman, mother, who was good enough to play escort in Naples that hot day we were tied up there."

"Mr. Richard-without-the-'s'?" Mrs. Wells inquired, and then went on, "Mr. Richard, I am indebted to you for looking out for my daughter." She was examining him with care. "She says you are a friend of that villainous-looking Captain. I am glad to see you such a peaceful-looking person. Please get back into your comfortable steamer-chair. We have been below deck ever since Naples and just must tramp a little."

"I'm sorry if you have been ill. The passage has been remarkably smooth."

"We have not been ill. I have a very sick boy."

"Oh, I'm so sorry!"

"He is better now. Pray sit down, Mr. Richard-without-the-'s,' and do put on your cap. I appreciate the deference to my grey hair, but I am also enough of a grandmother not to want to be the cause of a cold in the head. Later, I shall want to talk to you. Good-bye, until we get on our feet."

The incident of Mr. Richard, the Captain's friend, had been driven from Mrs. Wells' mind by the catastrophe to Walter. Now, as she walked arm in arm with Geraldine, she began to piece things together.

"That night in Naples," the mother began in a tone that put Geraldine on guard.

"Yes, mother."

"Why were you searching about the steamer only half dressed?"

When Geraldine had confronted her mother and Walter that night before her stateroom door, the easiest explanation was that she could not sleep and had been on deck to get the air. That excuse she had carefully tucked away for later use. But the mother did not ask, Why did you go on deck? but, Why were you searching about the steamer? Mother's second-sight was uncanny.

"Were you looking for Walter?" Mrs. Wells suggested.

"He had been acting queerly," said Geraldine. "He came to my room after you left."

"Of course he did not get the money from you?"

"Of course not."

They rounded a corner, bent themselves to the strong wind and turned for the trip back.

"There is something I want to ask you, Geraldine."

"Yes, mother; what is it?"

"I don't know myself. It is in the back of my head somewhere; it's an uncomfortable something-I-want-to-know, but don't know what it is. I trace it back to a question I was about to ask you when Walter began and blew everything else out of my head."

"Perhaps it was my prowling about the boat?"

"No; I did want to ask about that, but that is explained, and yet there is something else.... It will come to me suddenly some day, and then if you are not about I'll write it down."

Mrs. Wells was strong on Mind. Without being a Christian Scientist or a clairvoyant or a Yogi disciple, she was a little of all, including

Swedenborgianism. She claimed to be a free psychologist, interested in all spiritual and mental phenomena but above a label.

"That's most interesting, now—this concealed thought in my mind. Think of it, my dear, it is up there in my head hiding from consciousness! It was a question—I am sure of that—but about what I can't guess."

"Perhaps it was about Mr. Richard?"

Geraldine knew her mother. One might as well have the thing out now rather than later. This was a good safe time, while they walked alone.

"Yes!" Mrs. Wells called out triumphantly. "It was! That's a clue, at any rate. It was about Mr. Richard and—wait!... And it was about your kimono ... wait! Don't speak for a minute."

They walked along for the full minute.

"No," the mother shook her head; "it poked its head out; I almost put my hand on it, but it slipped back again. It was about this Mr. Richard, and about your kimono—oh, I can see your kimono plainly!—and about your search on the deck for Walter. I can see you bending over a man and saying something to him. What made you ever suspect that man to be Walter? Why, he had startling white shoes and white trousers, a get-up that Walter detests.... Oh! Wait!... No, it's gone again. I thought I had it."

Geraldine felt thankful that Mr. Richard had at least two changes of raiment. On the day of her adventure he had been attired in grey coat and white shoes and trousers. That is why she thought she had her man when she awoke the unknown sleeper on the upper deck and inquired, "Is that you, Richard?" "Is that you, Richard?" she had asked, she felt so sure that she had the right man; and when he had looked up with a "Eh, what?" the shadow of his cap was so dark on his face that she did not see her mistake until after she had said, "This is Jerry." The man had risen gallantly and came out into the light of an oil-lamp. He was quite different from Richard now; but when he saw the lady's face he was eager to be Richard or any other man the lady willed.

"Too excited over Walter, I suppose," Mrs. Wells answered her own question. "There! I won't talk to you any more. You look dead tired from these last few days. You are not yourself at all, my dear. You used to be such a chatterbox; now, you are becoming actually—reserved and self-contained."

They walked several deliberate steps before Geraldine said pleasantly, "Do you think so, mother?"

"There!" the mother exclaimed good-humouredly. "We walk five strides—plump! plump!"—and she counted out five more heavy steps with a "plump!" for each step—"before you say, 'Do you think so, mother?' And now that I think of it, such a non-committal phrase, 'Do I think so?' It throws the whole thing back on me. It doesn't admit anything." She squeezed her daughter's arm affectionately. "Now that's fine, Geraldine. I hope it is permanent. There's no use giving yourself away by incessant chatter. But, my lady, I'll have to study you all over again. This reserve and non-committalishness is very hard to read. I used to be able to look into your mind and see the gold-fish and count every one of them. It *was* like a sweet little aquarium, my dear, the kind with a tiny romantic castle—greatly exaggerated—at the bottom. I'm glad that's smashed. You got to be too pure and easy. I was aching for something harder, something— —"

Mrs. Wells stopped her talk abruptly. They walked on in silence, striding heavily to the heaving deck.

"Something what, mother?"

"Well." The mother was joyful. "That's ten 'plumps' before I can get a word from you. I'll have to watch you, my dear. You are getting deep."

Geraldine was elated that her keen mother had noted the change in her. It was all she could do to restrain herself from a voluble explanation. But here, fortunately, was a case where explanations would not help. She was practising her "latest self," as Mr. Richard had called it, and resolutely putting out the earlier tenant, that fluent, superficial, aquarium child. So she was restraining every impulse to speak, and when speech was necessary she chose words deliberately.

Already she had scored a fine point. As a rule she was limp before her mother's cross-examination, and the reason she never knew until now: always she had set the wheels of explanation flowing, sometimes without an interval between the mother's questions. On two occasions lately when Mrs. Wells had shot her questions, Geraldine, with a slightly nervous quaking, had begun deliberately to count five before answering. As a result Mrs. Wells had jumped into the vacuum created by the silence, even before Geraldine had got to three; and in each case Mrs. Wells herself had supplied a satisfactory answer to her own question. Q.—"What were you doing prowling about the deck that night in Naples?" A.—"Looking for Walter, of course." Q.—"Why did you disturb a man dressed in white?" A.—"You were so excited over Walter, of course."

Mr. Freneau, the university instructor guide, stopped the walk for a moment to make his polite inquiries. While Walter's condition was being made clear to him, Geraldine stepped back a few paces to "Mr. Richard's" chair.

"I must see you," she said, "before you talk with mother. Do you mind taking the name of Mr. Richard? I fear I have blundered in trying to explain our trip to mother."

"Not at all," he agreed good-naturedly. "It is a good old name. Shall I think up a pleasant Christian name to match it, or have you arranged that, too?"

"Yes, do. But please be careful. I see now how rash and impulsive I was to go off with you. Can you manage to be a friend of the Captain's, too?"

"I'll arrange that instantly. We have already passed the time of day. Fortunately I did not give him my name. He's the sort that doesn't ask for names. I know nobody on board. Except for your absence I have had delightful days and nights of hermitage. I'd make a first-rate Trappist. Since Naples I have spoken barely a word to anyone except the bathroom steward. Forgive me for being garrulous—I am just stored up with conversation now."

"Well, be careful what you say to mother. She thinks we went to the Museum and came right back. It would hurt her to feel that I had deceived her; and I'm sorry now that I did. Is this your chair?"

"Yes."

"I'll come up after dinner for a moment."

"Good! I have a very interesting story to tell you. It is about your namesake, Miss Geraldine Wells."

"Save it. Mother is looking for me. I must go. I'll come up when I can get away. Wait for me."

"Aye, aye, Madam."

After dinner Mrs. Wells insisted on going on guard to relieve the steward. Geraldine was, therefore, free to go on deck. Mr. Richard had arranged two chairs with rugs. It was a wonderful dark night.

"We have a little business to settle," he began.

"Oh, yes." She remembered that they had gone shares on the trip into Naples.

He produced her purse. She had forgotten all about that. It was a wonder that Mrs. Wells had not asked for it.

"Do you realize, imprudent lady," he said, "that you have turned over to a stranger—I am the stranger—the equivalent of very nearly one hundred dollars in gold?"

"Was it that much?"

"Don't you know?"

"No."

"You tempt me to be dishonest," he laughed. "And it is a great temptation, too; for not only am I broke, but I have lent some of your money to one of the passengers here, and, bless me, he seems to have fallen overboard. He hasn't been in his room, the bathroom steward tells me, and he hasn't been at his place at table."

"How much was it?"

"I'm awfully sorry, but it was forty gold lire. Most peculiar the way the thing happened. I was in the smoker watching a mighty poor game of bridge when I noticed a young chap beside me, odd sort of fellow, well dressed and all that, but consumptive looking. He was watching me with the strangest smile, as if he had some joke on me. Well, he had! When he caught my eye he leaned over and whispered, 'Good-evening, Mr. *Richard.*' Then he winked and stuck out his tongue in the drollest way. Of course I fancied he knew you and had heard about our little fun over names. 'My name's Wells,' he said, and leaned far back and nodded knowingly. 'And my sister's name is Geraldine Wells.'

"We shook hands and I made some remark about taking his sister's name in vain. I explained how we had picked a name at random, and asked him point-blank how he had found us out, but he winked at me and shook his head. 'I'm no squealer,' he said. 'Mum—that's *my* name,' he said very mysteriously. Well, I chatted with him for a while—he didn't say much himself; he appeared rather disturbed; kept asking me what time it was and getting up and looking out the door and coming back and shaking his head, until I asked if there was any trouble. I'd be glad to make amends for picking his sister's name out of the catalogue and christening someone else with it.

"'No,' he smiled, very plaintively, I thought; there was no trouble, only he wanted to go to bed and couldn't because the family luggage was tied up out there on the wharf with a lot of cash due on it. Mrs. Wells, his mother, was doing Naples and Pompeii and had taken all the money with her. Of course the trunks and things could wait until morning, but it was rather dangerous to wait. The boat sailed pretty promptly at six the next morning, you know.

"He said, 'Good-night,' and started out. I asked him if five dollars would do. He wanted to know how much that was in lire. When I told him he shook his head and said he would camp on deck and wait up for the mother. Forty lire was the amount due. I fumbled in my pocket and fell on your purse. He refused to take the money at first, but finally let me lend it to him. Of course he'll pay me, unless he got into trouble on the dock and failed to sail with the steamer. But wasn't it strange about the name Wells, the one I picked out from that steamer-list?"

"Walter Wells is my brother."

"Eh? The chap who borrowed the money?"

"Yes."

"Don't tell me that you are really Geraldine Wells?"

"Exactly."

"Well, of all occult happenings!"

She explained how the underscoring on the steamer-list had attracted his eye and forced him unconsciously to choose the name.

"And you knew all along?" he asked.

"Don't be silly. Of course I know my own name."

"But you said nothing, gave me no hint.... You are deeper than you look. And say," he recalled something; "what an ass I was to tell you all that rot about keeping silent and not blurting out all you know. And by the way, Miss Jerry, you scored beautifully on that stay-over-until-the-next-boat idea. I'll wager you knew all about that sailing hour."

She smiled mysteriously.

"I admit nothing," she said. "I'm complimented enough to know that you thought me game enough to do it."

"Never thought of you at all," he remarked frankly. "Should have, of course. I was thinking of myself solely. Dreadfully selfish, eh? I am an egoist, not an altruist at all.... But it would have been jolly."

"Thank you."

He laughed intimately. "We have a lot of personal vocabulary between us, haven't we? 'Thank you,' 'much,' and — —"

"And 'my dear.'"

"Oh, yes! Yes; yes. That little family luncheon-party with our own butler was charming, now, wasn't it?"

"Your ear-tips are reddening, Richard, my dear."

"Stuff," he returned. "You can't see them in this darkness.... Now, why did you suggest the plagued thing! They are beginning to burn like fury. Odd about those ears; they give me credit for modesty and honesty and a lot of virtues. Blushing is just a disease of the circulation, like pallor. Criminals blush as often, I suppose, as— —"

"Richard!"

"Eh?"

"Why do you let speech blur the finer self, deep-hidden and begging for expression?"

"Very good! Very good!" he cried; "a hit! Do you know, Miss Jerry, I am having an extraordinary rush of conversation. I haven't talked so much since I don't know when. But here goes. Shop closed."

For a minute or two they rocked gently with the steamer and cultivated the "unexpressed self."

"Oh, see here!" he was the first to speak. "I can't stop now. There is much to settle up yet."

"Please don't attempt to settle money matters on this boat," she interrupted. "I don't see now how you can ever pay me back without mother knowing; and I won't have that now. Forget about it. You can pay in many other ways."

Again they had a minute or two of silence.

"But there's something else," Mr. Richard insisted. "Where is this Walter brother of yours who took the—oh, I beg your pardon; he is the sick one, isn't he?"

"Yes."

"Is he better?"

"Yes."

"He got the luggage from the dock all right, I suppose?"

Geraldine counted five before replying and then five more. He had better know the truth.

"There was no luggage on the dock."

"What!"

"Our trunks and bags were taken on at Genoa and are all packed in the hold or in our staterooms. Walter was working you for money. He saw us together in the Naples Museum and was trying to blackmail us, that is all."

He said nothing.

Geraldine sketched briefly the story of this youthful derelict and of their seeming control of him lately. She told how their only safety was in keeping money from him, how they had warned everybody and how the mother had believed she had broken down his very will to beg. Then she gave Richard the result of the interview in the hall; and the frightful outbreak and their days of struggle with a drink-crazed man.

"My refusal to pay up," she said, "stirred his courage, I suppose. It angered him into action. He went straight to you."

"And I gave him money," Richard spoke thoughtfully, "the money that sent him down and out. That makes me responsible."

"You did not know," Geraldine excused him.

"Responsible none the less," Richard insisted quietly. "You surely don't believe that the events of this world depend on whether folks know or are sorry or even wish otherwise? I gave that boy the money that sent him back to the devil. Knowing or not knowing has nothing to do with the fact. I feel responsible and I'll make what amends I can."

"You can do nothing with Walter. Everybody has given him up. And it is such a pity. He's really a nice gentle boy who has been poisoned, that's all.... But he is frightful when the devil gets working in him. Mother isn't afraid of him, but I am. You can do nothing; nobody can."

"We'll see," said Richard. "I am terrifically strong. I can lift and pull and knock things about in a quite extraordinary manner. That gives me confidence. This drink business is largely mental. I've done a little mental-suggesting, out of curiosity merely. Let me have a try at the boy."

"If you talk that way," she laughed as she left him to take her turn below, "you and mother will get along famously, and she'll believe anything you tell her. Mental is mother's favourite word. With mother everything is mental."

"Everything is," he assured her solemnly. "Even you, now, charming as you are, even you are only a figment of my brain, a well-ordered complication of my optic nerve. See! I can close my eyes so—and poof! you vanish. To me you are a very pleasant dream."

"Thank you."

"And for me you would not exist at all," he went on, "if I ceased to hear you, see you, touch you, taste you and—I haven't tasted you yet, but I would know your scent in the dark."

"How dreadful!"

"Oh, no! No; no!" he sniffed the air delicately. "It is a faint orris and carbolic acid. Very pleasant, really; and perfectly antiseptic. You probably use an orris perfume. I don't know what the carbolic is. All existence is sensation and I am an epicure on the cultivation of the senses. I am right about the scents, am I not?"

"Oh, quite right," she laughed. "Carbolic soap is one of mother's manias. Keep up that pose and mother will love you!"

CHAPTER V
THE CARD ON THE DOOR

The time came when Walter, a very sick boy, could be brought up on deck and cared for. It is so easy to account for any sort of secret illness on shipboard that few except casual inquiries were made. The ship's doctor, a good old fellow using the trip as a vacation from regular practice, knew exactly what to do. Unknown to the mother Walter received his daily tipple, only a touch, to be sure, but enough to prevent the complete horrors of unrequited thirst. The grateful Walter lay on his chair disturbing nobody, and, in his weak way, lived. Mr. Richard and the doctor had good chats together, all of which were stored up by the layman for future use.

Mrs. Wells and Mr. Richard fell into each other's arms, figuratively, at the first encounter. Geraldine sewed tranquilly and listened to the contributions to the thesis of the ultimate spirituality of all material things, with side excursions on telepathy, hypnotism and dreams. When Geraldine later had twitted Mr. Richard (whose given name, by the way, they could not agree upon, she claiming it should be something simple and easy to remember like Robert or John, and he sticking up for a distinctive cognomen like Llewellyn or Gladstone)—when she had jested over his fine acting with the mater he had looked at her with his mildly-serious gaze. "I could not do that," he had said, "not with your mother. I am a Platonist, I suppose. This world, to me, is a beautiful illusion of the senses, a weak copy of the eternal verities. Your mother is a very remarkable woman. I could not fool her long on her favourite theme. No; we're in deadly earnest—both of us!"

In the middle of one of their discussions on the mystery of mind Mrs. Wells suddenly turned to Geraldine and cried excitedly, "I have it, my dear; I have it!"

Geraldine sewed on and waited. The mother struck an attitude of deep concentration. Somehow Geraldine felt apprehensive. No member of the family had ever attempted a prolonged practical joke on Mrs. Wells. She had plenty of good humour but no appreciation of fooling directed against herself. Therefore the palming off of a stranger under an assumed name had grown to be a burden to Geraldine, especially dangerous now that Mrs. Wells had received the said stranger into the intimate purlieus of her pet theories. One could not play jestingly with Mind! Geraldine was particularly anxious on this afternoon because Mr. Richard had appeared in grey coat and white trousers, white hose and shoes.

"Do you believe, Mr. Richard," asked Mrs. Wells, her eyes firmly fixed on his white trousers, "that conversation can be heard by the subliminal self and be transferred later to consciousness?"

"Oh, yes, indeed," Mr. Richard assured her. "That is a very common experience. Half our requests to repeat are not due to bad hearing. Our hearing is well-nigh infallible, like any other recording machine. Consciousness has been busy with something else, that is all. Give it time and it will get the message. When anyone asks me, 'What did you say?' I always wait a second or two. Quite often my remark doesn't need to be repeated; he picks it up out of sub-consciousness, where it has been perfectly printed."

"The white trousers bring it all back," announced Mrs. Wells solemnly.

"Yes?"

"I see the upper deck very plainly." Mrs. Wells closed her eyes. Geraldine moved to a seat back of her mother, from which safe position she raised a warning finger to Mr. Richard. "Don't fidget, Geraldine; I must concentrate.... Geraldine is in a kimono; her hair braided and wound around; she leans over a man in white trousers and she says, 'Is that you, Richard?' and adds, 'This is Jerry.' He says he is not Richard. Geraldine apologizes and moves away. The white trousers stare after her."

"Very rude of the white trousers, I am sure," Geraldine remarks, but offers no further help to clear up a situation she remembers only too well.

"That is what I wanted to ask you about, Geraldine,"—the mother ignored the comment—she had probably only heard it with her subliminal ear, "but Walter," she glanced towards the boy who appeared to be sleeping, "but Walter upset my mind completely. Now, Mr. Richard, I did not hear a word of that conversation at first, because it took all my mind to get to the fact that Geraldine, whom I had just left sleeping in her room, should be prowling about the deck nudging sleeping men. It was not until Geraldine had moved completely away that I caught up the words. When she spoke I heard only a murmur, absolutely nothing distinct; and yet it must have been recorded on the subliminal and lifted later into consciousness. I was going straight to Geraldine to ask her about her strange conduct and particularly to inquire why she should be asking about a 'Richard' whom she knew well enough to permit calling her 'Jerry'—why, bless my soul, Geraldine was looking for you, Mr. Richard! But she did not say *Mr.* Richard—I am sure of that; and she *did* say 'Jerry.' Geraldine, help us out."

"It's too deep for me," Geraldine smiled into her sewing. "You two work it out," she added serenely; "one of the party ought to keep sane."

"Nonsense!" Mrs. Wells was always irritated at the suggestion of any connection between mental mysteries and loss of mental balance; but it drove her away from Geraldine—as Geraldine intended—and set her questioning Mr. Richard.

"Don't you think it is possible that I heard correctly?" she asked Mr. Richard.

He pondered over the situation. The events of the night came before him. Suddenly he remembered that Geraldine had told him that she had sought for him after Walter had visited her room with suggestions of exposure.

"Ah!" he concluded suddenly; "I believe you heard accurately, Mrs. Wells."

Geraldine looked at him carefully. He gave her an assuring nod.

"Miss Wells was hunting for Walter," he said. "She told me later. She thought she had discovered me in the white-trousered sleeper and sought a helper."

"But she called you Richard, as if you were a butler or a chauffeur, and she presumed that you would know her as 'Jerry.'"

"Oh," Mr. Richard laughed, "didn't you know that my first name is Richard, too? Don't blame me!" he spread his hands out and shook his head. "Richard Richard, that's the label they gave me."

"Why, no one would ever— —"

"Oh, yes, they would. Look at Jerome K. Jerome."

"Yes, that's so."

"And Peter Peter," Geraldine helped.

"What!" the mother turned on her. She knew of no Peter Peter.

"The pumpkin eater," explained Geraldine as she thoughtfully threaded a needle.

Richard Richard bubbled with mirth. He had a hearty out-of-doors laugh. "Great character, old Peter Peter. He and I have many qualities in common. He was always hard up. So was his cousin, Tom Tom."

"Eh?" Mrs. Wells' mind could not catch up quickly with the jest. "Tom Tom?"

"The piper's son, you know," Richard explained. "He stole a pig," he added instructively.

"To be sure. To be sure," Mrs. Wells admitted. "How stupid of me." But her intent eye showed that her mind was still on the mystery. "There is no Mr. Richard Richard on the steamer-list. I am sure I should have noticed it."

"No," Richard answered slowly. "No-o. It wouldn't be. I came in late at Genoa. Didn't make reservations. Knew there'd be plenty of room in July; all the rush the other way, you know. So they didn't get my name in time to print."

Richard seemed to be enjoying the game. Every now and then he would look towards Geraldine for approval, but she gave him only a calm wide-eyed survey.

With cap drawn down almost over his eyes, Walter, stretched out in his chair, was observing the group with ferret-like eagerness. He knew a thing or two! They were not pulling the wool over his eyes. And he would show them, too; but in his own time.

The mother was not satisfied. "It sounds plausible," she admitted grudgingly. "Although how any sane person would name a child Richard Richard— —" She interrupted herself to gaze firmly into his honest, genial face. The absence of all guile assured her. Besides, here was a man who really knew mental phenomena, had taken courses under James and Münsterberg; had some hypnotic abilities himself; was familiar with what was to her an unknown region, Kant and Hegel; a man, in other words, who had the right attitude towards Mind. Yes; he was all right.

Then a horrid doubt assailed her, for she remembered vividly that Geraldine had said to White Trousers, "This is Jerry." An hour or two of strolling about Naples would not bring them to first names.

"But," she began, and stopped.

"Wait, Mrs. Wells," Richard sat up. "Do not speak. I am about to try a bit of mind-reading. You are wondering why your daughter should have called me Richard— —"

"And why she should have presumed you would know her as Jerry."

Mrs. Wells had taken the mind-reading as a matter of course.

"Exactly." Richard was quite ready with an explanation. "You see, my peculiar name struck Jerry—struck Miss Wells as absurd; which of course it is. She said she could not call me Mr. Richard, as if she were talking about me to one of the maids—'Mr. Richard will have his tea now; Mr. Richard does not go out to-day'—and all that sort of thing. She said, and wisely, that Mr. Richard was not, strictly speaking, a name at all; so she said— —"

This story was not going as well as it should. In the flash of planning it had seemed a first-rate explanation.

"What was it you said?" he appealed to Geraldine.

She counted her five before looking up from the sewing.

"You seem to be doing very well," she commented quietly. "Go on. I'm quite sure I don't remember what I said."

"You said something, I'm sure," Richard cocked his head sideways and tried to think of something she might have said.

Mrs. Wells was thinking, too. "If Geraldine made up her mind to call you by your first name she would not be a daughter of mine if she hesitated. I agree with her; Mr. Richard is uncomfortable; I think I shall drop the 'Mr.' too."

"By all means, do!"

Richard was glad to get out of the difficulty due to the failure of invention.

"And I won't press you," said Mrs. Wells, her fine face lighting up wonderfully, "to make up any more ingenious stories of how two young people off on a lark manage to call each other by their first names."

Richard laughed. "It was embarrassing," he admitted. "One drops into first names, sometimes, you know—uh—so easily and—uh—the explanation is deuced hard to make—uh—in public."

"I'm an old woman——"

"Oh, tut, tut; not at all."

"But I am not so old that I can't understand young folks. And anyway, young man, you are not built to lie—your ears give you away."

Geraldine broke forth in sudden merriment.

"Oh, see here!" Richard expostulated. "See here!" The large lobes of his ears were burning. "You'll get me all fussed up if you draw attention——"

"The whole ear"—Geraldine spoke a word or two between attempts to suppress her glee—"is crimson—and now—the back of your neck is on fire!"

In the joyfulness of the moment Walter slipped carefully from his chair and sauntered off; but he had not gone far before Mrs. Wells' watchful mind—the subliminal, probably—had noted his absence. Without a word she rose and trailed the boy. At the top of the stairs he looked back, turned about sullenly and waited for her.

"How did I do?" Richard asked earnestly, the moment they were alone. He was as eager as a boy. Although Geraldine was a strikingly handsome young woman Richard paid no attention to that. In her presence he was like a near-sighted man intent on his own ideas. Just now he was openly delighted with his own cleverness and appealed to her as co-conspirator to give him full credit.

"You're a better liar than I thought," she gave her judgment composedly.

"Ugh!" he shuddered at the word. "'Liar' is pretty stiff, don't you think? That's a fighting word, you know. Now, I should not call it lying, but diplomacy. Same thing, of course, but—uh—quite different, you know.

"But I say," he bethought himself; "what'd you think of my blushes, eh? Pretty clever, that. Gets you credit for a deal of innocence. I——"

"You surely don't give yourself credit for the blushes?"

"Why not?"

"You can't turn it on or off like a faucet."

"But I can," he insisted. "Been practising for years. Found it very useful when caught with the goods on."

She looked at him thoughtfully; he grinned back and nodded his head. As she gazed steadily at him the tips of his ears began again, and slowly the flood welled as before.

"I suppose you are giving me an illustration now?" she asked.

"Am I reddening up again?"

"You are—gloriously."

"The deuce you say!"

"The deuce I say."

"Well, of all—but it only shows how expert I am."

"You turned this one on, too; did you?"

"Did it a-purpose; just to show you I could, you know."

"You *are* a better—fibber than I thought," she announced.

From the stairway Walter's high-pitched voice made itself heard above the ship noises.

"I'm done with you; d'y' hear!" He was levelling a very bony finger at his mother. "No more! No more! I won't let you get *my* goat no more. No, sir! No, sir! Talk all you want! Oh, I'll look at you."

She had been quietly asking him to look at her in the hope that with her eye upon him he would wilt as before.

"I'm lookin' at you! I'm lookin'!" he shouted menacingly. "An' what good's it doin' yuh? I've got your number, O.K., and it's *all off*! *All off*, I tell you!"

Evidently she had asked him to let her go with him to his room.

"No!" he raised his voice a half-notch higher. A passenger here and there looked up. "You don't follow me about any more, you don't. I'm on to you, I am. No more! That's—final."

She kept steadily at him.

"Stop it!" he shrieked and began to sway back and forth, "stop it or—or—or I'll throw myself overboard. I will! Do you hear? I will! Aw!" he whimpered piteously, "can't you shut up!"

Suddenly he darted towards the side and began frantically to put a leg over the swaying rail. A passenger struggled with him and delayed his attempt, which gave Mrs. Wells time to reach him. She put out a hand towards his shoulder; he struck her savagely. Other passengers including Richard and Geraldine soon surrounded the frantic boy and tried to calm him, but certain unsuspected depths of passion had come to the surface and gave him strength. His eye never left his mother. He seemed anxious not to avoid her, but to fight it out then and there for the mastery of himself, or rather, for his freedom from the mother's superior will.

The blow had staggered her. He saw her falter and knew his chance. He fairly crowed his announcements that she would no longer settle on him and drive him here and there like a puppy. In spite of her magnificent appearance Mrs. Wells was no longer young. She was sixty and she had driven herself hard. The sudden fright at the boy's jump to the railing and the unexpectedness of the blow, to say nothing of the power of the sickening thought that her own boy should offer to strike her in public, had its effect. An unusual weakness caught her limbs, and her heart lunged forward.

Summoning her will she presented a semblance of poise and dignity. To the group about her she explained that her boy was ill. He interrupted constantly. She asked the passengers to let her manage. She knew how. He would go to his room and she would go along and reason with him.

All of this he denied shrilly; and in her heart she knew she had lost her grip, as he cried aloud his victory. No! No! He would never again go with her.

"Will you go with me?" Richard asked mildly. "Let's get out of this, old fellow, and talk it over. No use letting this gaping crowd know our business, eh? What d'y' say?"

"Sure I'll go with you," Walter nodded seriously, but there was no giving in in tone or manner. It suited him to go with Richard. He told everyone that it did. Richard and he were pals, he told them. They had things, they had, to talk over and come to terms on. Secrets, ha! Secrets that would make 'em all sit up and listen.

Richard agreed and led him away. As they went down the stairs, Walter leading eagerly, Richard cast one look back. Pity for the old grey woman, looking greyer now than ever, struck him hard. He pressed his lips together and wished he could requite in some measure the evil done her late years by this hopeless boy.

The hopeless boy turned suddenly in the hall.

"Richard Richard!" he cried and laughed. "That's a good 'un. Richard— hell! I know you."

"Of course you do. Of course you do," Richard agreed. "But don't bark it out to the whole ship. Come along to my room and talk it over."

"All right," Walter assented. He said "Aw ri'." One would think by his speech that he was still "not himself," as the Welsh have it. No doubt the passengers agreed upon that theory. But Walter's speech, drunk or sober, had become blurred and difficult.

"All right," he said. "I'm no squealer. I only want my rights. That's all.... Knew yuh wasn't no Mr. Richard. Knew from the first."

"H'm," Richard mused aloud as they walked with difficulty along the swaying corridors. "How did you get on to it, old fellow?"

"Saw your name on the door. Card."

"The deuce you did!"

"Yes, thass-ri'," Walter chuckled. "Saw yuh go in. Looked at the door. Saw your name plain as writin'. The card said——"

"S-sh!" Richard silenced him so thoroughly as to frighten the boy. "Never mind what the card said. Where do you think you are?" he demanded roughly; "alone in the ocean?"

Richard put on his fiercest face. Walter had a secret: very well; it should have value. "You're a fine pal," Richard growled, "a devil of a fine pal." He strode forward with an excellent assumption of ferocity. "Hang that card!" he added, merely to give verisimilitude, as Pooh-Bah would say, to an otherwise bald and innocuous situation.

That card was a mistake. He had put it up to make certain that his luggage would reach the room promptly, and with no thought of its being a permanent name-plate. When he reached his door with Walter he wrenched it off impatiently.

"Come in," he changed his tone. "Come in, old chap. Let's talk things over. Have something to drink."

Richard unscrewed a flask and poured out a good-sized "slug."

"That's all," he warned. "You're in a bad way, man, and I'm not going to have you kicking completely over. I'm good for a drink now and then, but you can't swim in it."

Walter drank eagerly. It seemed to set him up almost instantly. Some of the fight went out of him.

"You're all right," he commented sagely. "A wise guy, you are. And so am I, all right."

"Of course you are."

"And I'm no squealer, either."

"Of course you aren't."

"You can be Mr. Richard Richard if you want—or anything. Mum's me! But in my opinion you ain't either one."

"What's that?"

"Yuh ain't Richard and yuh ain't——"

"S-sh!" Richard glared ferociously.

"Well—you ain't. That guy," he pointed towards the spot where the card had been, "I've seen his picture in the papers, and he's an old man, old man with whiskers, he is."

A look of pain shot across Richard's face. He turned away and looked steadily for some time out of the open port-hole. Then he came gently to the stricken boy and said:

"Walter, let's be friends, you and me. You're right about both names. That man," his voice caught as he pointed towards the door, "I'm not fit to walk in his footsteps, much less bear his name.... There's nothing wrong about me, Walter. I want you to take my word for that."

"Sure there ain't. An' there ain't nothin' wrong 'bout me, either."

"Of course there isn't. That's why I am going to stand by you and keep you from jail."

"Huh?"

"That forty lire you got from me for the luggage which was supposed to be on the wharf. That's what they call obtaining money under false pretences. Good for five years, I think."

He gave the boy time to get the thought.

"Jail's not half bad," Richard looked up reminiscently as if he was speaking from experience. "They give you good grub and work enough to keep you feeling right and sleep enough—*that's* all right. But—there's not a drop to drink. Not—a—drop. Days go, and nights go—nights when you stay awake hour after hour with your tongue as hot and dry as a burnt stick, and you cry out for a little cooling drink, and all you get is a blow on the head. And the days pass and the nights pass; and when you begin to count up the months and maybe years yet to come— —"

He stopped suddenly. Walter was holding his head in his hands. The picture was too much for him.

"Well," said Richard soothingly, "you needn't worry about me, Walter. I wouldn't send a dog to a place like that—not unless I were forced.... I have my own reasons for being Mr. Richard. I'm going to trust you to forget all about that card. You keep that a dead secret, old chap, and I'll stand by you to the last ditch. Is it a go?"

"Sure," nodded Walter, but the brag had gone out of his voice.

They shook hands on it.

CHAPTER VI
ASSISTANT WIDOW

At Richard's suggestion Walter moved into the older man's stateroom. There the two men spent many hours together. Walter was glad enough not to have to appear among the others, and Richard wished to study the boy. It was not entirely a humanitarian interest. Here was a mental puzzle to study out, and just at the time when such studies were being made in the treatment of neurotics. Certain midnight talks with a good chum in the faculty of Columbia University were remembered; a lot of desultory reading of the Freudians came rushing into memory; and Roman bronzes fell to the background.

Walter's antipathy to the mother underwent no change, except perhaps to increase in intensity. It hurt her pride to have to give up her position of influence and she did not do so without a struggle.

No one else save Richard, or perhaps a professor of the science of mind, could have talked with her on the science of abdication. As delicately as needful, for she had not yet recovered from the shock of Walter's sudden attack, he made clear the psychological necessity of resigning if only temporarily.

"You arouse opposition. You make him strong to oppose you," he said to her one late afternoon as they chatted on the upper deck. "No one knows why these mental storms arise, but it is always wise to guard against stirring them up. He is in earnest about doing away with himself if you try to control him again. He and I have talked it over and on that one point he is unshaken. You must frankly face the fact that your boy is a neurotic. Back of that is always the danger of self-destruction if thwarted. Fortunately, there is the possibility of sudden cure. In fact, there is more hope nowadays for mental ills than for physical ones. You can't grow a new leg or a new lung, but you can completely remake the mind. Of course I don't have to tell all this to you."

"Are you a psychologist?" she asked. "I have never thought to ask about your occupation."

"I?" he laughed. "Oh, no; not at all. I'm not anything."

"You talk so well on so many subjects," she speculated, "ceramics, Roman bronzes, psychology— —"

"I'm a potterer," he explained. "I just dabble here and there. One year I'm daft on old printing, or the growing of white blackberries, or multiple personality—oh, I'm jack of a dozen things. But I have one real accomplishment. I kept at it once until I could read an Assyrian cuneiform brick in the Metropolitan Museum! There's an untranslated Assyrian dream-book in the British Museum that I am just itching to get at."

"You mean that you just try a thing for a while and— —"

"Not exactly. I keep a great number of things going. For instance, I'm tremendously interested in primitive religions, Shinto and ghost dances and sun worshippers and all that sort of thing; but I don't keep at it all the time. I drop one interest and take up another; give them each a turn. Just now I've grown interested in your boy, but that's an old interest: I've been thrown a lot with twisted-minded people, over in the West Side, New York, where I often live. There's a little settlement of social workers, Legal Aid Society folks, socialists, new poets—oh, a delightful group. That district has some pretty odd cases, too; and I've been up all night with some of them."

"And you have no regular occupation?"

"No; nothing regular, unless— —" he laughed at a thought that occurred to him. "You see, I've a pack of awfully good friends who have money and homes and all that sort of thing. When I get hard up—as I am just now; I've only five dollars to my name—I pay them a visit. I go only to places where they understand me and let me alone. So I suppose I might call myself— uh—a professional guest. I pay visits for my board and keep."

"You're not a sick man?"

"Lord, no! I'm terribly healthy. I've played football, rowed in a crew, polo, and I can swim a dozen miles. I'm so strong I'm ashamed of myself."

"Then why don't you work?"

"I wonder what you mean by work?" he asked mildly. He had long ago ceased to resent this inevitable question. Here was a man without funds who got along with the least amount of "work." He explained. "By work I suppose you mean making something to sell. I've no objection to that, for those who can do it and like it. The mass of people are working in that sense. Of course it's necessary, but the most of them look pretty down-trodden and driven, don't you think? It's a slave's life for most earth dwellers. Some of them never see sunlight: they drive away at some monotonous task under gas-jets or arc-lights; they burrow in wet mines;

they count up endless figures with green shades over their eyes; they shovel endless tons of coal, mix endless puddles of mortar or teach endless classes of somebody else's endless children. I can't do any of those things. For me it would be imprisonment, stifling, maddening. I must follow my will and, unfortunately or fortunately, my will does not lead on to fortune. Happiness is my goal, personal happiness; and in a very large measure I get it. Work? All my work is play and I play hard. You don't know what hours it took me to get enough information together to read that Assyrian brick! I lived for weeks on bread and tea and an occasional chop cooked on Father Maloney's cook-stove over in the West Side."

"But somebody had to pay for the chop and the bread and the tea."

"Oh, yes; that's true," he seemed to recollect that his story did not fit together. "Oh, I work, too, in your sense, to get enough funds together to do my own kind of work. I've wired houses, fixed up leaky roofs, cut grass on the big lawns—I've never had the least trouble in selling my muscles—but my real job when I get down and out and don't feel quite like playing up my professional guest business—I had almost forgotten my best money-maker!—I'm an assistant widow."

"What?"

"Isn't that good! Assistant widow, and you don't know the business at all, do you? Oh, it's profitable—I make several hundred dollars in a few weeks—it's terrible drudgery, but it's short and swift and soon over. At Harvard college a 'widow' is a professional tutor," he explained. "There's a famous one at Cambridge whose business it is to put fellows through examinations with the least amount of effort on the part of the student. Not a bad idea, eh? It's a rather sorry trade, I must admit, but it is very humanitarian. Old 'Widow' Knowells always has work for me whenever I want it at the time of the hour examinations and at midyears and at finals. He gives me careful notes of all the professor has done during the term, synopses of outside reading, etc., and I'm an expert in bottling it up. I can almost guarantee to put a fellow through, if he has enough memory to last him over night! Philosophy's my stunt. I boil it down—from Thales to William James—and make it palatable for the unphilosophic mind. I've had as many as two hundred men in one group for a three-night cram before the exam. Rather horrid; isn't it? But Knowells charged 'em five dollars apiece, and he generously gave me three. That was my banner group. I made $600, enough to keep me a year and save something towards this trip. But it took me a month to get the taste of the thing out of my mouth. Work? Ugh!"

American-bound steamers in July carry few passengers, so Mrs. Wells had been able to reserve a fine corner of the deck for her group, which now invariably included Richard. At this moment as they talked Walter lounged in his chair near the railing while Geraldine and two middle-aged ladies who had been with the Freneau party, and Mr. Freneau himself, were chatting quite near. Geraldine leaned forward.

"Excuse me for listening," she said. "Richard tells such interesting stories."

"Oh, this is all true, every bit," he told her.

"I don't object to its being untrue," she rejoined; "the only objection to bad fiction is dulness. This story of yours is not at all dull. What I want to know is what would happen to the world if everybody did as you. The stokers, for instance, live like condemned devils. Don't tell me they like it. But if they obeyed their own sweet will where should we be?"

"And that chap putting tar on the ropes," he pointed; "I'll wager he'd throw that job for a couple of good sovereigns."

"Of course he would," she went on. "What I want to know is how you manage to take care of the disagreeable jobs."

"Very simple," he said; "I don't manage at all. I am not my brother's keeper. My interest is solely in steering myself. I have no theory for the other fellow; I have only pity."

"How cruelly selfish."

"Exactly," he spoke quietly. "The cruelty of living is the most colossal mystery of creation. I don't pretend to understand it, and I know of no remedy for it. The struggle for existence is the acme of cruelty until you renounce it, as I do. I live my life as simply as I can. I try not to interfere with anyone else's chance. That's all I can do."

"What about the future?" the mother asked. "You will not always be strong."

"I take no thought for the morrow," he said simply. "I live entirely in the present. Who can take thought and prosper? Happiness is not to be saved, put in a bank. I live contentedly from day to day. When I cannot do that—well, the remedy then is equally simple, quietly end it."

"Rather gruesome," Geraldine shivered.

"Death is not gruesome to me," he said. "I am very sensitive of the shortness of life and of the inevitableness of death. Most of us ignore the topic; but it is constantly in my thoughts, as it was in Socrates'. That's the way to rid yourself of fear of the sure end; face it; every morning smile in your glass and say, 'Thou shalt surely die.' Then all the world spreads happily before you as a garden of delights, and the pettiness fades and all the discords of smallness.... Well! well! I grow poetic—as I should. It is the most magnificent event in life; the very thought of it blesses the present hour."

The steamship *Victoria* was moving through the placidest of twilight seas. The setting is very important to have in mind: the soft blur of blue on the horizons, the high-banked clouds fringed delicately by an unseen sun, the pure transparent grey of the zenith, and the cool, salt breeze. Some themes cannot be set in midday, nor amid the turmoil of business. A thousand miles from land with only the frailest tie to existence, poised in the centre of tranquillity, there without mockery one could speak of death, of man's mortality. Here, if ever, was Death's sanctuary, where one could perform fittingly the ceremonies of awe and praise.

Mrs. Wells spoke first. "How old are you, Richard?" she asked.

"Thirty-three."

"You have the thoughts that usually come with old age.... Are you a nihilist or—anarchist—or something?"

"I dislike labels," he said, "but why shouldn't I be called Christian? I take no thought for the morrow and I would do unto my neighbour as I would that he should do unto me—I let him alone."

"Isn't that just the opposite of Christian?" Geraldine asked. "Christians are rather aggressive; aren't they?"

"Yes," he agreed, "the altruists are. Now I'm an egoist. I always felt that Christ preached personal purity and renunciation of the world's goods. If each person were pure in heart and covetous of no man's goods, why, the millennium would appear."

"I don't understand your egoism," said Geraldine. "I always thought altruism was undisputed."

"My altruism is universal egoism," he said. "If each person on this ship were trained to take perfect care of himself there'd be no need of a sacrifice in case of shipwreck."

Mr. Freneau drew his chair nearer. He had been neglected pretty thoroughly by Mrs. and Miss Wells, and he did not particularly object. It was a tiresome job to pilot four women and a vagrant man through the cathedrals and art galleries of Europe. Mr. Richard was a welcome assistant, who had suddenly relieved the tension and had given the guide a needed rest. As the journey neared its end he began to recover and, humanly enough, had a desire to talk and be heard.

"That's very well put, Mr. Richard," he nodded approval. "We're all selfish naturally, and it's a really decent creed; only everybody calls it bad names but goes on practising it just the same. But isn't it often cruel? The essence of Christianity, I take it, is sympathy, brotherly love. Egoism, as you call it, fights all that, doesn't it? It is isolated."

The other two ladies drew into the circle. Richard became silent.

"I'm asking you, Mr. Richard," Mr. Freneau inflated his lungs and began a dissertation in ethics. At the end he appealed to Richard for confirmation of his analysis.

"I'm awfully sorry," Richard arose and worried through his excuses. "I have no doubt you are quite right. I have never studied such things. I only know my own life and I know very little about that. I have no really fixed opinions on anything. Who could have? But, excuse me, I must go. Walter and I are playing a most exciting tournament of cribbage. Hey, Walt, old chap; what d'y' say? Another bout, eh?"

Walter sprang to attention eagerly. He understood the code. It meant cribbage, of which he was desperately fond—Richard had found that out early—but it meant also a gill of precious cognac.

"Sure!" he said, and dragged himself out of his chair and followed.

Mr. Freneau talked on, but his argument smelled of the recitation-room. It was as far from life and living as a college debate. Mrs. Wells watched her boy as he went off so willingly with Richard, and wondered, a little enviously, what charm the piper played. As they made their way forward in the dusk she heard her boy laugh at a remark of Richard's, the first laugh from him in many a day.

Geraldine found it too dark for sewing, so rested her hands in her lap and looked out to sea. Before the interruption the conversation between the three had been quiet and intimate. She felt that they were just about to approach interesting and novel things, revelations about the common modes of thinking that would illuminate them for ever. It was not a doctrine of cruelty and selfishness that Richard was presenting, and in no sense had he the attributes of a doctrinaire. As he talked his face had taken on a wistful inquiry as if he were in the act of coming to curious conclusions, he knew not what. "Life is a strange land," he had said to her once in talking about Walter; "I always act towards it like a voyageur floating down an unknown river. At any turn may be a peaceful lake, a wonderful vista, an enemy in waiting or a dangerous waterfall. It is folly to predict too much on the sole basis of the journey done. And it is all wonderful to the curious minded, even the enemy in waiting—if you approach him right he may turn out to be a friend!"

Neither Geraldine nor Mrs. Wells was listening to the eloquent Freneau.

"I am sure you have a thought on that point, Mrs. Wells," Mr. Freneau leaned forward expectantly. This was the proper professional attitude to quicken interest among wandering students. "Do let us share it."

"Well, I will," Mrs. Wells arose. She got up carefully and breathed deeply to steady herself, for she wished to conceal the fact that Walter had struck her a hard blow. Her pride would never have owned to it, but it took serious attention on her part to rise and walk without a show of stiffness. "Well, I will," she spoke firmly: "I have been thinking very, very deeply on a matter that worries me much as I get nearer home. I'm thinking exactly what I shall do to George Alexander if he hasn't weeded my hardy perennials exactly according to directions. If he has permitted those sweet-williams and Michaelmas daisies to monopolize the whole patch at the expense of those delicate larkspurs, I'll—I'll—probably take away his corn pone for a month."

CHAPTER VII
GETTING WARM!

Meanwhile, in Richard's stateroom Walter had had his gill and was fighting hard at cribbage to count in a fine handful of "fifteen's." "Pretty smart," Richard remarked as he drew a card. "Now why did you let me have that eight spot?"

"Knew the five was under it," Walter grinned and rolled out his tongue foolishly.

"How did you know that?"

"Oh, I know the cards all right. And I know you got two eights and a seven which you aren't goin' to count in.... I need that five to make a 'fifteen-two.'"

Walter made good his boast in one or two swift plays that ended the game in his favour.

"Well!" Richard affected great astonishment. "You peg out. I always thought cribbage was a game of pure chance. You certainly can spiel 'em. Let's have another."

As they drew and played and pegged Richard asked questions. Sometimes he got the answers he wanted; at other times a series of stealthy probes into the boy's past brought nothing. Finally he struck a vein that brought the result he was after.

"What did you most like to do when you were a kid?" he asked.

"Fish, mostly; and climb trees. Wanted to be a sailor."

"Why didn't you?"

He darkened and twisted his face ferociously.

"Oh, I know," Richard soothed. The mother had said no, of course.

"And wouldn't she let you fish, either?"

"She didn't kick again' fishin'. Always glad to get my trout."

"Ah! She wouldn't let you climb trees, I bet."

No answer.

"Ah! I thought so! Still like to climb 'em?"

Again no answer.

"Play the game!" muttered Walter savagely. "Play the game!"

They played, but Richard could hardly see the cards before him. He made many bad mistakes. Once he really forgot himself, and began to peg in fifteen-two's; but he caught himself in time and let Walter finally peg out a winner of every contest. But his mind was not on that game; it was excitedly going over the ground of some interesting data that his friend in the Columbia faculty, Professor Galloway, had produced in one of their all-night chats on things mental. And here, if everything turned out well, was a parallel case in Walter.

Galloway was telling how the psychologists were turning into veritable wizards and healers. Beginning the study of abnormalities for the impartial purposes of science they had to do with all sorts of freak cases of mental derangement. Naturally the patients and their friends were more interested in cures than in the progress of science in the dim regions of psychology; and naturally, too, the investigator found his fame depending more upon a sensational cure than upon the discovery of psychic law. They had been forced into the practice of psychology; and with hypnotism, "suggestion," dream readings and casting out of inimical "personalities" their trade began to take on the character of the ancient soothsayer and witch-doctor.

Galloway had been telling Richard of certain sudden and unexpected "cures." In one case, a "dope fiend," emaciated and degenerate looking, had abruptly changed not only his mental personality, but had become physically transformed. Growth began in him like a garden after a drought. Healthy flesh multiplied on his brittle limbs, his back straightened, his eye took on intelligence. As if a bolt had been released that chained his real self he cast off the Mr. Hyde and became an uncontaminated Dr. Jekyll. Through accident they learned that a nervous mother some years before had peremptorily refused to let him run an automobile. There had been many violent scenes; the mother had become hysterical; the father, to keep the peace, joined with the mother. Seemingly the boy had acquiesced, but soon after, he had slipped many moral stages, until a bad crowd and cocaine had got him. To the normal mind it would be ridiculous to find a cause for moral degeneracy in so simple a matter as the repression of a strong desire to run a car; but the psychologist knows the wisdom of readiness to believe anything. They got the boy a car; they let him run it, take it apart, rebuild it; they even permitted him to let her out a peg in the open country and paid his fine for speeding. And—a miracle—the long-suppressed spirit rose and took possession and six years of vile living were cleaned out as if they had not been.

It was this case that Richard had strongly in mind when he took up an interest in Walter. It was a chance, he thought, but worth trying for; so he began from the start to probe. Tree climbing had come into the conversation several times before. Richard fell upon it as a clue; but Walter was wary. Like all neurotics he fought away from the cause of his trouble. When pressed directly he always denied any interest in the thing; but Richard had found him watching the men in the crow's nest; and when he talked about the trip at all it was about the height of the masts, and how fine it would be to crawl up there on the rope-ladder and fix the top lights. He was obviously disappointed when told that the lights were probably electric and were turned off and on by a switch in the engine-room.

Cases of thwarted will are engaging the attention of mind students nowadays. A youngster will grow physically ill, resisting diagnoses and medicines, and all because a dollar watch is denied, or because someone says no to a request for a pink dress. Most of us, fortunately, fall in easily with the pressure of convention. We are the lucky normal children; the ones who thrive under opposition and make the rules for the unlucky others.

When Richard asked Geraldine if she knew about Walter's desire to climb trees, she could not recall anything of value. The mother on her part said he had never expressed a desire to do such a thing. "He climb a tree?" the energetic mother had ejaculated; "he was always too lazy. What nonsense is this he has been telling you?"

But while Richard was disappointed he felt it unwise to press the mother for further information. He tried once to hint of the newer development of body cure via the release of mental suppression, but, interested as she was in mental phenomena, she would not connect anything of the sort with Walter. "He has had every freedom a boy could desire," she had said firmly; "he has had too much. What he needs is a strong, resolute hand."

Geraldine, however, was taken with Richard's point of view and set herself to help.

"Let me ask you questions," Richard said. They had gone off together to the mass of machinery at the stern of the boat. "Don't mind how silly they may seem. Galloway told me you can't ignore anything. He did a fine stroke once on a half-witted kid by noticing the way she pulled at one ear. It's a good story, but I won't tell you now. What I want from you is a list of the things that Walter has been forbidden to do. I know your mother well enough to see how she would take mighty good care of her son and heir; and her plan would be to make fast rules. Am I right?"

"On the contrary," Geraldine replied thoughtfully, "she was most indulgent. Everyone says that she gave him too much leeway, and she feels very conscience-stricken over it now. That's why she is trying to make up by extra vigilance. I'm the one she always held in check, but I never objected seriously; mother was usually very sensible in her exactions."

"Is there any other member of the family who may have coerced him?"

"No; father died when we were very young. Mother has managed the household ever since I can remember. She was firm in small matters; but she was always kind and reasonable. That's why," she hesitated and then went on, "that's why we always feel so dreadful when we deceive her."

For a moment he gazed in his mild way far out to sea, at the great churned path made by the vessel.

"You begin to make me feel guilty, now; an experience I very seldom have," he said finally.

"It wasn't your fault."

Without being specific each knew that the reference was to the day in Naples.

"Why should it be anybody's fault?" he asked. "I don't believe in 'faults.' If you are a true Whitmanite there is no blame. One might as well feel guilty over cold and heat as over the acts of our nature. There's Whitman and Spinoza rolled into one! I don't feel conscience-stricken because my diaphragm moves up and down or because my appendix is inflamed; why should I be concerned, then, if my will takes its next appointed step and attempts to go off with you and your purse?"

"I don't know why," she spoke after a moment's thought. "It's my training, I suppose. But let us get back to Walter.... The only time that I remember when mother seriously attempted to control Walter was several years ago when she scolded him in public for something he had done in one of the sailing races. He sulked around the house for days afterward, and he never would go in the races again, although I am sure he was awfully keen for them."

"Jove!" Richard was suddenly eager. "We're getting warm. When was that—the exact date?"

"I can find out. I don't know exactly; but it was the year the *Tecumseh* won the cup. Every other boat was either wrecked or blown ashore or filled with water. Walter was helping sail the *Tecumseh*. He can't swim, you know."

"What was the thing he did that made your mother scold him?"

"I don't remember. Possibly I can find out. My feeling is it was something to do with the spinnaker. He used to be very clever at getting it out in just the right minute when we came about and went before the wind. But I can't recall. All that I know is that a terrific blow came up and sent those boats on end. It ripped the masts out of two of them; and the *Tecumseh* was so sprung she never was the same boat again. I was time-keeper, I remember, and I know they did the twelve-knot course in less than an hour. It was a record, I think."

"That's fast sailing."

"Oh, you should see those 'Class A' boats. They're the fastest sailing boats built. I'm not boasting. They're scows, you know—centre-board—and they just slide over the water. We took the inter-lake cup the next year. You must come up and have a go at it. It is fascinating sport."

"I think I shall." He spoke as if he had already made up his mind.

"Mother is going to ask you to pay us a visit—as a 'professional guest.'"

"Fine!" he laughed.

"I believe you planned to have her ask you."

If you had told Richard that he had planned to forge a cheque he would have considered the matter with an open mind and have rendered an impartial decision.

"Quite possibly," he admitted, "although I am not at all conscious of doing it. I thought I had intended to visit a good friend in Montclair. In fact, I wrote to him yesterday; but all the same I may have been planning to go with you. I want to go with you. That's a very important clue. Trust your desires every time; they tell which way the mental wind blows."

"What could be your motive, then——" she began.

He interrupted. "Motive? I have no motives, no conscious ones. I don't know why I do things. That's what makes me such an interesting phenomenon to myself. I unfold like a plant; and it's very exciting—I am always eager to know whether I'm going to blossom into a sunflower or an apple tree or a wild strawberry bloom."

"Or poison ivy," she interrupted.

"Quite so!" he agreed heartily. "Motive? I've long ago given up trying to discover my motive for anything. And, by the way, we're usually wrong when we do discover. Listen to the bragging of folks around you, to their cock-sureness in knowing why they do this and that. Sometimes the holiest of men have the unholiest of motives, and many a rascal would be surprised to know how really Christian he has been acting. It is the same with nations and elephants and earthworms. Life will have its way whether we understand it or not. All that I know about myself just now is that I very much desire to go to your Penn Ying——"

"Penn Yan, please," she corrected.

"You don't know how curious I am," he looked at her frankly, "to see what will happen next."

"I am not sure that I want you to come," she answered thoughtfully.

"Why?"

"I am hoping you will go quietly away altogether after we land. If you come up to Keuka, sooner or later, mother will know you are not Mr. Richard and—it is a small matter, but I know her: she will not think it small. It will strike her like a blow ... and she is getting old. She tries to conceal it, but I know. The whole family have sat back and let her carry the burden, but it has always been done so well that we never inquired.... I'm just beginning to see what it has meant to her. At 'Red Jacket'——"

"What's that?"

"We call our place 'Red Jacket' after a local Indian chief. 'Red Jacket' is really a huge plantation. We have farm land, vineyards, gardens— wonderful gardens!—and a big household. She manages every inch of it and has always done so. It's beginning to tell on her now.... She wouldn't understand our studied deception. It would break her; I'm sure it would."

"I understand," he agreed. "All right." Silently they watched the swirling water. "Walter interests me," he explained, "interests me more than you can guess, but I can give him up.... Well, we've got a day or two left. Let's make the best of it. The boy stirs me like the answer to a hard puzzle. I'm built that way. I throw my whole life into the next thing that attracts my curious mind.... To be honest, I'm afraid I don't care anything for the boy. Does that seem brutal?"

"No; I understand. You are like a surgeon performing a fine operation."

"Exactly. I think I'm on the way to fix that boy up! Really! I'm tremendously excited about it.... By the way, wasn't there something in that yacht race about climbing—I mean in the thing that Walter did that set the mater off?"

"Why, yes!" she exclaimed, catching some of his excitement. "I remember now. He went aloft to disentangle the peak halyard. That's it! Mother was watching the race with a glass, and she nearly fainted when she saw him leg up. She knew he couldn't swim. The boat was scudding down the Lake with the wind back of her; he did that leg in less than a minute and she was heeling over nearly to the water. And Captain Tyler said that that's what won the cup, Walter's shinning up the mast."

"By Jove!" Richard seized her hand and wrung it fervently. "We're getting warm, Jerry! We're getting warm! That's what he meant by climbing trees— —"

"Of course!" Jerry was equally excited. "When he couldn't— —"

"You have it!" he broke in. "When he couldn't climb masts, he sulked and wouldn't race at all. Then he went off and climbed trees all by his little lonely— —"

"Just to show her that he wasn't going to be bossed!" she helped quickly.

"Sure! Then he got taking a drink or two just for company— —"

"I don't think he ever really liked the stuff. None of us do."

"Of course he doesn't. If his primary interest is drink," Richard flung up his hands, "the Lord help him, for nobody else can. That's what Galloway says. I'll get in touch with Galloway soon as we land. Perhaps I can get him to come up with us— —"

"Where?" She was sobered suddenly.

"To 'Red Jacket,' of course." He laughed at her stupidity. Her expression puzzled him for a moment. "Or is it 'Yellow Jacket'? I'm no good on names. Well, never mind the colour, old girl. We'll all work on it and we'll bring that kid around as sound as buckwheat. Aren't you excited about it?"

"Yes," she answered quietly. With her head resting in her hands, she was frowning at the great swirl of water left by the receding boat.

CHAPTER VIII
"MAN OVERBOARD!"

Professor "Jawn" Galloway was of a different "caste" from Richard, but they matched up equally as chums. Galloway had been one of the West Side group; in fact, he had been a West-sider from birth, one of those clever Irish lads who can rise to distinction out of the soddenest of homes. Dan Galloway, the father, was a hearty, noisy—and it must be admitted—dirty Tammany helper. Dublin had brought him forth and he had seen troublous times there. A lucky immigration and a still luckier political situation saved him the trouble of working and gave him lodgings, beer and victuals. "Jawn" Galloway, the son, inherited nearly every trait of his father save two—he was the farthest removed from a loafer; and he hated uncleanliness. By the dint of sheerest personal push he had gone through school, college and university and was making a name for himself in the newest of callings, psychotherapeutics. At twenty-eight he held honorary doctorates from honourable universities; but to look at his rubicund Irish face, to hear his laughter and to see his joy over the coarser delights of life, one would never guess all that.

As the S.S. *Victoria* neared New York, Richard prepared a letter to John Galloway. It read:

> "Pal Jawn—August will be your vacation month, I am a prophet and foresee much. Besides, you admitted when I left that you would be free in August. You are to go to Penn Yan (not China), New York, and thence to 'Red Jacket'—which is a house—and inquire for your hostess, Mrs. Emma Wells. Some time to-day I shall let her invite you.

> "The daughter, Geraldine, will interest your Irish heart. She sheds flattery as if she were used to it, as I suspect she is; but she has never met your subtle blarney. I'm on tiptoe to see the effect on her.

"But that isn't the point. It may turn out to be. We'll leave it to the gods, who manage beautifully if we are not too presumptuous. The point is a boy, neurotic, just your kind; idiot with gleams of sense; drinks, perfect guzzler, but not primary, you know. *And I've got hold of the primary interest!!* It's climbing trees and furling spinnakers. Aren't you itching to get at it?

"I bet I've spoiled your vacation, O.K.! I hope so.

"Yours,

—"Wait. I'm travelling incognito. It's a glorious experience. Wonder why I never thought of it before. Accident—I mean the gods did it. Of course, we know there ain't no accidents, just incidents! My first name is Richard and my last name is Richard—Richard Richard. Can you beat it? Monotonous? Not at all. There's Dick Richard and Richard Dick and Dick Dick. I wanted to have a middle name, Richard, too, but got scared off.

"You don't know the joy of incognito. To be free from the everlasting questions. I'm beginning to see—data for you— that the name hampered me, drew me into myself, made me shy and backward except with good old pals like you, Jawn, who know what's what. If I ever have a boy I'll not junior him. Fancy a George Washington, Jr. Think of the life of that kid! And it sounds like George Cohan, too!

"Practise my new name. There must be no slips. More data— the boy (name, Walter Wells; age, twenty-two; specialities, tree climbing, spinnaker furling and wood alcohol) knows about the name, my name. He's holding it over me! I let him and we thrive together. Also (more data) I give him two drinks a day. Bring (more data) some superfine cognac.

"Lots more, but it'll keep.

"On second thoughts you'd better stand by in N. Y. until I
'phone you, which means that you're to pay the train fare
to Penn Yan. But amn't I after getting you free wittles for a
month? And you know, Jawn, there has been days when free
wittles was not to be sneezed at!"

With the characteristic directness of an egoist who knows what he
wants, Richard lost no time in searching for Mrs. Wells. He found her in her
accustomed place in the lee of the bridge. She was propped up with more
than the usual number of cushions, and the pallor of her face struck him
instantly.

"My dear lady!" He sat beside her, his voice genuinely sympathetic.
"Don't tell me you are succumbing now, after going through the main part
of the voyage."

"I am never seasick," she said, with an imitation of her old firmness;
"just a little weariness, that's all.... That's a good boy——" He was tucking
her in dexterously. "You are making me very fond of you."

"Of course I am," he cheered her; "it's a plot."

"You remind me of what I've missed by being so independent all my
life. Sit down. You're not going to run away just because I look a little seedy,
are you?"

He sat down on the foot-rest of her chair.

"Here I sit, your squire to command," he joked.

A little colour came into her face. She reached a thin hand and patted
him on the arm. There was not a particle of doubt as to his interest in her.
She was twice his age, but their minds were contemporaries. They had met
in tournament mentally and jousted for the sport of the thing; they had lent
their minds out to each other and had made broad paths towards intimacy.
And at the same time it was sweet flattery for her to know that this strong
youth—his thirty-three years sat lightly upon him—was paying a kind of
court to her intelligence. As a rule the young men had hovered about out of
politeness, but were off at a nod from the daughter.

"You're a good boy," she said. "I shall miss you; unless——"

"I accept in advance!" he cried gaily. "You know I'm a professional
guest!"

"And also some sort of a widow," she smiled.

"Assistant widow," he corrected; "but please don't remind me of that. I won't have to think of that until the November exams. begin. Let's talk of 'Red Jacket.' You're too tired to talk, so let me talk for you, tell you what you were going to say. Gracious! You don't know what a silent crab I am usually. You have brought me out, introduced me to speech, you and Jerry."

"What was I going to say?" she helped him, amusement in her quiet tones.

"Oh, yes," he remembered. "You were about to invite me to 'Red Jacket'—Jerry let the cat out of the bag—and I'm coming. We'll have great old pow-wows, won't we?"

She closed her eyes wearily, but the contented smile remained.

"You don't know what a flutter you're putting me in." She looked at him tenderly. "Women of my age don't often get such genuine attention from young men. It's so rare that—well, you'll have to be careful. Don't give me too much of it. I'll be getting jealous of Geraldine next; begin to fool myself into thinking I'm young again."

"Young? Pooh!" He tossed his head. "Why all this silly eagerness to be young? Age is the thing, the goal. 'Grow old along with me, The best is yet to be, The last of life for which the first was made.' You remember your Ben Ezra, don't you? Well, that's the best of sense. Youth? It's a time of folly and bad thinking. You don't catch a successful business man sighing for the days when he had a tuppenny shop with more debts than customers. We don't pine for green blueberries, do we? What's all this march forward of growth if it doesn't mean something mighty fine? Why, lady mine, I'm just eager to push on to forty and to fifty and to sixty—to a hundred if I could. Life's a climax—always a climax; don't bow for a minute to the world's sentimental nonsense over youth."

"Well," she said thoughtfully, "you are right, of course. I wouldn't go back even five years."

"Who would?" he questioned triumphantly; "which proves my point perfectly. The world doesn't believe its own nonsense; and that's a text for an enormous arraignment of the world in all its beliefs. The credo is the act, not the pious patter of the mouth. What a man does, that is his belief, whether he knows it or not.... Don't you think you'd better close your eyes and take a little nap? You look knocked out; has anything happened?"

She opened her eyes resolutely. "Go on," she said, without answering his question. ("Ah!" he said to himself, "something has happened," but he gave no sign.) "Go on. I've often thought that thought. It's not what you say about yourself; it's what you do that tells the story. That's very true. Very true."

What she was thinking—and some inkling of it was in her voice—was that this young man was really interested in chattering with her; that Geraldine often protested interest, but her neglect was the truth; that her boy Walter had never expressed either dislike or affection for her, but his act in striking her in public was eloquent. Richard sensed a specific application but, naturally, he could not apply it exactly. So he went on cheerfully:

"I've spent many delightful hours writing out the creeds of various men. I've followed them to their churches and into their businesses and, sometimes, into their homes. This man who professes Christian humility openly, who begs the world to turn the other cheek, to forgive seventy times seven, who cries out that the meek shall be blessed and shall inherit the earth—oh, it is great fun to judge him by his deeds. Arrogance and self-sufficiency rule him. He is merciless to wife, child and employee. It takes a destructive and criminal strike to squeeze decent wages from him. He links himself with corrupt politicians for personal gain. He connives at shady legislation. Oh, he is meek—in after-dinner speeches and in addresses before the Sunday school—and verily he well-nigh inherits the earth!... And I have seen rough-spoken men whose acts are the heart of humility."

"Your arrogant man," Mrs. Wells took up the discussion, "I am interested in him. I am an arrogant person myself, and I'm often sorry.... Within the past hour I have been arrogant, and I am suffering for it."

Richard said nothing. Instinctively he knew she would tell him, if it were proper for him to know.

She continued after a moment's pause, "Could not your arrogant man be sincere in all his professions; fool himself, as it were?"

"Oh, yes, indeed. Yes, indeed. That is the interesting thing to me. I'm an onlooker merely. I do not condemn. I condemn nothing. Sincere? Undoubtedly. But sincerity is no great virtue. Every persistent burglar is sincere. He has no pricks of conscience. Question him—as I have done—and he justifies himself every time. Sincerity is the cheapest possession, and the world values it too highly. The Spanish inquisitors were sincere; so were the scalping Indians; and Boss Tweed. And so were Lincoln and John Wilkes Booth. So is the devil, for that matter."

She laughed weakly. A little more colour came back into her face.

"Your incongruous company is very amusing," she smiled, and began to sit up. He helped her with pillows.

"The only point, isn't it," he said, "is not whether a man is sincere, but whether he is wise or ignorant. Now your boy, Walter——"

A flash of pain that came suddenly across her face told him much.

"You have been talking to him?" he asked.

"Yes."

"Was that wise?"

"No."

"Was he—violent?" he asked anxiously.

"I shouldn't have done it. I was—sincere, God knows; but, as you say, I was ignorant——"

"Did he touch you?"

"No."

"What did he do?"

No answer.

"Let's be frank. I'm trying to get him out of the slough he's in. I must know everything. Treat me as if I were his physician, as I believe I am. He was nasty to you?"

"Yes; he called me the vilest name.... We've talked about that, I know; names should not affect us. 'Sticks and stones,' etc.—I know that is true; but, man, you can't know the surging, overwhelming emotion that covers a mother when her boy calls her something low, unmentionable—horrible."

"Let's forget that," he said, "and get the gain out of it. It means you must give up trying to control him. Don't care about that. It's just like a doctor when something that should stimulate depresses. He changes the medicine as one would change a coat, and with no more concern. You had to try this out, to see if you couldn't hold him. You could not give him up without one more trial. That's all right, and now you must leave him to me. We're getting along. He lets me scold him. It's my luck not to get on his bad side. I may; nobody knows. But I've been able to suggest lots of good habits. We walk miles together on the deck, you notice. He's getting some health back; and I'm chucking him full of confidence. Cheer up. Don't let a name or two bother you. That's just the devil in him talking. Oh, he's got a devil, all right, and I'm the boy to exorcise it. You leave it to me. You will; won't you?"

"I am not sure that I should." She turned her face away.

"Ah, that's pride, I fear."

"I am sure it is." She turned her face to him with a wan smile.

"Good!" he cried. "Honest confession is good for the soul."

"It is," she admitted. "I don't often practise it. The puzzle to me is why I do it to you. Pray tell me, O youth, what makes you so fascinating?"

"Am I?" He appeared hugely gratified. "How jolly!"

"*Now* who is proud?"

"Me! I own up. I'm bloated with pride. But I always own up. It's part of my creed."

"Then, pray, own up something to me."

"Name it."

"Why—precisely why—are you willing to give up your plans and your other friends and stay with us at 'Red Jacket'? No fooling, young man; nothing but the truth, the whole truth."

He crossed his heart.

"Hope I die." He imitated the children's formula, the charm to insure truth. "I want to come because I like you—you and Jerry."

"Humph! Me and Jerry. Not just me?"

"Nope—both of you; and the reason for that is that I talk to you. I can always tell. I have only two joys in life—curiosity about life itself, and talk. I've stayed up all night for a good confab with the right person. But only certain persons can I talk with. Don't know why; but I trust the instinct. With you and Jerry I am garrulous and contented. That's enough for me. There is another reason why I want to go—I'm extremely interested in Walter. Curiosity about life, as I told you, is one of my passions. I want to unravel his mental puzzle if I can; and I think I can. I'm on a most exciting clue——"

Should he tell her the whole truth; that she was directly responsible for the boy's downfall; that her impatient arrogance, her stupidity in not realizing that a sensitive man does not enjoy a public reprimand from even his mother, was the beginning of all the evil that followed? He looked at her aged face and decided to say nothing.

"A most exciting clue," he repeated.

"Those reasons don't seem adequate to me." She looked at him with smiling suspicion.

"Oh, there are other reasons, no doubt," he agreed; "only I don't know them. They'll come out later. They always do. The subliminal—the self inside, deeper than consciousness—it is at work, I suppose, here as everywhere.

I am expressing my predestined self. But, of course, I don't hold myself responsible for that. That's in the hands of the gods. My soul-mate may be up on that lake of yours—dispensing soda in one of Quackenbuster's drug stores."

"Quackenbush," she corrected, amused at his air.

"Is it? All right. That's one thing I don't have to remember. Quackenbush or Quackenbuster, it's the business of destiny, not mine. Although, I suppose, when the time comes I'll crow a lot about my good judgment. Every blade of grass, no doubt, believes it has chosen green for a colour.... But, why aren't my reasons adequate?"

"Well, they are not normal——"

"Ah!" he interrupted. "That's exactly what I claim to be, normal. It's the rest of the conventional world that's abnormal."

"Do you remember the Quaker," she commented, "who said to his wife, 'Martha, all the world's queer, excepting me and thee—and thee's a little queer'?"

"Honest Quaker!" he rejoined. "I've much admiration for him. It's the way we all feel. To me all mankind is deliciously comic, all except me—and I'm a *little* comic."

Far off towards the stern of the boat someone uttered a cry. It sounded at first like the gulls, which were beginning now to follow the boat. But it was repeated with a clear human suggestion. Mrs. Wells, with eyes contentedly closed, heard nothing. Richard had performed his office well; she was cheered and heartened. So he deftly tucked in a stray corner of the rug and slipped quietly away. Far off he had seen Geraldine, her face in agony.

Fortunately the majority of the passengers had gone down to early dinner. The deck was free as he sped forward at full speed.

"Quick!" she called to him. "There! Walter! Oh, quick! quick!"

The stern of the boat was narrow and almost cylindrical, like the hull of a tank steamer. Only a hand-rail and a life-saving raft or two gave any protection against sliding off into the sea. Stumbling over the odds and ends of ship machinery usually lashed down here, Walter was making his way to the extreme end of the boat. His unsteady gait and his occasional sprawl at full length told the story.

"The rest of my cognac!" thought Richard, as he leaped to the deck below, ran across a space full of dismantled derricks and winches, and clambered up the ladder which brought him back again to Walter's level.

"Hi!" Richard called commandingly. "Come out of that!"

He called to gain time. At the call, Walter steadied himself on a life-raft and slowly turned himself about.

When he saw Richard climbing over a railing he waved a hand and shook his head.

"Sta' back!" he demanded thickly. "Going to stop whole business. Sta' back, I say. She wo' let me 'lone. Tol' her I'd do it. 'N' will do it. Sta' back!" he screamed. "Do y' hear me! Damn y' soul, I tell y', sta' back!"

Just before Richard reached him his slow mind realized that whatever he was to do must be done quickly. On either side of him bulked the life-rafts, but beyond, near the very end of the boat, was a cleared space of several feet. Nothing but a low guard-rail of rope protected one from the rounded hulk of the vessel. Towards this open space Walter threw himself, clutched the rail and flung his leg over.

At this end of the boat the ship motion was marked. She would lower a dozen feet every few seconds and fling herself up again rhythmically. It was the sudden lunge up as Walter's leg went over the rail that prevented Richard from pouncing upon him in a single leap. The two men were only a yard apart, but the tilt of the vessel made Richard's progress a climb uphill, and when the ship started down again Walter's body had already begun to roll slowly over the rail towards the deck. Once on that wet slant and he would have shot bounding off into the churning sea.

With the tilt of the steamer downward, Richard leaped forward, and seizing the hand-rope, which he gripped like iron, he catapulted completely over the rail and on to the curved iron deck. The lunge carried him against Walter's slipping body, which his arm encircled. As the steamer rose and fell Richard clung to the guard-rope and hugged the boy to him in a terrific grip.

"Le' me go, damn you," whimpered Walter, although his head was nearly smothered against the deck. "Le' me go, can't yuh? Tol' her I would; an' I will. Le' me go. Wo' let her boss me. Le' me go, I say! Aw! Le' me go!"

Richard tried to draw himself up, but stopped, fearing that the boy might struggle; and besides, he did not wish to risk losing his grip on the rail. Looking off to the side he could see the curving edge, and beyond was the white-capped sea.

Of course Geraldine had followed swiftly, and with her she had brought a burly sailor. Someone had cried, "Man overboard!" A small crowd began to rush towards the stern. It was a simple matter to get both men back on the platform.

"Come along, old fellow." Richard lifted the boy and encircled him with his arm. "You're just feeling a little blue; that's all. Come along down with me and we'll talk it all out."

The soothing voice, where he had expected reprimand, had an amazing effect.

"Aw ri'," he agreed cheerfully enough, as if risking two lives was a matter of every-day happening. "Guess y'r ri'; but she ought never come at me 'at way—spesh'ly after I *tol'* her. You know, Rich'rd, I *tol'* her. *Didn't* I tell her?"

"Of course you did." Richard drew him farther on. "And what's more, she won't do it again."

"Oh, yes, she will. You do' know 'er."

"She promised me she wouldn't."

"She promis', did she?"

"Gave her word she wouldn't."

"Gave 'er wor', did she?"

He pondered over the fact.

"Tha's fine!" he said. And after a few steps further, he nodded his head vigorously and repeated, "Tha's fine! Good ol' sport, mother; aw'ways keeps 'er word. Tha's fine!"

In a few moments after, with the help of the ship's doctor, Walter was sleeping blissfully in Richard's room. Richard sat on a camp-stool and Geraldine sat on Richard's berth.

"Seems comfty, doesn't he?" Richard gazed with smiling interest at his charge and then looked into the face of Geraldine.

"Has mother been after him again?" she asked.

Richard nodded good-naturedly, as if that did not matter.

"He said he would jump over the side," she shivered at the thought, "if mother pestered him again. I told her to look out. But she laughed at me. Does she know about this?"

"No."

"Are you going to tell her?"

"I can't make up my mind. Not just now, at any rate. She's pretty spent. Something has happened lately to take the spark out of her."

"Yes; I've noticed that. She has aged frightfully."

"That quarrel on the deck upset her. She'll get over it. We must wait. Meanwhile I shall not let this determined youth get out of my sight.... I'm sorry," he added, as a thought occurred to him, "but you see now that I must go on with you to 'Red Jacket.'"

"Has mother asked you yet?"

"Yes; this afternoon—and I accepted.... Do you mind?"

"Yes." She looked up at him frankly. "You like the truth. Yes, I do mind; but this thing of Walter's has scared me.... I'm sick at the thought of it.... I see that you must come with us.... My only fear now is—is that you won't."

"That's all right, my dear——" A faint smile visited her whitened face at the remembrance of her jesting on the top of the hill back of Naples.

Then tears came suddenly into her eyes, the after effect of the scene she had just witnessed. She brushed them away and smiled at the same time, a sunshine and shower effect.

"Lord, how I have aged since Naples!" She spoke with low emphasis.

"Of course you have," said he. "You've grown up, just as I predicted you would. And you're much nicer as a young woman than as a pert kid who knew she was good-looking.... Now, don't worry about mother. She and I are irrevocable chums. I could tell her the whole story—real name and all—to-morrow and she would forgive me. But don't fear her discovering anything. I'm having the greatest joy out of Richard Richard. I'm going to keep him alive as long as I possibly can. It's more to me than a new name; it's a new personality.... I'm just discovering something."

He stopped to think.

"What is it?"

"Names are important. Galloway told me once that the police changed the name of a street which for years had been a veritable reproach and that instantly the street took on a new tone and in the end cured itself. He was indignant when I scoffed. But I see he was right. This new name has transformed me. I don't know myself."

"You, too, have grown up."

"Really, I don't seem to be the same person. I used to be a recluse, a member of the Independent Order of Glum."

"You were."

"Eh? Oh, this was before you knew me."

"Was it?" She looked across at him tantalizingly.

"Oh, yes. The moment you came along I changed my name and slipped out of my shell.... See here, what are you grinning at?... Say, have I ever met you before? I'm awfully forgetful."

"I sat beside you for a full day on the way from Genoa. First days out are never agreeable to me."

"You did!" he ejaculated. "Why didn't you punch me?"

"I felt like it. A half-dozen passengers tried at one time or another to talk to you, but you froze them off with what seemed like malice."

He laughed.

"I wanted to be alone. I'm in fine company when alone."

"So when I saw you on deck that morning in Naples, I made a little bet with myself that you wouldn't snub me."

"And, by Jove, I didn't!" he cried. "Give me credit for that!"

"No," she said, "you didn't, but perhaps I deserve a little credit for that."

"You do," said he speculatively, as if trying to get the exact facts; "the evening before, I had seen you counting a huge roll of bills. When you came towards me that morning at Naples I decided to be friendly, tell you my predicament and get funds for a visit to the Museo Borbonico. It worked out splendidly."

She smiled at what she believed was just playfulness, and looked towards the sleeping brother.

"I'd forgive you anything now," she replied quietly, "but you fib too well."

"A fib in time saves nine," said he.

"Remember that, please, when mother gets too inquisitive at 'Red Jacket,'" said she.

The unusual ceremony of shaking him warmly by the hand as she left the room was not misunderstood by either. He returned the grip with equal fervour. Both stood a moment and gazed at the boy. Then she slipped quickly into the corridor.

CHAPTER IX
"WE SHALL SEE"

Geraldine went directly to her mother. She found her in her usual place, forward under the bridge. Evidently Mrs. Wells had had a little nap; she looked refreshed and immeasurably better. An empty tea-cup and a plate of toast was beside her, a sign that she had had her dinner served on deck. It occurred to Geraldine as she came forward that dinner would be out of the question that evening. Indeed, it took all her resolution not to go to bed from sheer weakness. But the sight of her mother's cheerfulness and obvious return to health gave her will to go on.

"Hel-lo," the mother sang softly, the two musical notes that had been a family call for a generation. It was the first chirp she had uttered since the scene with Walter on deck. It encouraged Geraldine in her determination to be frank.

"My dear," said Mrs. Wells, "where have you been? Writing letters? I do hope you have jotted a few postcards for me. I have been shamefully lazy. Where is Richard? I owe him an apology. He was talking away beautifully, giving me all sorts of little thrills with his absurd poetical views, and I only closed my eyes so that I could hear better—I did take a teeny nap, but don't ever tell the dear boy—when, pop! he was off without my hearing a sound."

Geraldine stacked the remains of the dinner in a pile near the rail, convenient for the approaching deck steward.

"It was so comfortable up here this evening," the mother explained, for fear she might be accused of weakness, "that I just had the steward bring me a bite. The dining-room is abominably stuffy."

"You are much better, mother, aren't you?"

"Better?" She looked up sharply. "You talk as if I had been ill. Nothing is the matter with me. I get tired—the same as others, sitting around on this boat with nothing to do but stumble over steamer-chairs. What made you think anything was the matter?"

Geraldine was expert enough in signs to know that this topic had better be dropped, so she began on a new line.

"Have you seen Walter this afternoon?" Geraldine asked casually.

Mrs. Wells knew she was under cross-examination. Perhaps it was clairvoyance; undoubtedly she had a kind of ability in reading the intentions of others that amounted almost to mind-reading; but more likely it was the consciousness of guilt that led her to avoid this topic too. But she was unusually clumsy. She fussed with her pillows, asked why the steward did not remove the tea-cup and plate, and, finally, when Geraldine, with calm persistence, came back to Walter, Mrs. Wells pretended at first she had not heard, and then asked petulantly, "Yes, I have talked with him. Why shouldn't his mother talk with him?"

"Do you think he is any better?"

"Oh, he's coming along as well as I expected.... Aren't those sunset clouds wonderful?"

"Mother, aren't you afraid of him?"

"Afraid of whom?"

"Walter."

"Still on my Walter," she parodied, and took great amusement out of her deft sally.

"I'm afraid of him, mother. I'm dreadfully afraid he'll go out of his mind and——"

"Tut! Tut!" Mrs. Wells interrupted. "Put that out of your head, girl. I know Walter. And I know how to bring him around. Afraid of him? Nonsense. The fact is, I have been indisposed ever since we came on board; therefore I have had to give way to Richard. When we reach 'Red Jacket' I shall be myself again and will take Walter in hand myself."

"I wish you wouldn't, mother."

A group of men came out of the companion-way beside them. They were smoking their after-dinner cigars and talking about the narrow escape of a passenger from falling overboard.

"What's that?" Mrs. Wells asked the man nearest her. "A man overboard?"

"They got him as he was falling," the man replied. He had a big voice and he seemed to relish the horror of the incident. "They say a passenger was back at the stern, a man it was, and he fell afoul of a coil of rope or something and pitched over the railing."

"I heard something," Mrs. Wells remembered. "It sounded like someone screaming for help, but I was taking a little nap at the time and thought I had dreamt it. Dear me! Isn't it dreadful?"

Geraldine watched the mother, whose placid face showed no hint of her intimate and personal connection with the recital now going on about her in several keys.

A shrill-voiced man scoffed at the theory of a "man overboard." It was the usual false alarm on board a ship. Passengers have nothing to do, and therefore they're always glad to get themselves all fussed up; they'd scream "Man overboard" if they saw a flying fish.

Another person felt differently about the matter. And he knew what he was talking about. He had his information on the best authority. There was a man really overboard—the second-officer was the authority—a man overboard while the steamer was stoking ahead at twenty knots an hour. And did they stop to hunt for him? No. What would be the use? He'd be a mile astern before we could turn about.

While Mrs. Wells from her throne among the pillows cross-examined the men—a favourite rôle of hers and a sign that she was coming back to her control of things—Geraldine had dropped back into her chair, seized by a horrid suggestion of nausea. Every vivid detail of the struggle was made more vivid by the heartless narrators. There had been much interruption as the men rehearsed various versions and, worse, a lot of the senseless witticisms that men employ to show that they are a devil-may-care lot.

Mrs. Wells scoffed at the notion that a man, a passenger possibly, had really fallen overboard and that the vessel had gone on its way without any concern in the matter. Had the second-officer himself told the gentleman? Well, no; not the second-officer himself; but he had told the thing in confidence to the quartermaster, who had passed it along to the crew. It was the bathroom steward, in fact, who had given out the details.

"Ah!" Mrs. Wells was highly pleased with her quiz. "On the authority of the bathroom steward!" she chuckled. "You men know what the day's run is going to be, on the authority of the bathroom steward; you tell us exactly when we shall dock, on the authority of the bathroom steward. The male bathroom steward, my dear sir, is the exact equivalent of the female hairdresser."

A quiet Englishman came into the group while Mrs. Wells was expressing her suspicion of the theory of "man overboard." As others emerged from the companion-way, which led up directly from the dining-room, they stopped to listen. About six or eight passengers lounged in chairs or stood about.

From her enthroned position under the bridge Mrs. Wells was naturally the centre of the group.

"But, really, there was no man overboard, you know," the Englishman told Mrs. Wells. "I saw the whole thing and helped to get the poor chap on his feet. He wasn't overboard, but he was jolly well close to it."

Questions overflowed on the reticent Englishman.

Oh, no; he had done nothing—merely helped one of the crew pull the two men up over the rail and upon the deck. It was a tall, blue-eyed chap, the big fellow with the hearty laugh, you know, the one who is everlastingly tramping the deck—he's the boy who gets the medal. Why, he sprang right over the rail, depended solely on the grip of his hand to hold himself from sliding overboard!

"Back aft, you know," he explained, "the vessel bulges out like a flattened cylinder. There's a little foot-walk on the top of the cylinder with a bit of rope on each side. The foot-walk's quite safe, you know; but one step over and you're on a smooth, round slide. A man might hold on if he'd lie flat and if the boat didn't jolly well wobble. But it does wobble, you know; up and down with the rollers and then a side shake or two; and, besides, it's wet back there from the spray and all that. Not much of a lark to try to hold your own on that bit of tin.

"I was standing against the rail," he went on, "just off there, where our deck stops. A man and a woman were quarrelling around the corner of the house. I couldn't see them, of course, and I couldn't hear all they said, but they were having high words, the man was, rather, I should say. Well, the man's voice stopped. I heard the woman call after him. She seemed to be begging him not to do something or other. I couldn't get it. Then she screamed. She screamed twice. Quite startling, you know. Not loud, but— penetrating. Went quite through one. Of course I——"

Mrs. Wells interrupted. The man's leisurely style irritated her. She suggested, good-humouredly, of course, that he might shorten the melodrama and get to the tragedy.

"Quite so," he agreed; "but this is the first act, you know. Quite necessary, I assure you. For if the lady hadn't screamed I—well, I might have seen the chap drive out aft and topple half over. Of course, I did see him, you know. What I mean to say——"

"Prompter badly needed," remarked Mrs. Wells grimly. She had not relished the Englishman's quiet turn of her theatric figure of speech.

"Prompter?" he inquired blandly. "The lady called and, being a gentleman, I ran to her assistance. Nothing could have been prompter." The Americans, who love a pun, applauded, but the Englishman went on as if he had not scored. "She was calling to someone and pointing aft. Then I saw the man. He had got down among the life-rafts and had stumbled over something or other. He lay sprawled out on the deck. I started after, of course, although I saw no reason to hasten. Between the life-rafts it is perfectly safe. It's just beyond where the trouble begins. Then I saw the big chap. He was lugging it up the ladder and calling, 'Hi! Come back!' The first chap, the chap who had stumbled, he got himself up and ran farther aft, and for a second it seemed like a race. But the vessel lurched badly, or something, and the first chap—I hope I am clear—the first chap smashed up against the ropes. The impact carried his leg over. You could count five while he slowly turned up and on top and then began to fall over that rope rail to the deck, you know.

"Of course all this happened while one might say Jack Robinson; but it seemed to me he was devilish leisurely—the first chap, I mean—in getting over that hand-rail. Good thing, too. The second chap, the big chap, was coming full steam ahead, charging like mad. He needed every second and he knew it, so he put one hand on the rail, gripped it, swung over, came smash against the sliding body of the first chap, and pinned him against the deck. And there he swung, with an arm and a leg around the other chap, hanging by one hand to that blooming, sagging rope. He's the medaller. I? Like a silly ass, I stood there watching it all and let the woman pass me. She was on them like a shot. Strong 'un she is; she had them both fairly well up before the sailor chap and I could lend her a lift. I hope I've made it all clear, but I fear I have mussed it up. Rather beastly thing, you know, two men dangling over the side and the old ship tossing like a mad bull!"

The Englishman was an effective narrator after all. His quietness; his hesitations—he puffed on a pipe during the recital—and his child-like candour gave a horrid suggestion of reality to his picture.

By this time Geraldine had recovered sufficiently to watch her mother. Mrs. Wells' swift mind had visualized the scene; she saw the deck rise and fall and the two men hanging over the depths. The horror of the thing was on her face, Geraldine noted, but there was no suspicion of Walter.

"I saw the two of them coming back," a lady announced. "They passed right by my chair. The smaller man was fearfully wobbly at the knees and he seemed dazed. He talked thick, like a drunken man, and he smelled horridly of whisky. Of course that's what the doctor had given him to revive him. He mumbled and talked foolishly. If I hadn't been told I'd have taken him for an intoxicated person."

This clear description of Walter came to Mrs. Wells with the cruelty of a shock; but she did not utter a sound, or move a muscle. Rigidly she watched the speaker, but Geraldine saw the colour fade from her face, and her heart beat in pity.

Summoning her energies, Mrs. Wells rose slowly and moved towards the companion-way. At the top of the swaying stairs she pulled herself together, and went straight to Richard's room and knocked.

Richard opened the door softly, peered out and let his face lighten up at the sight of Mrs. Wells.

"Come in!" he whispered, but in the tone of gay mystery. "Walter's taking a nap. Come in!"

She looked into the room. Walter was sleeping soundly, thanks to the doctor's morphine.

"No," she said.

"Can I do anything?" he inquired; "pull out steamer-trunks, open a port-hole or—mix you a glass of orange juice?"

His cheerfulness assured her. It was not Walter, after all.

"Nothing, thank you," she said. "Just passing by and thought I'd tap and see if you were at home. I've missed you. Why did you run away from me this afternoon?"

"My speech put you to sleep," he laughed; "so I just tucked you in and slipped off."

"I wasn't asleep at all," she said. "Just dozing."

"And I didn't run away at all," he mimicked; "I just slipped off. But, isn't there something you want?"

"No." She moved on. "Good-night. I'm off to bed. It'll be a hard day to-morrow with customs and trunks. Good-night."

She was assured, but she would have given much to have been able to ask him questions. She could not; her pride forbade, that pride which Richard had accused her of more than once and which she had confessed to no one but herself and Richard. Obstinacy was a good name for it; so was independence and strong will and masterfulness. It was the quality that made her dominant wherever she moved and, at the same time, often mastered her and kept her from what she desired most. Having gone so far as the man's room in her fear, and having found, as she thought, that fear to have been groundless, she was too proud to admit her praiseworthy weakness.

Richard followed her down the corridor to a door that opened on the lower deck. "Good-night," he called after her softly. "Call again!"

She waved a hand lightly in recognition of his playfulness. But she did not go to her room. With confident step she ascended the tipping stairs and took her accustomed seat among the pillows.

The group had dispersed. Only Geraldine remained, crouched in her chair in the same position.

The mother hummed an air as she adjusted the pillows and rugs. Everything was all right. The unfortunate stoker or passenger, or whoever it was, was not Walter. So spoke the external Mrs. Wells, backed by a pride that never admits defeat. After all her interest in the two selves, the self of consciousness and the subliminal self of our deepest instincts and beliefs, Mrs. Wells did not know that all her assumption of serenity was a bit of acting. She really did not know. When the cry from within told her that no one but Richard could be the "big chap," the "blue-eyed chap," the "chap with the hearty laugh, who is always tramping the deck"; and that no one but Walter could correspond to that thick-voiced small man with the suggestion of an inebriate—when her strong instinct for the truth cried out to her she shut the door, would not listen, summoned her wishes and willed them to be the truth.

So she hummed, and appeared serene. Evidently, thought Geraldine, Richard has fibbed to her. Richard meant well, but it was man's mistaken chivalry to woman and to age. He did not know her mother. He did not know that her life had been a series of notable successes against hard conditions and that every success won by her will had made her invincible against opposition. And he did not know that with the successes had gone unspeakable blunders. After the event Mrs. Wells had often admitted frankly that she had been wrong, but always after the event. It took one year's failure of the grape crop to convince her, against every authority, that her spray mixture was faulty. It took the breaking of old Israel's leg to convince her that a certain nervous mare was dangerous. And so on and so on. Her answer always was, "We shall see"; and if anyone had had the courage to flaunt her with a list of the failures of judgment, she might have invited such a one to strike a balance of her successes. Six hundred acres of land, mostly under cultivation, besides interests in mortgages and shares in local wine companies—these had engaged her judgment also, and to show for it was what seemed on the surface to be a sound financial success.

"We shall see," the mother would say. Well, she must be shown. The only question was how to go about it.

"Mother," Geraldine began resolutely, "what are you going to do about Walter?"

"Aren't you well, my dear?"

"Yes, mother."

"You really look quite knocked out, Geraldine. Why don't you go to bed early to-night? You know we'll have a bad day to-morrow landing. You know what the New York customs is. I've had such a good nap this afternoon that I think I'll just sit here and moon. You go down, that's a good girl. I'll be dropping along soon."

"You haven't answered my question, mother."

"Eh? What question? I beg your pardon, dear."

"I asked you what you were going to do about Walter."

"My dear, you are obsessed about Walter. He's a care, I'll admit; and it's bad enough that I have to have him on my soul, but I do wish you would be happy and not concern yourself about him. Even I don't wish to have him in my mind all the time. When we get back to 'Red Jacket' I shall bring all the force of my will to bear upon him. I shall force him into good habits as I've done many a-time with a hunting dog. He'll 'charge' or 'heel' at my command."

"But he hates it, and he has threatened to do away with himself," the girl implored.

"Naturally he hates it. So does the dog; but he gets the right habits eventually and doesn't spoil the shooting by a lot of barking and prancing around. There's not a flaw in my theory, my dear. Of course, I am sorry we must do this. I don't like to treat my boy like a dog. But we must face the fact. He is a dog. He has got himself into the ditch; and we mustn't mind the mire—we must get him out. You wait in patience, my dear; we shall see."

That "we shall see" made Geraldine determined. To the great relief of the mother she seemed to drop the subject altogether.

"That man overboard," she suggested.

"Yes; horrible, wasn't it?"

"They say he deliberately threw himself over the side and struggled and fought against a rescue."

"Why should he do that?"

"He was trying to kill himself."

"Who says so!"

"Richard."

"What does Richard know about it?"

"Richard was the man who leaped over the side and held him until help came."

"Richard!"

"Yes."

"And the man who— —"

"That was Walter."

It was cruel, but was there any other way? Cruel and pitiful. In the July twilight Geraldine could see her mother age perceptibly. In a moment she seemed to shrink and fade and grow a shade greyer. The firm lines about her mouth loosened, giving her the look of genial senility. It happens often to those who have led rigid, muscle-tense lives; when they finally go, the result is not a gradual growth but a horrid transformation. Geraldine was frightened. She summoned help from the passengers about her and sent someone off for the doctor.

There was enough fighting spirit left in the aged mother to object to all this attempt to help her, but weakness finally conquered determination; she was forced to give in and let herself be put to bed.

CHAPTER X
THE FAITH OF A TREE

Early the next morning Mrs. Wells appeared as usual on deck and, with apparently the same imposing mien as of old, watched the docking of the S.S. *Victoria*. Externally she had altered little, but in a moment of conversation with her it was clear both to Geraldine and to Richard that she had "suffered a sea-change into something rich and strange." Had she packed her bags? Had she locked up the steamer-trunks, paid off the various stewards, arranged for the porterage of trunks in the hold? Not at all. Why should she bother about all that? What were husky young folks for? And what was age for if not to levy tribute upon youth?

Never before had she permitted anyone to do for her. Now she shifted to the other extreme. She would do nothing. And it was not at all unreasonable, she assured Geraldine. Nor was it weakness, but rather the result of strong decision. She willed now to have others take charge of things, she said.

And so she fooled herself into a pleasant attitude of mind. Indeed she joked about it. Sitting snugly in a deck-chair she watched Geraldine and Richard as they superintended the bringing of luggage to the surface and having it stacked properly, labelled and lettered.

"Now I shall begin to be appreciated," she announced cheerfully. Geraldine had dropped beside her, spent from the exertion. "When I did everything, nobody knew what it cost me. I could worry over every hair-pin, but nobody cared. That's because nobody knew the price I paid for their comfort. That was a mistake, I see. I did too much. Now I'm going to take a rest for awhile and collect. What a fool I was to slave the way I did! And the blessed relief, now that I've passed it over to you, Geraldine! I never remember feeling so lazy and comfortable and—beatific!"

No doubt it really was a blessed relief to give up the fight. Many dominant persons are like that; they spend three-quarters of their lives bullying their families into nervous servility, and suddenly plop down on the said families for the remaining one-quarter and invite themselves to be taken care of.

About Walter she said nothing. One never would think that only the evening before she had been literally struck down by the news of the horrible method Walter had taken to rid himself of her constant espionage. The shock had been terrific, for her confidence in the eternal rightness of her judgments had given her no preparation for the revelation when it came; but the very severity of the shock served a good purpose: it drove the whole incident into the depths of her mind. It was now something far away, a grief that distance and time had assuaged; something to be aware of, of course, to ponder over sadly, but whose sting was gone.

When Geraldine had told Richard of the graphic description of the struggle as related by the quiet Englishman, and then made clear the surprising manner in which Mrs. Wells had abdicated, he said it was quite normal so to act.

"Of course the shock did its work," he said. "It knocked her out completely. She may recover, but I doubt it. She has held a mild despotism for the strong years of her life. This is like a successful revolution breaking out against her. Otherwise she acts in quite a natural human way. In his lectures, James used to enjoy telling about these freak shifts of character. When we give up an ideal or an ambition it is really a great relief. Instead of disappointment we actually have happiness. James used to be fond of describing the lady of thirty-five who at nine-fifteen of a certain evening decides that she no longer cares to be thin. That will be her first night's perfect sleep. The struggle is over. She tosses the dietary to the winds, lets out her waistband, and takes to a rocking chair and sets loose the springs of laughter. Your mother, it seems to me, has been living on a strain; she really carried herself a notch or two above her strength. It will be a great joy to her to let down and be natural. I predict you will find her a much more agreeable companion after this."

For the present at least Richard's prediction was verified every hour. Instead of the semi-querulous person who checked off every article of personal belonging and bossed stewards, porters, and even customs officials, she walked down the gang-plank with only a slender handbag and cheerfully sat on a trunk and permitted Richard to superintend the irritating job of going through the customs. She offered no advice, but she was not slow to see the humour of the situation and to proffer broadly satiric suggestions to the workers.

Walter, too, was in splendid spirits, splendid for Walter. He tagged along with Richard and showed a sort of weak interest in the formalities of customs inspection. The fact that the mother had given her word that she would let him alone made the day seem to him like the first day of vacation. He was almost cheerful.

He followed Richard willingly enough because, he assured himself, he had that man in his power. An assumed name is not taken up without a lot back of it. And Richard permitted him to think so, even going so far as to take him aside more than once and have him pledge all over again his vow of secrecy. Walter, too, was fooling himself, pretending to himself that he was a clever man, but all the while he was mortally afraid of jail, and the unexpressed thought of it was the controlling power in his attachment to Richard. No one had ever suggested jail before. Like an irresponsible child he had always been allowed to work his little game for money. Of course they had scolded, but always they had let him off.

When Freneau had come along to help he discovered Richard in full charge of the Wells' affairs.

"You run along, Professor," Richard laughed him aside. "You've done your job, but I'm looking out for the two ladies and the boy now. No! I won't have you even find a customs man for me. I'm enjoying this. It's the first time I've ever really handled a family. I'm feeling delightfully domestic—a brand-new experience—and I want to get the last morsel of enjoyment out of it."

"Oh, very well," Freneau had agreed with his adversary quickly; "that will be a great help, and I will toddle off and see to the other members of the party. Thank you so much."

When all had been done that could be done the group sat about on trunks and bundles of rugs to await the heavier baggage, which was now being derricked out of the hold. Mrs. Wells on a pile of rugs spent the time chattering her farewells with the two other ladies who had made up the Freneau "party." Walter sprawled beside Richard on a trunk, and watched the derrick pull up trunk after trunk. Geraldine had found a more or less comfortable suitcase. They could see the heavy baggage as it was being lifted out of the hold. Richard had managed his trip on a commodious handbag, which he had not permitted to go below in the hold. It was Walter's job to watch for Wells' trunks, black with an enormous white "W."

A noisy insincere set of farewells were going off directly beside them. Richard and Geraldine exchanged glances which showed that they appreciated the banality of every effusive phrase.

"It's might cosy," she said, "to have you going right along with us to 'Red Jacket.'"

The quietness of her tone and the sincerity of her straightforward gaze was in contrast to the noisy group breaking up beside them. And she not only meant it to convey a contrast but a sign also that she had given up her disapproval of his coming along.

"You don't have to say that," he said; "I know it."

"How?"

"I sense it; you know I have cultivated all the senses in order to extract the last drop of elixir of life. I sensed you from the very beginning—not very well, I admit. I made some blunders there, but I got you essentially, nevertheless."

"Got me? Sensed me?" she smiled up at him. "Excuse me for being amused. You talk as if you were a hound and I—a pheasant!"

"I am a hound—I cavort around with my nose in the air, eager to search out things."

"But how did you sense me from the beginning?" she came back.

"I knew you were the kind of woman you have turned out to be. I did not judge you to be simply an astonishingly healthy animal—your health is uproarious; it shouts at one!—vivacious, gabbly, frothy——"

"Thank you; oh, thank you!"

"I thought you had a mind," he went on. "I sensed it. Your broad forehead showed it; the eyes wide apart and large; the way you held your head on your neck; the judgment and taste in your clothes; the inflection of your voice; your choice even of slang; your laugh; your frown; the care you spent on your body (no woman is better than her hair!); your forced volubility; your woman's smile which belied the girlish chatter—and so on and so on. That's what I call sensing you. Most persons go on words, but speech is of very little use in judging persons. That's why the legal witness-box is so absurd."

"I'm trying to think of that quotation—'Twelfth Night,' isn't it?—where Olivia gives an inventory of herself; item, one nose; item, two eyes; item, one mouth.... You gave me no impression you were taking an inventory of my charms. But you are right about words. I often mean the opposite of what I say."

"Yes! Speech is not natural. It's an acquired skill and a poor exponent of the self within. We are always being fooled by it; and yet words are causing all the trouble and misunderstanding in the world. We should be able to look beyond words. That's how I came to give up being insulted."

"How did you manage? I'm very sensitive to a snub."

"I got to looking beyond the words to the real person speaking. Do you remember Tittbottom's spectacles?"

"No."

"It's in *Prue and I.*"

"Never read it; thought it was sentimental."

"It is, but in a good sense. Tittbottom's spectacles are the best thing in it. He had only to put them on and he saw the inner-self of anyone on whom he looked. Well, I have cultivated the Tittbottom habit. I see the impatience, the illness, the ignorance, the misunderstanding, back of the words, and then I can't be hurt. Might as well be insulted because a leaf turns brown."

"I believe you would forgive a criminal for being bad!"

"Quite so. I would even forgive a good man for being good!"

The racket about them was most persistent: the rattling of hand-trucks, the bumping of trunks, the roaring conversation of hundreds of embarking passengers—more than one steamer had arrived that morning—and the shouts and whistles that gave direction to machinery. But the noise instead of interfering with the dialogue cut the two off from the rest of the world, isolated them, as it were, in their own private room with invisible walls.

"Well," she said, "whatever you are, I'm glad now that you are coming with us."

"I knew you wanted me to come with you to 'Red Jacket' even when you said you didn't."

"You 'sensed' right then. I did. But I was fearfully afraid of exposure. I am yet. That's why I'm going to ask you to be very nice to mother on the train, and then when you 'sense' the proper moment tell her the whole story of our trip to the top of the hill in Naples, your real name and everything."

"But——"

"Oh, you must. I can't stand the deception. You can do it beautifully. Make her laugh: I can't do that."

"Oh, very well. All right. If you wish it, but—Jove! I was enjoying my incognito! I've taken on a sort of new soul. All my instincts say to keep it."

He looked at her for permission to go on keeping it.

"No," she shook her head. "My instinct says, no."

At that moment Walter slid off the trunk and stared hard at a black trunk marked with a prodigious white letter, swirling around in mid-air. The letter turned out to be "M," but it took him a moment or two to decide.

"Jove!" Richard exclaimed again; "I must! It's part of the cure." He nodded towards Walter. "The only reason he listens to me is because he thinks I'm a bad man like himself. I'm travelling about under an *alias*," he lowered his voice; "he thinks he has me in his power. We talked it all over and swore each other to secrecy. He'll be talking about a percentage of the swag soon! Oh, it wouldn't do! We must leave things as they are. Don't you see my point?"

She did, but reluctantly. Walter came back to his perch before she could reply; and a banging trunk, turned end over end by the American system of porterage, stopped all conversation temporarily.

The incident at Naples was a trivial thing, now that she could look back upon it. Why had she not told the mother the whole episode, omitting nothing, on the very evening of the happening? Why had she feared to own up? Here was another of those "mental facts" which Richard was so curious about. Mother would have looked at her with mild disapproval and then, probably, would have laughed at the whole affair. But instead of being frank, Geraldine had been secretive; she had literally created a situation that had had no real existence. She had made a mountain out of a little Neapolitan mole-hill. The evil lay not in tripping off with an unintroduced male but in the careful and prolonged system of concealment. It is easy to see life in review; why cannot we be equally wise in the midst of events?

When she propounded this mental obtuseness to Richard he was full of illustrations to show how common is that human experience. But he was glad it had happened. It gave him a medley of new sensations; and here he was, finding his greatest adventure at the end of his adventure-seeking journey! Of that she was glad too, she said. And he was glad she was glad; for he admitted that he had become attached to the Wells family like a mongrel dog.

"First you are a hound and now you are a mongrel dog!"

"We're very much alike, dogs and us. The skeletons are strikingly similar—don't you think—especially when you set them up on end. Oh, we're near cousins! But I'm really mongrel. I go here and there. I have no fixed home. I attach myself to all sorts of persons, and—alas!—leave them for other persons. Like the mongrel, I go where my spirit moves me."

"You really are a sort of Quaker."

"Oh, I am very sensitive to the call of the Spirit—I spell it with a capital because I believe we're all part of the same mysterious Impulse—I spell that with a capital, too. We're like good microbes in the blood, working out our selfish ends, but all for the unknown glory of something greater of which we are the unconscious molecules."

She accused him of being a pantheist. He admitted it. Then she labelled him an old-school Presbyterian, but he admitted that.

"The main point in the old Bluestocking," he explained, "is that as God had arranged it all, why worry? They didn't always stick to the main point, because they were artistic creatures and loved the sensation of startling pictures—infants broiling for ever in hell, and the elect, who had done their darndest on earth, safe in heaven be-harped and be-winged with the fright of the pit still in their faces. But their main point is unassailable. You can't argue it away. Predestination? Why not? We are observers, merely: it is only an allusion that we act. I have no more choice in going along with you to 'Red Jacket' than I have in liking you immensely or being a biped or sitting on this trunk."

"Oh, we can do some things of our own free will."

"Name one."

"We can do what we want to do, certainly."

"That's all."

"Don't you ever do something you don't want to do?"

"Never; although I fool myself into thinking that I am making a decision. Do you think, for instance, that you could stand on that trunk and sing 'The Star-Spangled Banner' at the top of your lungs?"

She shuddered at the thought.

"I could if I wanted to."

"Ah! But you can't want to! I won't ask you to sing; but I defy you to *want* to.... There! You can't want to. It is predestined that you couldn't want to.... Now, what next am I?"

"Do you mean to say," Geraldine was intent on this old problem of free-will versus determinism; "do you mean to tell me that I cannot choose between, say, simpering at a man—like that fool of a girl over there—oh, she knows what she is doing, all right, and why she is doing it!—or being just myself?"

"I tell you simply that you cannot choose but be just yourself. Vain persons choose vanity; greedy persons choose to be greedy; simpering female adolescents"—he turned to look at the young girl who was flashing herself at the young man—"do their best to choose a healthy male. And Easter lilies choose to grow tall and slender and water chooses to run downhill. Oh, Presbyterianism is a great faith for an indolent chap like me— you cease to worry about the whirligig of time; you didn't make it nor set it agoing; and you can't direct it nor stop it. You leave it to the Maker and go about your blessed selfish business free of all responsibility."

"I don't believe you half believe all your beliefs."

At some hour in the day or week, he assured her, he believed many of them. He wobbled about a lot and had a good time wobbling. The only fixed belief he had was the belief that he should always be open to a new belief.

Walter leaped to his feet; he had discovered a Wells trunk, and was as delighted as a child.

"'At's one!" he shouted.

"One what?" Mrs. Wells was startled.

"Trunks!" cried Walter.

"Goodness! I thought it was a fire!"

"'Ere's 'nother!" cried Walter again. "'Ere they come. All of 'em!"

"Good work!" Richard slapped him on the back. "You're the boy! Now let's rustle up a stevedore and a customs gentleman and put them through."

Mrs. Wells had given Geraldine the family purse, and she in turn had passed it over to Richard. Like a veteran tourist-guide, he paid small duties, fee'd the draymen, arranged for expressage, called taxis, bought train tickets and established his party in the rear seats of an observation car. Not until they were speeding out of the Lackawanna Station did he realize that he had not telephoned Galloway. "Well," he thought, "he has my letter mailed on shipboard. He'll find us, all right."

Then a ridiculous thought seized him. He took a seat beside Geraldine and pulled from his pocket a thin wallet, the one he had shown her on that first day at Naples; from it he produced a solitary five-dollar bill.

"Look!" he waved it.

She did not comprehend until he had brought the family purse from another pocket and dangled the two before her.

"I've bought my ticket out of your money!" he cried. "Now wasn't that clever of me! I still have my five dollars to windward and good free meals ahead! Oh, it's a wonderful thing to have faith. The Lord will provide."

"Did you say 'faith' or 'nerve'?" Geraldine knew her man thoroughly now.

He looked at her with mock incredulity. "Woman," he said, "don't you know that to have faith requires the greatest nerve on earth? Nerve! Phew! Just you try to live in this world on faith alone. Then's when miracles begin to happen—they just have to!"

"I believe our part of the country will just suit you—the country you are now being predestined to on our predestined money."

"'Your reason, most excellent wench! Your exquisite reason!' That's almost Shakespeare; so it's all right."

"Penn Yan was first settled by a Quakeress, Jemimah Wilkinson, who called herself the Universal Friend. She believed in faith, just as you do——"

"All right; I'll be a Universal Friend, too."

"But she put her faith to a severe test," Geraldine continued; "she announced a day when she would walk on the waters of Lake Keuka as an exhibition to her many disciples. And when they had crowded the shores of the Lake and she had offered a silent prayer and walked to the water's edge, she turned to her followers and asked them to renew publicly their confession of faith in faith. As a test she asked them to assure her before she should step out on the surface of the water, that they had faith that she could do all she professed in the name of the Lord. They all had absolute faith, they cried. 'Then,' said Jemimah, 'I need not prove aught to ye who believe.' Having said, she turned from the Lake and went home."

"Good for Jemimah!" said Richard. "I wager she was a keen one. That was a bully rebuke to all that side-show crowd. But my faith is different. I don't ask for miracles, since every breath I draw is a miracle. I don't think about it at all. I have the faith of a dog——"

"What sort of a dog this time?"

The train spun suddenly around a curve, throwing him quite over against the lady.

"Almost a lap-dog," he laughed. "But I've been working that dog too much lately. So we'll change the figure. My faith is the faith of a tree."

"That's a very beautiful picture," she contemplated the thought, "the faith of a tree—I wish I had it. That's what gives you your serenity—just like a great, strong, shady tree."

He was pleased and told her he was pleased; and then defended himself from the charge of vanity by admitting it and proving from his favourite Whitman, not only the joy of vanity but the universal practice of it.

And so they "pow-wowed," as he called it, for many a mile. On shipboard it was Mrs. Wells and he who had displayed to each other the eloquent wares of their minds. Only once or twice had he and Geraldine talked together, and then but for short intervals. The strong-minded mother had seized on this man like a mental vampire. But after Walter's crazy adventure, the spring had gone out of her mind; it no longer snapped at ideas. On this journey she was content to doze in the chair car, or drowsily read.

Mrs. Wells had claimed the attention of Richard after the change of cars at Elmira which had broken into one bit of conversation begun on the observation-platform.

"We're going to have good times together at Keuka," Geraldine had said; "better times than you dream of. We have a big roomy place at 'Red Jacket,' with horses and good riding roads; we swim, canoe, tennis, and sail; there's fair trout fishing and a bully good summer climate. Later there is good pheasant shooting and fine skating. And we're absolutely secluded among the hills. I live in a bathing suit until October. You'll enjoy tramping over the hills; and you can be alone to your heart's desire."

"Oh, I'm going to like it! I sense it all." He pretended to sniff the joy in advance.

"Do you know what I like about you most of all?" she suddenly confessed.

"No! Tell me. My egotism needs feeding."

"You treat me like a human being."

"Well," he looked her over with great care, "aren't you?"

"You treat me like a human being, not like a woman."

"What's the difference?"

"I'm grateful because you don't seem to make any difference. I like to talk to men—some of them; they do so many interesting things. But all that I ever get is a lot of—fluttering. They won't talk to me as you do. They twitter and fly away."

"Birds of passage, eh?"

"Worse," she pondered, as if out of deep experience; "vultures."

"Exactly," he dropped the bantering tone; "I understand precisely what you mean. You're right; I'm not that sort. Do you know, I have a suspicion that I am sexless. I always treat women as if they were men.... But they won't have it that way," he shook his head ruefully, "even the old ones.

I'm tremendously interested in many women, but sooner or later they misunderstand my interest. Sooner or later they shame me to the core. Are my ears burning?"

"Yes."

"I thought so. The very remembrance is awful. Sooner or later they begin ... making eyes at me, or they write me outrageous confessions and then—I decamp! Of course I understand the law of the thing, and if I could reciprocate I suppose it would be all right and natural. Lord! I am interested only in their minds! You know Shakespeare advocated the 'marriage of true minds'; but I haven't found a woman yet who took to it for long.... I can't afford to marry.... I won't let the thought get in my mind. I have closed my life to the things that tie me. 'I celebrate myself' with good old Walt and decline to attach myself to anything. Detachment—that's the only means of happiness. One must be an observer, never a participant. That's the artist's point of view. With wife and children would come a sort of pleasant, altruistic slavery. Thank the Lord 'Jawn' Galloway is a gentleman—I never need fear that some day he will fall in love with me."

At this point the break in the journey had begun. For some unaccountable reason this speech had inflamed Geraldine with anger. It was seemingly so pointed, so carefully aimed at her. It was, as she took it, a notice in advance not to trespass; indeed a hint that inevitably she would trespass. Make eyes at him? Write him confessions? Egoist? Egotist, rather! The colossal vanity of the man! Well, she would show him. She would prove an exception to his experience. And so she fumed, but kept her outward calm.

As they stepped out of the train at Penn Yan and moved towards black George Alexander, who stood grinning and bowing before the door of the Wells' family carriage, she managed to draw Richard aside for a moment to say:

"You need have no fear, my dear charmer, about this woman. She has no intention of falling in love with you, exquisite sir."

The smile that came to his face puzzled her. His mild eyes seemed to be looking into her very "subliminal."

"How can you be sure?" he asked searchingly.

CHAPTER XI
TSHOTI-NON-DA-WAGA

Instantly Geraldine knew that she had blundered. The lesson of the value of silence she had not quite learned, although she was making strides. After two weeks of "non-committalishness," as Mrs. Wells had styled it, she had committed herself thoroughly. It was now the turn of her own ears to burn. During the late dinner and after she went to her room she flamed at the thought of her silly speech. And it was not as if the thing had come from her impromptu; she had thought it all out carefully; planned even the order of the words! With a phrase she would squelch this exquisite self-centred gentleman. In the silent rehearsal on the train the words appeared to have a smashing, annihilating power. It seemed almost too cruel to use them.... And their effect had been a comic confession of girlish inability to take a general discussion impersonally! In a smile and a look the man had accused her of laying her mind bare, of giving herself away by protesting too much.

In the morning the anger was gone, evaporated; chagrin and mild humiliation took its place. In that mood she met Richard at breakfast.

"I was outrageously angry with you last night," she confessed. They sat opposite. Mrs. Wells was too busy getting into domestic harness again to have even a subliminal ear open; and Walter, as usual, remained aloof.

"Yes," he appeared to have forgotten the cause; "so you were. Was it my fault?"

"I don't suppose it was anyone's fault," she replied; "that is, according to your view of things. It was like a gust of wind. It swept over me. I present it to your collection of interesting 'mental facts.' Your suggestion that all women eventually make eyes at you——"

"Oh, did I say that? Not all! It wouldn't be true to say all."

"Well, the majority of them, even the old ones, you said——"

"Oh, no; not all," he gazed out of the window towards a rolling view of the Lake several hundred feet below them, "for I distinctly remember a good old coloured cook who didn't.... But then I was only a child."

She laughed. "Last night I couldn't have seen the humour of anything. Do you know, Sir Richard, I could have struck you last night? If I had had my riding crop in my hand I would have lashed you across the face. Now, psychologist explain that brain storm, if you can."

He did not turn his head from the window. The scenery took all his eyes. In the darkness of the previous night he was aware that the carriage had been travelling up a considerable grade, but he was not prepared for this elevation of about four hundred feet above the level of the Lake. The house—the Southern mansion type—turned its four enormous Ionic columns half-way about so as to enjoy the vista down the blue Keuka and the far ridges of high, misty hills.

"How can you keep your eyes away from that wonderful view?" he asked.

"It is wonderful, isn't it?" She moved her chair. "And don't believe for a moment that I think lightly of it. I was born in the room just above this—my own room, now—and that view has coloured my whole life. Nothing in Europe was half so good to me, because *that*"—she threw a touch of a kiss to the Lake—"that is home."

"I quite understand you," he spoke appreciatively, "although I never had the sensation of home.... It must be thrilling ... to be able to come—home."

"You poor boy."

Curiosity about his possible past came over her. It was not the first time, but she withheld the question that rose to her mind. Besides, the mother was hovering near. And, besides again, he must not now be asked to tell anything, not while he was a guest in this house.

"I don't intend to exhibit 'Red Jacket' to you," she covered her exclamation quickly; "it must unfold itself. There are dozens of views, but you must come upon them unawares; and each has an inexhaustible pack of scenes—I am always discovering new ones. 'Red Jacket' is a crafty old Indian; he'll remain stolid and silent as stone until you are ready to commune with him. Those four great columns outside, for instance; they are never the same. At first you will glance at them and pass under, unless you wonder why they put such huge columns on a dwelling-house. Maybe you'll make the usual joke and ask if this is the post-office or the Carnegie library. You'll be here a long while before they grow big and you grow small; and then you'll pass them some moonlight night with a little reverence; and on stormy nights you'll be glad of them and feel, oh, so protected when you are safe inside."

She talked with a smiling casualness—hesitating here and there for a word—which took the eloquence out of the speech, but left all of the affection and all of the poetry.

"You are very dangerous," he spoke with decision abruptly. "Your song of home is stirring primitive instincts in me. Look out, or I may stick a bread knife in my belt and stalk down that long hill to the cottage I see at the edge of the Lake and run amuck among some good man's daughters. You are arousing my domestic instincts. Please don't force me to marry somebody in self-defence."

"What's this?" Mrs. Wells caught a word. "Marry in self-defence? What an ungracious remark, Richard. I trust, if you do marry, you'll marry for the good of your immortal soul. You know it isn't good for a man to be alone; therefore it is bad; and therefore, a lost soul."

She was recovering some of her old spirit. "Red Jacket" had done that. Since five o'clock she had been wandering in and out among her hardy perennials, and every blossom had given her courage. But the old vim and assurance was gone; only the external imitation remained. She looked almost as imposing and masterful as of old; but the aggressive force was no longer there. In its place had come a permanent yielding sweetness, a charming thing; and, better still, a long-belated sense of humour.

"Bravo!" cried Richard, "you are a theologian, Mrs. Wells. Any seminary would pass you, except possibly Union and Harvard Divinity; and they might, because they believe in everything. Jerry has been letting me into some of the secrets of 'Red Jacket.' It begins already to domesticate me. But I see that 'Red Jacket' has deep roots."

"You don't ask questions and bring us out," Mrs. Wells beamed at him. "'Red Jacket' was built by my grandfather. He came with his slaves from Virginia in 1818. George Alexander's great-grandmother was my grandfather's 'Mammy.' You'll find black folks all over this country who are the result of that migration. Grandfather Wells was a close friend of Red Jacket the Seneca Chief. Red Jacket—the Indian, not the house—was born just below us on the Lake; he was a friend of the whites, you know, and was most helpful in thwarting old Tecumseh. Grandfather was made a member of the Seneca tribe. We have a heap of mementoes of that in 'Grandfather's Room' upstairs."

"Really!" Richard's eyes widened. "When may I see them?"

"Wait, I'll get you the key." The mother was on the way when Geraldine interrupted.

"Now, mother, you're spoiling it. Don't let's get the key. Let it wait. I don't want to personally conduct Richard about like a Freneau party. Let him find out things for himself. If we tell him everything it will spoil the surprise."

The mother agreed reluctantly, and so did Richard.

"All right," he settled back. "I'm game. I hate to be told things. I do like to find them out for myself. May I go anywhere?"

"Yes," said Mrs. Wells; "only be careful of the under——"

"S-sh!" Jerry warned.

"Ah-ha!" Richard cried. "Mystery, plot and underground passages! I am in luck. And I do hope there's heaps of danger."

"Don't be too sure you've guessed," laughed Geraldine. "'Red Jacket' was one of the 'stations' of the Underground Railway which spirited negroes from the South. This was one of the last 'stations' before Canada. No! I won't tell you any more. You are free to go anywhere you please, but I wouldn't try to walk off Bluff Point after dark. It is only an eight-hundred foot drop to the Lake."

Richard elected to go first to the porch and sit in the guardianship of the four Ionic columns. The Lake is nearly a mile wide at this point and the view swept southeast over a lengthened vista of water and rolling vineyards.

"Would you like to be introduced?" Geraldine nodded towards the great columns, which shot straight up to the roof-trees. "The farthest one is 'Tshoti,' the second is 'Non,' the one to your left is 'Da,' and the last one is 'Waga.' Put together they say Tshoti-non-da-waga, 'People of the Mountains.' That is what the Seneca tribe call themselves, and here among the mountains they lived and ruled."

"My Indian history is rather shaky—but I'm eager to brush up," said Richard. "The Senecas were one of the Six Nations, weren't they?"

"Yes; they were the leaders of the Six Nations!"

She was standing as she spoke, gazing off far across the Lake. She was brown and broad-cheeked, as so many Virginians are. In that setting she took character; and her pride as she said, "They were the leaders of the Six Nations!" caused Richard to wonder. Great-grandfather Wells, friend of Chief Red Jacket, had been received into the Seneca tribe. Could it be a touch of Indian blood that gave the erect figure, the dark skin and the swart hair?

"Are you a Seneca maiden, I wonder?" he asked.

She turned swiftly and posed like a statue.

"You should see me in my birch canoe," she spoke after a second or two. "For your private joy I'll braid my hair in two thick plaits and put on a genuine Tshoti-non-da-waga costume out of 'Grandfather's Room.' Then you *will* wonder. Oh, my dear Sir Richard, you are not the only one to have mysterious pasts!"

Instantly he took up the jest—if it were a jest—and parodied Longfellow at her:

"Tell me, tell me, lovely maiden

Of the Tshoti-non-da-waga,

Do you still sneak up behind one

With a scalping-knife extended

For to—uh—lift one's curling ringlets?"

She was quick to answer in equally bad doggerel:

"No! nor does the lovely maiden

Of the Tshoti-non-da-waga——"

She stopped for a moment to get the next lines smooth, and then went on swiftly:

"Roll her eyes or fall in love with

Every thing that struts in trousers."

"Good shot!" he cried. "Hey, Walter!" Walter had lunged along after Richard. He seemed to enjoy being present, so long as he was not bothered. "Hey, Walter, what do you think of that for poetry? It's enough to make old Ralph Waldo Longfellow turn over with envy."

"Huh!" Walter sniffed in a very, very knowing way. "You're all right— you two!"

There was something almost sinister in his look. He had sized them up, it said.

"What do you mean?" Geraldine began to flame again.

"Jerry!" Richard caught her arm and pressed it significantly.

"Oh, I'm on!" Walter snapped. "Go to it, you two. It's all right. It's *all* right, I tell you. I don't care. I'm no squealer, I tell you. Go ahead; on'y no use puttin' up no bluff with me."

In a moment Jerry was standing before him, her eyes blazing. She was about to seize Walter and shake him. But Richard followed quickly and put his arm completely about her shoulders and held her to him.

"There now, Jerry," he soothed. "Of *course* Walter's on. Why shouldn't he be? He's a good sport, and he might as well be in this, too. I'll have no secrets from Walter. I tell him everything. It's the only way to treat pards— —" Richard's pressure on her arm was telling her to join in the stratagem, that it was the only thing to do; but it took her several bewildering seconds before she comprehended. Then she made amends; her dramatic instinct came to the fore, and she laughed softly.

"Walter, you're a keen one," she nodded towards him, and slowly disengaged herself from Richard's grip. "You've got the mind of a— —"

"Tshoti-non-da-waga," Richard put in quickly for fear she would spoil all with a too ironic figure.

"Well, that's not what I was going to say," she considered, "but it will do."... She moved briskly to re-enter the house. "Prowl around, Richard. I've a duty or two in the house and then let's all go down to the Lake. I'm keen for a swim in real water."

"But Walter doesn't swim," Richard objected. She stopped at the doorway. Geraldine was not always considerate of Walter, but Richard remembered that the care of Walter was his chief claim to "Red Jacket."

"Never mind me," Walter crouched in his chair sullenly.

"Haven't you a boat?" Richard turned to the boy.

"No!" he growled. "Can't have nothin' 'round here."

"Mother would not hear of owning a sail-boat," Geraldine explained; "we've always had to go passenger on somebody else's."

"Who owns that sloop over there?" he asked.

"That's George Alexander's. And it isn't a sloop," corrected Geraldine; "it's a cat-boat."

"Well, let's confiscate it for Walter."

Walter looked up with interest. His "pard" had the right spirit. Alone the boy would not have had courage, but the big man's blue eye spoke a determination that was contagious.

"All right," said Walter, and got on his feet.

"I'll make it up with Mrs. Wells," Richard explained. "Walter's got to have a boat, a real boat—what do you call them—class something or other?"

"Class A scows."

"That's it. We are going to have one, Walt, if I have to crib the money somewhere. But for the present you fix up that 'cat' down there and let her go. If you don't come home alive, I'll break the news to the home folks. Go along, old boy." Geraldine had gone into the house. "And when you get back, feeling just right for it, we'll have a little nip, eh? Just a teeny one—or maybe two teeny ones, eh? When we changed cars at Elmira I blew myself— Jerry's money; good joke!—for a quart of something guaranteed all pure food."

"I know," said Walter, and added, "saw it in your room this morning."

"Did you! Good! Well, go to it, old man; and don't forget to work up a proper thirst."

Walter grinned and sauntered down the hill. He understood. It was a bribe to keep him quiet. Oh, that Richard Richard was a smart one, a good fellow to keep next to! He wasn't straight with others, but what did Walter care? Something crooked about this Richard Richard—too glib and good-looking to be anything but crooked—but Walter was done with good people. He was a bad man and Richard was his sort. All right. He would not squeal, but he would have to get his "divvy." That's all he cared about. So long as they let him alone and gave him his share, they could make off with the whole shooting match.... Nice little revenge on mother, too; she thought herself so smart, and now she was being taken in all right.... Go to jail, eh? He wondered if Richard Richard was clever enough to keep out of jail. He hoped so. He would never "squeal." As far as Walter was concerned there'd be no killing of golden-egg geese.

From the porch Richard could see the boy—in spite of his twenty-two years one could think of him only as a boy—as he stumbled slowly down the hill, disappeared for a few minutes in a growth of striking Lombardy poplar on the very water's edge, and pushed out in a tender to George Alexander's cat-boat. He watched the tender made fast to the floating buoy, saw the sail go creaking up, fill and send the boat like a live thing out towards Bluff Point and the main branch of the Lake.

Lake Keuka—Keuka is Seneca for "crooked"—is shaped like a bent-over "Y" with Penn Yan at the right-hand upper tip, "Red Jacket" at the left and Bluff Point protruding into the stem. From the porch Richard could see the whole length of the left-hand branch of the Y and a mile or so on to the farther shore of the "stem." It was a soul-filling sight; but he had room enough left in his soul to consider Walter and to begin the perfecting of a plan for getting him on his feet, first physically and then mentally.

He was in the midst of what looked like splendid strategy when Geraldine appeared dressed for a swim. She wore an easy-fitting suit which stopped at the knees, a brown stuff—like taffeta silk, guessed Richard, it being the only silk he knew by name except *crêpe de Chine*; and as it melted down into brown stockings and brown moccasins and up into a brown band about the hair, Jerry stood revealed an Indian princess. That is what he told her—that and other things—after he had recovered from the delight of looking at her. He said all this in the presence of Mrs. Wells, who had come out under the shelter of Tshoti and his three sentinels to take an enforced rest in a "rocker."

"Your bathing suit, Richard, is down at 'Lombardy,'" said Jerry, "just back of that row of Lombardy poplars, Mrs. Norris' cottage. She keeps extra suits for us and lets us track our wet feet all over her house. Mrs. Norris is a gem and a saint; if you don't worship her we'll all hate you, won't we, mother?"

"Oh, yes, indeed," mother rocked away. "Phœbe Norris is a saint, if there ever was one on earth. She lived ten years with a crazy husband, took care of him and kept him easy in his mind until he fortunately died for her. And now she lives for others. She rents her vineyard out on half-shares, which gives her all she wants in this world."

"So she spends her time preparing for the next?" Richard queried.

"Oh, she's not that kind of saint!" Both women laughed at the thought. "She's——"

"Mother!" admonished Geraldine. "Please let Richard discover us properly. You are for ever guide-booking him. Phœbe Norris could never be explained with words."

"Quite true, my dear," the mother smiled at the thought, "quite true.... It does my soul good to get into an American 'rocker' at last." She shifted the topic easily; and then shifted again at the vision of Jerry before her, one of the many signs of the change that had come over her. "Isn't it strange, Richard, that my girl should be the athlete and my boy should not even be able to swim?"

"Why should he need to swim?" Richard had laid his plan and went resolutely to put it into execution. "Very few sailors can swim. Walter's a born sailor. Do you know that you are going to buy him a boat and let him lift the Lake cup?"

"Eh?" she turned to this confident man with a touch of her old resentment towards being managed. "I said he should never own a boat or sail it alone until——"

"Of course you did," Richard interrupted, glancing down upon the Lake where Walter was plainly coming about on his second tack. "We all say a lot of foolish things. And now you're going to buy him one and let him employ that mind of his. If you don't," he raised his voice to drown the beginning of a protest, "you will send him to the devil as certain as if you had signed his commission. Weak as he is, he's got your Virginia determination; and when he goes to the devil it will be on the gallop. I know; for I am a strong man, but he almost succeeded in breaking down my grip on the rope rail on the *Victoria*—all by sheer will, too—and if he had——"

Mrs. Wells ceased rocking. She looked helplessly at Richard, mutely begging him not again to force that picture into her mind.

"Well," he spoke calmly, "you are going to give up, aren't you—for the sake of that boy?"

Walter had broken a tack suddenly in the middle of the Lake, obviously to take quick advantage of a change of wind.

"Yes—I suppose so."

"Good! Now let's go the whole way forward. Not only are you going to let him have the boat, but you are going to tell him so—without a word about the past; just as if the matter had never come up before—and you are going to give him the money so that he may buy it himself."

She protested faintly that that would only be tempting him.

"It's a risk, I admit," Richard agreed. "I'll be frank; we run a chance. But my conviction is that what that boy needs first is our faith in him. I have a bottle of whisky in my room, put there purposely to see if he would keep his word with me. He told me he wouldn't touch it except when I—well, uh, he said he wouldn't touch it. I had faith and put the stuff right out in the open; went off and left him alone with it. Not a drop touched!... You will do this, won't you?... It's part of my plan to put him on his feet."

The splotch of white, Walter's sail, was growing increasingly smaller; evidently he was making for the narrows which led into the main body of water.

Yes, she would do as he suggested, although it went against the grain to give in.

"Of course it does," he cheered her; "we're all built that way, but, let me tell you, the joy you will experience in giving up will compensate you for life. Blessed are those who occasionally give in, for they shall inherit the joy of living."

They left Mrs. Wells silent and stationary on the porch. Down the driveway and across the State Road Jerry marched on silently. She was disturbed more than she wished to express. So she kept slightly in advance of the man and started ahead. He had achieved his little victory so easily, but he had no conception of what that surrender revealed to the daughter. She had never before seen her mother so weak, so mentally benumbed. Who in the past would have dared accost her as this guest had jauntily done? The sharp satiric tongue would have withered him; he would have been struck in a dozen vital spots before he had half been aware of any attack at all; and the indescribable "manner"—poise, bearing, what you will—would have quelled him.

But this worried woman on the porch had seemed eager to give up and get rid of a vexing gentleman. There was something very pitiful in the contrast and it filled Jerry with foreboding. She stopped as she crossed the State Road and looked back. Mrs. Wells had begun slowly to rock; soon she was going her regular pace, a sign, Richard hoped, that she had cast upon him all her burdens. Farther down the hill they could see her bobbing forward and back between the massive stolidity of "Da" and "Waga."

Concerning her mother Jerry could not bring herself to speak aloud; nor would she disclose in feature or tone any hint of her fear. There were other things on her mind, however, which could properly be brought forth to the light of familiar conversation.

"We've been interrupted horribly lately," she began. "If it keeps up I'll be irritated and show my claws at you again."

"I see you have claws;" but his eyes were on the steep road.

"I blow up," she admitted.... "If I had struck you last night it would have hurt, and I should have meant it to hurt; but the moment after I should have been terrifically sorry. Why should I have flared up so, I wonder?"

It was the traditional female attitude, probably, he suggested, carefully keeping from the suggestion made to her at the time that her vehement protest of independence was the sure sign of the beginning of dependence; the female bristles most and kills less, because, he supposed, they grow angry for protection and not as hunters. Traditional female attitude and also the common human sensitiveness to words. He need not tell her what he thought of that. She was insulted again! Always permitting herself to be insulted. Even the gods should not be able to insult via words. But humans like to be insulted. She protested. He insisted; it feeds their pride, he said, and arouses their combativeness, both great human delights. Every human and every nation is eager to be insulted; it's the hard job in life not to insult them.

Well, perhaps. But he had been so irritatingly calm; so serene; so confident of his ability to charm.

But why not be confident if one does charm?

Who is proud now?

Not he! No more proud of his ability to charm than he is of his ability to eat an omelette. Why should one be proud of so universal a quality? Look about you, he adjured her, at the successful matings—he did not mean marriages. The dog's-meat man is fondling the hand of the cook with the scraggly hair! "Beefy face and grubby hand!" Men kill one another for the veriest drabs of women, and women grow desperate with jealousy over the blankest of males. Everyone has charm; the Lord knows why he distributed it so generally.

"Mawnin', M's Geraldine!" a happy, shining darkey plumped at them from among the grapes.

"Good-morning, Bolivar," she waved a hand.

"Mawnin', M's Geraldine!" called a voice a little below on the other side of the road. Through the corn another black head peeped out.

"Good-morning, Saul."

There were several other "Good-mawnin's," to each of which Geraldine responded with the name of the black salutatorian.

At table and near the house Richard had noted the coming and going of many negroes. Mrs. Wells had said that nearly one hundred years ago her grandfather Wells had brought his slaves with him from Virginia. In that time there must have been much marrying and giving in marriage. Had the progeny of this prolific race stayed on at "Red Jacket"? It seemed so. He was about to ask her, but her mind was tenaciously on her flare-up of the night before. With the greatest attempt at tactfulness she was trying to show him how lightly she had conceived the matter—she would cure her blunder of speech by more speech!

"Well, you made me angry, and I showed my claws. I'm glad I didn't scratch, because it is all over now and I am not in the least angry with you."

"You must be angry with me often," he talked and slid along the pebbly incline; "it's a sign of affection. I believe the Serbian word for darling is almost the same as 'I'll strangle you.' Loving and strangling are very close together. I don't know why. The two electric currents are charged, I suppose, and the slightest contact starts a flash and a shock."

"But I was angry with Walter, too," she said, "a few moments ago, when he made that absurd suggestion about us. And here we are combining for his good—not our own."

There were many things he might have said here. He had his own opinion of the cause of her anger, but he did not care to broach it. Was she going to make eyes at him after all, and hardly before he had got settled in this beautiful place? He did not care to leave just yet.

He decided to avoid the dangerous topic, over which she fluttered with such obvious interest.

Mrs. Phœbe Norris was not at home, but her house was open to the four winds. In a neat little room Richard found bathing suits of many sizes, and managed to discover a fitting combination of upper and nether garments.

A whir and a splash told him that Geraldine had taken her plunge and was throwing herself about in joyous abandon. Out of his window he soon saw her, going at a swift pace, hand over hand, a splendid "crawl" stroke.

The sight gave him a quick thrill. Here, too, was a swimmer, not a dabbler in pools, but possibly one who could do a long journey with him. It was pleasant to swim for miles alone; but it would be a new and rare experience to troll along with a companion. He hurried his preparation in anticipation.

She was swimming past the floating dock when he prepared to dive.

"Come on!" she challenged, and struck out into the Lake.

He dived and followed. Both were using the long side-stroke, and after several minutes there seemed to be no diminution of the space between them. As she swung her head from side to side she would look back occasionally and smile at him tantalizingly.

"Come on!" she seemed to say; "if you can."

As they got out beyond the shore trees she noticed about a mile away the white spot of Walter's sail coming down towards them before a light breeze, and altered her direction and made towards it.

CHAPTER XII
SAINT PHŒBE

The sun was shining pleasantly over Bluff Point, and the temperature of the water was absolutely neutral to the swimmers. It was glorious swimming, thought Richard. He was enjoying it and he knew that Jerry was equally happy. As they drew near the boat—Walter had seen them and had trimmed his sail to meet them—he lengthened his stroke. Instantly Jerry lengthened hers. The space between them had not changed a foot. He wondered if she could hold the new stroke, a slow but powerful overhand; but his wonder increased as she held it without effort. There was not a splash or an ungainly movement in her swing. When he slackened for fear of pushing her too hard, she imitated instantly. It was as if she had determined exactly how much distance should be between them.

Walter brought the little boat into the wind with such expertness that Geraldine had but to reach out her hand for the stern. There she waited triumphantly for Richard. She counted with satisfaction the fifteen long swings which represented the amount of her victory.

As he reached up beside her and caught the edge of the boat she waited for him to congratulate her. She was an exceptional swimmer, and he had just found it out. This time she would not blunder by speech.

But his eye was upon Walter. "Good work, old man!" he exulted. "You turned that boat about with the precision of a Dutch watchmaker. That's what I call skill!"

Walter laughed, the excited laugh of a boy pleased with an earned compliment. It was his second laugh in Richard's remembrance, the first genuinely hearty one.

Jerry clambered into the boat. Richard followed. Walter eased the mainsail and went on his course towards the dock.

"Bully good work!" Richard went on. "You've certainly got the number of this skiff, all right!"

The two swimmers had gone forward, where they lounged and rested in the full warmth of the sun. Walter sat by the tiller, one hand controlling the mainsheet, ridiculously proud.

"Thirsty?" Richard called back.

"Sure. And hungry, too. Puts an edge on you, this does!"

Hungry! That was a fine sign.

"Well," Geraldine was forced to bring up the topic, "I beat you."

"Oh," he affected great surprise, "were you racing?"

"Good sport, you are," she smiled ironically. "Own up; you tried to overtake me, and I wouldn't let you. I saw you lengthen out and then let up. I've been waiting for this ever since you boasted that you could swim. I had lots more left, and in a spurt I can 'crawl' like an express train."

"Knew she'd win," Walter nodded proudly. "She's beat all the men 'round here. That's what scares 'em off. She always asks 'em to go swimmin', an' 'en she makes 'em look sick.... Can't blame the fellows for scarin' off."

That was a long speech from Walter. Richard rested and reflected on it. This boy was no hopeless case. It was just a question of letting him lead a natural healthy life, he thought. But Geraldine, full of her victory, rejoiced that she had humbled the big man into silence. Was he wrinkling his face on account of the sun, or was it sullenness?

"You wanted to win," he answered her thought quietly.

"Naturally. A woman likes to beat a man, occasionally. That's the latest female sport."

"Why should anyone want to win?" he asked.

"Pooh! Philosophy!" She would not let him take her victory up into the empyrean where it would disappear into insignificance. That was the way of these clever argumentative chaps. After they slap you in the face, they cry loftily, "Think of all the millions of years that are gone and are to come, and what matters a little slap!" The answer is to slap back, a little harder—twice, if you can get it in—and echo, "Aye! Mere dust on the wing of eternity!" He had tried to overhaul her; she knew he had tried; he gave up because she was the better swimmer. "Pooh! Philosophy!" she ejaculated. "Let's be practical for once."

"Philosophy is always practical; philosophy is simply trying to think straight, even against our best wishes. It is disinterested and terribly curious. So when I ask, 'Why should anyone want to win?' I am disinterested and tremendously curious. Do you really know?"

In her own case she knew exactly. The calmness of this man had begun to irritate; he was so sure of himself; he could not be disturbed. She wished to humble him, to drag him out of his secure serenity. Few men can stand a beating from a woman. She hoped to punish him a little by winning. All this she knew, but she said:

"Instinct, I suppose. I never inquire about instinct. Might as well ask why we eat; the answer is, because we're hungry. Why are we hungry? Because we need food. Why do we need food? Instinct!"

"A philosopher come to judgment!" he laughed. "You reason exactly like a philosopher. The average man does not bring up at that answer; he says, 'I am hungry because I am a wonderful creature, the exceptional thing in the universe—I have an appetite!' Haven't you noticed the pride people take in their appetites? When philosophy tells you it is a common instinct over which we have no control, it is very helpful and very practical. It saves us from a deal of comic pride."

"You have no instinct to win, I suppose?" she taunted him.

"No," he replied thoughtfully; "that's why I am a failure."

Some of her throbbing aggressiveness slipped away from her at this speech. She remembered the deck scene on the *Victoria* when she had listened to Richard's announcement of his occupation as "professional guest" helped out by occasionally acting as "assistant widow."

"It would be much better for me," he went on, "as the world judges values, at least—if I could want to win. But I can't want to. You see, I am an individualist—I obey my own law. All the world is eager to win; I find that I am not. Fortunately for me there is plenty of chance for the fellow who doesn't care about getting ahead of some other fellow. There is practically no competition. He has a kind of monopoly!"

"Everybody wants to win," Walter contributed determinedly. "Racing, now—what's the good of racing if nobody wanted to win?"

"One could enjoy the race, striving to the utmost, without wanting either to win or lose."

"Can't see it," said Walter.

"The struggle is the thing—not the result. The result is with the gods, but no one can take from you the delight of contesting all your powers. Then there is a joy in giving up to others, an exquisite joy which few people seem to practise.... Yet Christ taught it."

"Like Phœbe Norris," suggested Walter.

"Ah, the saint!" Richard remembered.

"She's a young woman," Jerry explained, "only twenty-eight, yet she gave the ten best years of her life to an insane husband. He went out of his mind while they were half-engaged to be married. Phœbe insisted upon the ceremony. Talk about giving! Yet Phœbe is the cheerfullest red-head in Jerusalem township."

"'Tain't so red," Walter objected.

"Oh, it's a torch!" Jerry laughed.

"Well! Well!" Richard showed interest. "Saint Phœbe attracts me mightily.... I thought she was an old woman."

"She ought to be, considering the sacrifice she has made of her life—but she isn't; not by a jugful. Wait till you see her!"

"I don't need to see her," Richard stretched himself out more comfortably. "It is enough to know that you who know her know nothing about her. Sacrifice? Why, you talk of sacrifice like a Quaker paying a bill.... I wager that Phœbe Norris is no saint at all. She's had the finest time of her young life, that's all—doing the most selfish act in her character—giving up to others."

Objections came from both ends of the boat, Walter's suspiciously vehement.

"Listen, my children, and you shall hear true philosophy," Richard broke in. "For some persons the only joy is having and holding; for a rare few the only joy is giving. Find out what a man wants, the givers say, and give it to him quickly. But first want nothing yourself—or want everything equally. If he covets your watch, give it to him; you can tell time by the sun and by the stars; or better still, do without knowing the time at all. 'Give all thou hast to the poor,' the poor devils who cry so loudly for the baubles and gewgaws."

Sailing before the wind is like not sailing at all. Wind and ship are in perfect balance. Except for the swish of water flowing by, the sensation is of standing still. Suddenly the silence was broken by a rapid flapping of the sheet. Walter swung the tiller over and pushed the boom out with his foot and held it there steadily.

"What's up?" Richard inquired languidly. He was enjoying the rest and the sun and openly drank in the sensation of living.

"Dead," explained Walter, referring to the abrupt failure of the wind.

"Dead? Good!" murmured Richard, stretching himself full length. "O Death, where is thy sting?"

The wind had not died out completely; there was just enough breeze short of a complete calm to pilot the boat by inches and enable Walter to tack squarely off towards the farther shore.

"Hadn't we better get in?" Jerry inquired.

"Sure!" grinned Walter; "wind over there."

Richard shaded his eyes.

"How do you know?" he asked. The unrippled water seemed everywhere.

"Always is, with clouds going that way," he pointed overhead.

"But there's no sign on the surface. Seems just as dead as here."

"You'll see."

In a few moments wind struck the top of the sail. A fair breeze seemed to be floating along four to five feet above the water. Soon Walter came about and tacked straight for the dock. A good sailful was his all the way.

"Magic!" Richard cried as they sped along through the glassy water.

"Wind-pocket," grunted Walter. "Comes off the hill, I guess. This Lake's full of them. Got to know 'em if you want to do any racin'."

Was this a good time to tell Walter about his mother's change of mind on the subject of the ownership of a "Class A" boat? It seemed so. Richard was turning over in his mind the proper phrase to use—one had to be cautious, for the very mention of the word mother might easily drive all that eagerness out of the boy's face—when Jerry harked back.

"We're always having half-conversations," she said. "I like to finish things; get 'em over and off your mind."

"Get it off, then."

"You think you let me win?"

"Can't tell," he drawled lazily; "haven't tried to race you yet."

"When will you? This afternoon?"

"Let's wait."

"I like to get things done."

"Better put it off," he advised, "you've a better chance if you get into trim. You can't jump at these long swims without tuning up for them. You've been out of the water for several months— —"

"I swam in the Seine three weeks ago."

"You mean in the shore baths?"

"No; in the river."

"In the July races?"

"Yes."

"Glory be to Peter! Did you win?"

"Fifth place—out of forty-two entrants."

She exhibited the edge of her bathing suit, whereon was sewn a tiny silk badge showing that Jerry had entered as a member of the "Club du Siècle" and that she had achieved fifth place.

"Did mother——" he began.

"Not till it was all over; I had hard enough trouble bribing my way into that 'Club du Siècle.'"

"Jove!" he exclaimed; "you unfold beautifully! You don't show yourself all at once. It's just like a magnificent strange flower coming out of the bud. I must make a new set of judgments on you every little while."

He ignored Walter, although the little boat threw them close together. Jerry gave a significant glance towards the boy, but Richard would not have it.

"He's all right" he laughed aloud. "Walter is on; he might as well hear everything."

Walter leered at them knowingly.

"It makes my flesh creep," said Jerry. Walter's simple brain had no translation of that speech, but Richard understood. Walter's dark statement of the morning that these two before him were merely clandestine philanderers had irritated the woman almost into blows; and even yet, when she understood that this mentally ill-balanced brother of hers had to be humoured, the low interpretation put upon the very wholesome and natural relationship between Jerry and Richard was nauseating. It was the knowing leer that made her flesh creep; and, of course, Richard understood.

"It is necessary, I fear," said he appealingly.

"I understand. Go on; I'll try to get used to it.... You were saying something sweetly pretty about me which I shouldn't want to miss for anything. You were comparing me to a budding sunflower, I think."

"A sunflower, yes; provided one had never seen a sunflower," he explained. "In a flash I understand something about you which has puzzled me heretofore. You know, I began by analyzing you—on the hill at Naples."

"Yes; you told me I had the deportment of an octogenarian and the language of an infant."

"Precisely," he grinned; "since which time you have improved wonderfully. But that's not my point just now. Now I understand why you flared up so when I suggested that all women eventually made eyes at me."

"Oh, dear!" she affected boredom; "why are you always bringing up that topic?"

It was the first time he had brought it up; in fact he had been all morning diplomatically diverting the lady from just that topic. But he made no remark about this characteristic feminine disavowal of facts.

"Because I have just discovered why you were angry——"

"I was angry, angry enough to strike you, because without waiting to find out what sort of a woman I was you hinted that before long I'd be—— Well, sir"—a little flash of her old anger came back—"I am not the sort to make eyes at anyone or write anyone letters of confession!"

"I believe you!" he agreed, so firmly that she knew he was speaking from conviction. "And that's why you interest me."

He didn't know why at first, he said. Deep within the "subliminal" the reason of his interest was hidden. She had giggled and spluttered like an over-grown child, he told her. (Thank you, she said.) Kid-women he had never taken any stock in—those that gabbled without thinking or whined like spoiled babies, or substituted flippancy for conversation. Indeed, at the very start on the starboard rail of the *Victoria* she had exhibited all the female qualities that ordinarily sent him flying; but he was interested from the beginning. Always he trusts his interests, not his reason; reason is only useful in analyzing what is already done; his "interest" led him to ignore the personality number one which she presented at the starboard rail. Result: Keuka and personalities numbers two, three, four and five!

She listened contentedly. There is no glow warmer than that which comes on being understood!

"Of *course* you wouldn't go soft like all the others!" he announced. "I treated you like a man, and you responded like a man. You have the point of view of a man and the physique of a man. The arms fool one," he looked critically at her rounded arms. "One forgets that muscles don't show on a woman. It's the feminine layer of fat that all the magazine doctors have been talking about lately; but the muscles are there. That silk medal tells me that, even if I didn't know," he made a wry face, "from experience."

By this time all her resentment had vanished, had oozed beautifully away. She had lost even her desire to beat him in a swimming match. While Walter was making the dock, she confessed some of her athletic abilities, one of which was long-distance walking. They would swim across the Lake, take early morning canters. He chimed in like an old comrade. They would do stunts together! Meanwhile, he reminded her, they had responsibilities with Walter.

That youth brought his little boat around, fished up the mooring float and dropped his sail almost in the same act. Then he clambered into the tender and got ready to row ashore. A queer impish look was fluttering over his face; his mind seemed on the point of expressing something. Once or twice he opened his mouth, but thought better of it and pulled a stroke or two. Encouraged by the slight distance, he rested on his oars.

"You two can swim in if you want to," he announced; "or you can go below!" When one considers that George Alexander's cat-boat had not so much as a cabin on it, this was a stupendous jest from Walter. The two swimmers were appalled at the unexpectedness of the witticism, but they were bowled over by the remark that followed. "Do what yuh please, you two. That 'cat' won't squeal!"

Then he pulled sturdily away.

"It's a joke!" cried Richard.

"I bet it is!" echoed Jerry.

"He's alive! Any man who can make a jest is still alive!" he exulted.

"I don't know," Jerry shook her head. "It sounded uncanny to me. That's the first sign of humour I've seen from Walter for a 'coon's age.' Even when he's drunk he's surly. I'm afraid it means the breaking up of what mind he has."

"Don't you think he is improving?" he asked.

"Wonderfully. He talked two or three consecutive sentences out there on the Lake. It gave me quite a shock to see him so garrulous. And then, this joke——"

"Don't you think this would be a good time to tell him about his boat?"

"Perhaps."

"You don't seem much interested."

"I hate to discourage you," she shook her head; "but Walter is no good."

"Oh, don't say that."

"He's better now, I'll admit. But you should have seen him when he has been drinking for a week. Ugh! The very smell of him is piggish and loathsome! He is twenty-two years old, and he hasn't done a stroke of work all his life."

"Neither have I, and I am older by a decade."

"I don't think you always tell the truth about yourself." Her quiet tone searched him. She seemed suddenly to peer into the privacy of his mind, and to discount all his gay philosophy.

"You are right," he answered soberly; "I don't."

This was Richard's nearest approach to moodiness. Troublous thoughts showed on his face.

"I try to be honest," he turned to her.

"I believe you," she replied sympathetically.

He thought for awhile. "I talk everything out," he explained. "It annoys folks, I see."

"I like it."

"I know you do."

"Even when it is just silly." She would not let him feel too secure!

"That's what I most fear, that all my honesty is leading me to no honesty at all." He was too absorbed in himself to notice her gibe. "Sometimes I wish I could foresee the future and gather what my life really means after all. Deep within me I feel there is a tremendous change coming. I feel almost like a caterpillar grub just before he bursts into a butterfly. All my philosophizing may be just caterpillar-views; I'll laugh at it all when I take my first winging flight across the hills. Don't take my sayings too seriously."

"Gracious! When have I ever done that?"

"Good point!" He recognized the hit. "Let's get back to Walter. He's not hopeless. Didn't you see the way he manœuvered that boat? Didn't you notice his eyes? The first signs of intelligence I have seen in them. He was interested in that boat and vain as a rooster when we flattered him. Given interest in something decent, with a little vanity, and anybody can be saved. Let's swim in and break the news to him. I'm awfully hopeful."

"Walter's lazy beyond belief," she said as they swam.

"So am I," he admitted promptly, "and proud of it! 'Lazy' is a much-abused word. In a world of work it has got a bad name. But it is the ideal of all workers, after all—the state they save and strive for."

Walter was sitting on Phœbe Norris' little porch, which overlooked the water. Now that the trip was finished he seemed to slump into despondency. His jaw dropped and his eye took on the stare of an idiot. Certainly he looked a hopeless case.

Richard took a rocker beside him. Jerry stood back and watched.

"Can't get over that wind-pocket," Richard tried to stir him into mental wakefulness. "Still looks like magic to me."

Walter's face became animated. He had cat-boated all over the upper part of the Lake, he told Richard, ever since he was big enough to steal away from home. He knew a lot about that Lake that the other fellows did not know. Upon being pressed for further information, he said that he had sailed with the two best skippers on the Lake, Captain Fagner and Captain Tyler, but he could tell them a thing or two. Tyler was a careful man; he knew the Lake pretty well, but he took few chances; sailed a steady race and often won through sheer sticking to it. Fagner was more daring; he broke all the rules—split tacks when there seemed to be no good reason; dared shallow water when the sail was full; declined to reef until the stick began to pull out the back stays, and won often through sheer pluck. But there were some things about the Lake that neither man knew.

"Good!" cried Richard; "when you get your own boat, Captain Wells, we'll make those fellows hump themselves."

At that the light gleamed a moment in Walter's eyes, and then went out.

"Wouldn't you like to be your own skipper on a regular Class A boat?" Richard asked.

"Sure," Walter mumbled; "but," he jerked his head toward "Red Jacket," "what's the use of talkin'?"

"None whatever!" agreed Richard. "We're beyond the talking stage, old boy. Mrs. Wells is going to stake you for a real boat."

The idea did not get into the boy's head. He rose unsteadily and said, "When are yuh goin' up?" meaning "When am I going to get my promised drink?"

"But you are really going to get a yacht, Walter," Jerry told him. "Mother said so, this morning."

Jerry had been astonished at the intelligence Walter had exhibited in his story of the two skippers. The kind, somewhat grim Walter she used to know had appeared fleetingly on his face. She began for the first time to have hope that this disgrace upon the family would disappear. She, too, had to change her opinion of persons; the value of Richard's plan for the regeneration of this youngster began to appear.

Walter sat down, frankly disturbed.

"She s-said so, did she?" he asked incredulously.

"Yes!" Jerry cried enthusiastically. "Richard got her to promise. How soon can we get one?"

Nervousness seized him. He turned to speak, but stuttered and stopped.

"They're made in Wisconsin, aren't they?" she asked.

He nodded.

"We'll telegraph," Richard suggested. "Perhaps they have some already built."

Walter shook his head. They waited for him to get control of his voice.

"Fag—Fagner," he managed, "has one, new one, ordered. Said—said this spring he'd let me have it."

"Good!" cried Richard. "Where is it now?"

"On the w-way," Walter stuttered. "Saw him last night in Penn Yan. S-said it was on the w-way." He took a brace and went on more smoothly. "Said it had won races out there. Said I could have the *Moodiks* if I wanted it; could have my choice."

Jerry explained, "The *Moodiks* is probably the fastest boat on the Lake."

"Gave you your choice, did he? Well! He's a real sportsman, now, isn't he?"

"He—he's all right," nodded Walter. "Ev—everybody's fair 'n' square up here."

There was a certain tilt to his head and an odd look at Richard that both he and Jerry noticed.

"All right, Walt," Richard spoke softly. "Got you your boat, didn't I?"

"Sure," but he shook his head doubtfully.

With the steadiest gait Walter had shown in many a day he trudged up the hill.

"He seems to suspect you of something," said Jerry.

"Poor boy!" He watched the retreating figure.

"Why should Walter suspect you of anything?" she asked.

He turned to her inquiringly.

"You don't, do you?"

She hesitated; he laughed.

"No!" she spoke quickly. "You misinterpreted me. Only—Walter's tone seemed so—significant of——"

"Has Walter's tone always been significant of anything?"

"Oh, forget it," she spoke hurriedly. "Go in and get dressed. I'll wait for you."

"All right," he said quietly.

An unaccountable suspicion took possession of her—unaccountable because Walter's brain was not worth a burnt sulphur match, and any thoughts he might have should be laughed at. But for the moment he had seemed so sane—just like his old self—steady and dignified. He seemed to be warning Richard. And Walter was her brother—pshaw! but an idiot of a brother. Still.... After all, what did she know about this Richard Richard? Not even his name. Clever? Undoubtedly, but the cleverness that has employed itself often before and knows all the answers. Might he not be a clever impostor trying to gull two country women and a half-witted boy?

Appearances were all in his favour; but swindlers were no longer the villainous-looking desperadoes of the old melodrama. Certainly he was different from any man she had ever known—but then she had known only good men.

Then she thought—it came to her in a stunning flash—of the scene on the stern of the *Victoria*, the two men swaying up and down on that slanting iron deck; and remorse seized her. When Richard came out, she went swiftly towards him and held out her hands. He took them inquiringly.

"Forgive me, my dear," she smiled up at him, sure that the endearing term would recall their domestic playette at the top of the hill back of Naples.

"For what?"

"For suspecting you of being a villain," she smiled.

"What made you suspect?"

"Walter must have got on my nerves," she explained. "You see, I really don't know anything about you, and you *are* peculiar, and I had no experience with villains; and so putting nothing and nothing together I was trying to make a total.... Well! What are you puzzling over? We're even, that's all."

"How, pray?"

"Didn't you suspect me of being a flirt?"

He disengaged her hands carefully.

"And still do," he spoke gravely.

"You *are* a villain." She jokingly struck at him.

"I admit it." He caught her hands and warded off the blow. "All good-looking women are unwitting flirts, and all men are potential villains—the one beckons and the other—doesn't the classic song indicate that it is the villain who ever pursues her?"

"Villain?" cried a hearty voice from within the Norris cottage. "Who's tryin' to play villain on my front lawn?" A magnificent head of red hair parted the curtains that served for door and mosquito protectors. "Jerry!" cried Phœbe, "you angel-child! Come over here and hug me! Who's your young man?" she asked as the two young women rocked together. "Do I—or do I not—hug him too?"

Richard opened his arms.

"Decide, O angel-child. Quick, decide!" he cried.

Jerry emerged laughing from Phœbe's strenuous embrace.

"No!" she decided.

"Pshaw!" cried Richard.

"Don't it beat all?" echoed Phœbe, with a fine imitation of a disappointed damsel.

CHAPTER XIII
THE HOME FOR INDIGENT DRAKES

"Well, if I can't hug him," Phœbe resigned herself briskly, "tell me his name and let me get acquainted as quick as possible. Although I think you make a mistake, Jerry darling, not to let me hug him and get over with it. He's the most willin'-lookin' creature I ever clapped eyes on, and I'm sure we'd be both enjoyin' an innocent bit of lovin'. And mebbe if we had it out now right before your eyes we'd have done with it and not go hankerin' after it behind your back." Her rapid-fire tongue gave no one a chance. But, meanwhile, as she talked she pushed chairs out and arranged comfortable cushions. "There! Sit ye down and tell me all about it. What's his name and where did you find him? Here! Sit here! I'll half turn my back on him, he's that temptin'. Why don't some of you be talkin' and not make me do all the entertainin'?"

"Isn't she a wonder?" cried Jerry to Richard. "Look out! She's always up to mischief when she begins dropping her 'g's.'"

Red-head she was, and eyes of absolute blue; and her lips curved in perpetual merriment.

"Saint Phœbe!" ejaculated Richard.

"The same," she agreed. "Me halo's in the wash. But be quiet, young man, until you're introduced. I'm a respectable widow, and awful seductive—I mean, susceptible. Ach! Don't look at me that way like a Gibson pen-and-ink sketch! Do you want me to be eatin' out o' your hand?"

She turned her chair and faced Jerry.

"Who is the handsome creature?" she asked pathetically; "and how did he ever get out of his picture frame?"

"Mrs. Norris," Jerry took up the spirit of the game, "may I make known Mr. Richard, Mr. Richard Richard?"

"Is that his name?" she asked without turning around, "or are you stuttering from nervousness?"

"His name is Mr. Richard Richard."

Phœbe looked over her shoulder at him incredulously.

"That's not a name," said she; "it's the chorus of a song. Do you mean to say your last name's Richard?"

"I do."

"And you say your first name's Richard, too?"

"I do."

"You talk like a wedding."

"I do."

"Your middle name isn't by chance Richard, is it?"

"I tried to have it that way," he explained, "but— —"

"The family voted you down, I suppose."

"Exactly. You see, Mrs. Norris— —"

"Drat Mrs. Norris!" she interrupted. "A man with only front names can't have any advantages over me. You'll call me Phœbe, young man, as everybody else does. You don't suppose I'm goin' to delay our intimacy by Misterin' you, do you?" She turned abruptly to Jerry. "Just what claims have you on this beautiful person, Jerry? I want to know at once. The look of him sets me all a-flutter."

"None whatever," laughed Jerry. "But don't make him any vainer, Phœbe. He's stuffed with pride as it is."

"Ach!" Phœbe tossed her head. "I'll take that out of him. My method is to puff him full of flattery till he explodes—feed him till he's sick of it."

"If flattery be the food of love, play on," cried Richard.

And so they joked and grew acquainted. Amid interruptions and laughter Jerry managed to piece out an explanation of her meeting with Richard, of Mrs. Wells' interest in him, and of Richard's plans for the saving of Walter.

"Poor lad!" Phœbe grew serious. "Walter spent the night out on this porch just before you sailed. He had got hold of a quart of whisky somehow and was beginning on it, but I wheedled it out of him. He was going to toss it into the Lake, but I tried other tactics on him. I told him to put it on that shelf up there." She pointed to a small projection near the roof of her small cottage. A brown bottle obviously three-quarters full was in ample view. "I told him that he must fight the devil a stand-up fight. He slept out here all night, and there it is—just as he left it."

Phœbe might have told more; but she did not. She was the garrulous sort, the old "sanguine type," who keep their own counsel in the midst of much chattering. She might have told of Walter's maudlin love-makings; of his fierce attempts to force Phœbe Norris to run off and marry him; and of her struggles to keep him from slipping completely into the wallow. It would have made a great difference in the theories of both Mrs. Wells and of Richard if they could have known this side of the boy. And it would have been another blow to the mother if she had realized that it was the expert management of Phœbe Norris that had kept the boy straight during his journey abroad, and that the two lapses, in London and on the steamer, were brought on by the irritating surveillance of the mother.

Richard was tremendously interested. He probed Phœbe with questions, but she turned them off adroitly. When he persisted in asking her where she got her knowledge of how to treat Walter she explained frankly.

"You see," she said, "I have served my trade as an expert attendant upon twisted-minded folks. Perhaps they have told you, Richard Richard, that Seth, my husband, was out of his mind the larger part of ten years. I was his wife as far as the ceremony goes, but, as everyone knows, I was really only his hired nurse."

"I beg your pardon," he apologized. "Believe me, I did not mean to probe you——"

"Shucks!" she tossed her head. "There's not a thing to be fussy about. Seth was just a man with a child's brain. The real Seth, the one I knew, died before I married him; so I took care of the boy Seth—if you understand me—gave him his food, bathed him and put him to bed. When he was too violent I threatened him with a whip. I struck him only once—when he gave me that." She pulled down the collar of her gown and showed part of a livid scar. "He always remembered that whiplash and was a good doggie ever after. Of course I had to watch him when he got into his fits; but I have had less trouble with bulldogs. Poor old Seth, I got to be almost fond of him; but he was just a faithful two-legged animal; there's nothing to be sensitive about."

Again, this was not the whole story, as everyone knew. Seth Norris had changed from a fine young grape farmer into a violent crafty brute. Phœbe had mastered him with the whip, but she had been forced to barb-wire a considerable enclosure to keep the lunatic from doing damage to others. She had made a comfortable house for him away from her own dwelling, and there he lived and roamed about within the limits of the barbed fence in the finest kind of savage contentment. But there were wild nights when she had no sleep, and there was more than one struggle before she was sure of her physical mastery. And yet, except for the scar, which did not show, she bore not the slightest evidence of her gruesome experience.

"I'm a widow at twenty-eight, with land of my own and income enough to buy the winter praties." She struck an attitude out of *Monte Cristo* and exclaimed, "'The world is mine!'"

"You must have married young?" Richard persisted.

"Eighteen," she said. "Seth died this spring. You don't suppose I'd wear black, do you? Lord love you! I 'phoned up all the neighbours when he— —"

"She's just trying to shock you, Richard. Don't believe her," interrupted Jerry.

"Shut up, hussy. And I tried to inveigle them to come to a wake, but they all had previous engagements."

"You're Irish!" Richard guessed.

"Young man," Phœbe eyed him, "you are too smart for these parts. You remind me of the wisdom of our chief-of-police Casey. A German tourist-party motored into Penn Yan one afternoon and interrogated Casey. The German said, 'Bleeze, I sprech not Englisch. Mine name ist Schmidt. Bleeze, *who* is Elm Street?' And Casey looked hard at him and exclaimed, 'By Golly, you're a Dutchman!' Irish? Of course I'm Irish— —"

"Oh, you'll enjoy 'Jawn,'" exclaimed Richard.

"Mebbe," said she. "Wait. I'm Irish and I'm English and I'm Scotch and the Lord knows what else. How do you expect to keep a strain pure in this country where everybody pens up together and eats out of the same dish? It's hard enough to keep the feathers off the legs of my white Orpingtons and get any kind of ribbon at the Yates county fair."

"She's strong on chickens, Richard," said Jerry. "Look out! She's awful touchy on white Orpingtons!"

"And so would you be if you paid good money for the pure stock, penned them in until they couldn't breathe, and then watched them grow all kinds of things on their legs, things that are not in the books. I've only got six clean-legged hens out of a batch of forty. It gives me the jumps every time I see a dandelion thistle blow by. Pfitt! Is that one?... Well, what are you laughing at?"

She had made such a delicious face as she grabbed an imaginary thistle that laughter was compulsory.

"Sure, and isn't it the wind that carries the pollen and spoils your best flowers by mixin' 'em— —"

Jerry screamed at the thought, and covered her face.

"It's hardly the accepted theory!" roared Richard.

"Well!" Phœbe kept a serious face; "what I'd like to know is, *what* put the bad fuzz on my Orpingtons' legs? Anyhow, I kill every dandelion I see before they get bloomin' and gallivantin' about."

"Oh, you're Irish, O.K.," cried Richard when he had recovered. "Deliciously Irish."

"Didn't I tell you you'd love her?" exulted Jerry, drying her eyes.

"I fear I shall," said Richard gallantly.

"Fear is the word, me lad," said Phœbe. "For Seth's 'pen' is still there for the next one, and the barb-wire, too. It worked so well with himself that I couldn't be content with any other system. And the whip's on the rack within easy reach. So count your beads carefully, Richard Richard, and pray to be delivered from Phœbe Norris."

"It would just suit him," said Jerry. "He's a professional loafer. He'd just enjoy being fed and bathed and put to bed."

"Oh!" said she. "He's that sort, is he! Then I'm doomed. They're the kind that get on my soft spot. All the derelicts in Jerusalem township find my door somehow, and they know I can't resist them. Well, each man to his trade, I suppose. Whenever you're ready, Richard Richard, trot into the pen. Shove the door to; it locks itself."

On other topics Phœbe was serious enough; but the moment the subject touched herself she lifted it to rollicking nonsense. So before they left she spoke a quiet word or two to Richard.

"I'm interested in Walter," she said. "Some day I want to know what you are doing with him."

He sketched his plan briefly.

"And I want your opinion, too," he added eagerly. "You can be a great help, I feel sure."

"Do you think so? I don't"

"Why?"

She pondered for a moment and then shook her head.

"I'm telling nothing. I don't want to put things into your head. Let me hear what you can do first. He's a good boy. It seems a shame to have him go to the bad."

"Do you think he will come out all right?"

"I don't know."

"You don't think he's done for, do you?"

"I don't know."

"But you believe there's a chance, don't you?"

"Y-es," she admitted reluctantly. "There's a chance to save him."

"Tell me about it." She said nothing. "Please, do. It may help wonderfully. I must get clues everywhere."

"I'll tell you this much," she came to a decision. "You go on with your theory of boats and racing and all that. You may succeed. Lord knows I hope so. If you fail, come to me. I have a theory, too— —"

"Why not try yours first?"

"No—oh, no!" she protested. "It wouldn't work that way. If you fail— then I'll try my medicine. And the best of luck to you, Richard Richard."

The moaning yelp of a dog on the scent broke into the conversation.

"That's 'Count'!" said Jerry. "He's after me. Someone must have let him loose." The baying broke forth near at hand. There was a terrific swish of nearby bushes, then a huge liver-and-white pointer nosed into the cottage and leaped upon Jerry, whining and talking frantically. She had to beat him down.

"Charge!" she called again before he dropped at her feet and half chewed at her moccasins.

"Why, I believe the pup is crying," said Phœbe. It seemed so. His brown eyes looked pathetically tearful.

Jerry knelt beside him, stroked his head, talked baby-talk to him and let him take her wrist in his big mouth.

"I'm ashamed of myself, Count," she purred; "I never went out to see you after all these weeks away. Poor old faithful doggie! did he think his muzzer had left him for good and keeps?"

At the kinder tones he crawled nearer and nearer and thumped his long tail joyously on the floor; then he leaped to his feet and tugged at her short skirt, saying plainly, "Come along home. I'm afraid you'll get away again."

"I'll have to go," Jerry shook her head. "My baby wants me. Look how he trembles. He just suffers when I'm away; and here I went and forgot all about him. You faithful old brute, you make me ashamed."

She moved out towards the road.

"Are you coming up now, Richard, or do you want to stay longer and get acquainted with Phœbe?"

Richard was about to speak, but Phœbe forestalled him.

"Take him with you, Jerry," she called. "I'm afraid to be left alone with the man. He has a greedy look. If he finds out, somehow, that I admire him, the Lord knows what he might be tempted to do to me—kiss my hand, probably. Oh, them innocent blue eyes!" she fell purposely into the colloquial grammar. "And by the holy cross of Saint Michael, if it isn't blushin' he is! Take him away! I'll be liftin' him into me lap and singin' him sleepy songs if you leave him here!"

With much more chatter of the sort, broken into by replies in the same spirit, Phœbe drove them out.

She stood laughing in the doorway until road trees hid them; then her face relaxed into uncanny thoughtfulness. There she stood for some minutes gazing ahead at nothing at all, and twisting Seth Norris' gold band around and around her wedding finger.

Slowly she turned and walked into her garden to the side farthest from the Lake. A rustic one-and-a-half story building was before her. The windows were numerous but small, exactly arranged so that a man's body could not squeeze out. Almost anyone would have taken the hut for an imitation log cabin, but a closer view would show that it was built of genuine logs, huge, heavy fellows that could stand an Indian siege or, better still, do service as a frontier lock-up.

She unchained the door and stepped inside. It was a pleasant clean-swept interior. The articles of furniture were massive, in keeping with the general architecture, and all were fastened securely.

A farm helper was cradling oats in the field beside her. When he saw Phœbe's company depart he had gone on to the end of his row and then came over the stile into the garden. He found Mrs. Norris looking thoughtfully about the log hut.

"I could move the hull thing easy enough," he took up the conversation where they had left it a little while before; "and saw the winders out bigger and put a porch on this end. The only question is——"

"I've changed my mind, Henry," she interrupted.

"Hey?"

"I think I'll let it stand where it is for awhile."

"Y'll leave it stand, hey?"

"Yes."

"You don't want any winders cut, the way y' said?"

"No, Henry, thank you."

He laughed softly.

"Make a nice rabbit hutch," he suggested. He knew that Phœbe was too good a gardener to love rabbits.

"No doubt." Her mind was not on the man before her.

"Or perhaps," Henry was quite ready for a resting "spell"; cradling oats is not a sinecure. "Or perhaps," he speculated more seriously, "you're thinkin' o' raisin' guineas; they say they's heaps o' money in guineas."

Phœbe became suddenly aware of Henry.

"No, Henry, not guineas—nothing so useful and domesticated and industrious as guineas. Breathe it not to others, Henry; I shall keep this place as a home for indigent drakes who have lost their pia mater. But keep it dark, Henry."

"Hey?" called Henry, to whom all this was dark enough at the outset. But she had vanished into the house; and he knew enough of the sting of her Celtic tongue not to delay longer on the oats.

The next morning at breakfast Mrs. Wells capitulated handsomely.

"Walter," she smiled towards him beautifully, "Richard has won your hard-hearted old mother over. You shall have a yacht, the kind you want, to do with as you please. I just won't get used to the fact that you are grown up. All mothers are that way, I suppose. So you run along and buy yourself one and win some of those races the *Chronicle's* always talking about. And you can climb up after peak halyards or birds'-nests or whatever you want! Geraldine will make you out a cheque. She's in full charge of the money now."

"But, mother——" objected Geraldine, to whom the new office was a sudden and unexpected promotion.

Mrs. Wells laughed almost boisterously—a most unusual performance. Small things had begun to amuse her out of all proportion to their entertaining powers.

"No 'buts,' my child," she began before Geraldine could voice a further protest. "You've just been elected, and I've resigned—or the other way about. I've plumped everything on the library table—deeds, bills, mortgages, cheque-books, stock, everything. Look them over at your leisure, child. Study them out. You'll begin to appreciate the work your mother's done for you— —"

"But I do, mother! I do!" Geraldine protested. "Of course, if you wish I'll— —"

"Tut! tut! child!" she soothed; "don't get frightened. I'll sign things when you bring them to me. But I find I need a rest. Little things annoy me. I want to get free. You don't know how jolly I felt the moment I came to that resolution. Really," she puffed a little, "I am perceptibly growing stouter! Expect any minute to see the hooks and eyes start from their roots!"

Here the laughter verged into happy tears.

Many sobering things had happened to Jerry recently, but none more serious than this. It was the sudden abdication of a beneficent monarch, and therefore, to the crown princess, unbelievable. But it was something more: it was a strong mother cut down by the swift approach of old age. Some of the old fear of the dominant woman lingered in Jerry's attitude—it never quite left her—but it was mingled now with pity. Those puffy cheeks and the simper were ghastly when one thought of the past years of firm dignity. And a patch of pure white had appeared beside the grey of her temples.

Almost as abruptly as the mother had put off her responsibilities Jerry took them up. As the older woman had grown child-like, the younger woman had matured. But Geraldine Wells had always been older in thought than she ever had expressed in word or action; and now she quietly assumed her proper years. Richard had had a large share in that transforming, but the pitiful picture of the smiling, contented mother had hastened the process.

Richard was intent upon Walter; as much as he could he diverted the boy's attention from the extraordinary transfer of authority just being promulgated so carelessly. It was a great relief to see that Walter's interest was in the forthcoming yacht, and not at all in the change of management of the estate.

Richard got him to tell all over again the fine offer of Captain Fagner.

"Got a name for it yet?" Richard had then asked.

"Sure!" Walter spoke up guiltily.

"Have you! What'll you call her?"

"Sago-ye-wat-ha."

"Goodness, man, what's that? It sounds like a curse."

Jerry had finished the conversation with the mother by this time.

"That's Red Jacket's name in the Seneca language," she explained. "Red Jacket was a wonderful orator, perhaps the greatest Indian orator known in history. Sago-ye-wat-ha means 'He keeps them awake.' Pretty clever name for a good talker, isn't it?"

"Splendid!" agreed Richard. "And a bully name for a racing yacht. 'She keeps them awake'! Good! Here's hoping that she also puts them all to sleep!"

Mrs. Wells, as usual, had her coffee served on the terrace. Walter was soon making for the Norris cottage. He half explained as he left that he was going to sail round the Point in the "cat" and see Fagner about the new boat. Walter had no money for trolley fare; and he was never a youngster to take much to horses.

"This financial business has unnerved me," Jerry confessed when they were alone. "It was a shock."

"You'll love it," Richard commented shrewdly.

"Oh, that's all right," she corrected his view-point. "I'm crazy to get into it. I'm not lazy like you. What worries me is mother. She's getting sleek and fat and silly-minded. Did you see the way she laughed? Like a foolish old woman.... She's ill. That collapse on the boat meant more than we thought, I fear. I think I'll have Dr. Sampson drop in for a call. He's the only man about here who can manage her and prescribe for her without her ever being aware of it. Dr. Sampson can laugh a bone into setting properly, and over the telephone, too!"

"Those Sampsons could always do wonders with bones," he joked; "remember the historic jaw-bone?"

He told her not to worry about Mrs. Wells, that she was going through a very natural transformation. The old will show age. Jerry must get used to the fact that her mother was sixty years old in years but nearly eighty in performance. No doubt the shock had done its part in making the change abrupt, but there was nothing alarming. The point was, he insisted, to take her at her word before she became querulous—age is not at all consistent; and further, he suggested that she should see the family lawyer and have papers made giving Geraldine complete control of everything.

"Why, how absurd!" she began, but he pointed out to her the consequences to Walter of having an estate on his hands.

"Do you suppose for one minute that you could control him?" he asked.

That sobered her.

"I am not thinking of your mother's death," he assured her. "She is the type that lives on into a long peaceful dotage. But I am thinking seriously of what she might rise up some morning and do, just as she did this morning. She might hand over the whole thing to Walter, or present him with a dangerous sum of money."

"That's very true," Jerry agreed. "After this morning I'll believe anything of her."

"See your lawyer without delay," he repeated. "There is such a thing as 'power of attorney,' I think they call it. It gives you authority over everything without having the mother relinquish her title to anything."

"But she can always withdraw such papers—I know that much law."

"To be sure," Richard explained; "but lawyers know how to delay. What we want to stave off is any sudden on-the-minute decision."

Jerry agreed that the idea was a good one. For her own gain she would not have lifted a finger, but always Walter was forcing decisions.

"I'm really growing enthusiastic over Walter," she remarked abruptly. "He has picked up wonderfully. Doesn't it strike you as odd that mother's complete surrender and Walter's change have come about at the same time?"

"Not at all. It agrees with my theory; and whoever heard a man going against his own theory? Mrs. Wells had a sort of mental strangle-hold on Walter's mind. I believe that she clutched his mind and held it as literally as she could have held his wrist. When she gave up, he was set free. That's not only my theory, but it's the belief of 'Jawn' Galloway. Wait till you see him! He'll make it clear to you. He's coming, you know."

"Oh, is he? No; I didn't know. Did mother invite him?"

"Jove!" Richard remembered. "I wrote him that I was about to ask her; but I clean forgot it. But we can't expect him for several days yet. There'll be plenty of time to break the news that she has invited 'Jawn' up; and when she sees 'Jawn' she'll rejoice. I'm dying to see Phœbe and 'Jawn' get together. They're a pair of Irish comedians.... But I've good news for you. Walter declined his nip last night."

"What do you mean?"

He explained to her his system, backed up by the authority of the ship doctor, of permitting a small drink a day to keep down the agonies of thirst.

"Walter refused?" She was incredulous and happy.

"Absolutely!" cried Richard. "Said he would have to cut that out now. He said a skipper would have to keep himself pretty straight if he wanted to show in a race against men like Fagner and Tyler. Isn't it glorious?"

"Glorious?" echoed Jerry, her eyes shining. "It's—it's uncanny."

CHAPTER XIV
"JAWN"

It took a long part of the morning for Walter's "cat" to arrive at Fagner's dock. The skipper was in Penn Yan, he was told, at the N. Y. C. tracks, unloading his new yacht. So more time elapsed before Walter was able to sail into the Lake "outlet," tie up, and saunter over to the scene. Willing helpers enough were eager to assist in setting the mast, fastening the stays, adjusting this and that preparatory to dropping her into the Lake. Walter stood by, too shy to let them know that the boat was his own.

Finally, just as the last heave dropped her into the water, where she floated like the proverbial cork, Fagner noticed Walter.

"We're getting your boat ready for you," he chaffed. He had not the faintest notion that the boy's talk at various times was based on anything substantial. He had joined in with Walter's scheme out of sympathy and good nature. Walter's whole life and future were an open book to that locality. "Or would you rather have the *Moodiks*?"

"This 'un suits me," Walter remarked. "Whe' 're the sails?"

"They'll be along later; ordered new ones from Boston, and they had trouble with a strike down there."

Except for the sails the yacht was complete. The group on the dock stood off and admired while Fagner tuned up his motor-boat and arranged a tow-line; but meanwhile Walter had hauled George Alexander's cat-boat alongside and was fastening his own tow-line.

"Goin' to take him up, Walt?" someone asked. Unknown to Walter it had been a town joke among the men that Walter Wells, who never had a cent, had offered to buy a yacht. Fagner's offer to sell had been made in public, but the spirit of the offer was equally well known.

"Sure!" said Walter.

The operation caught Fagner's eye, but before he could say a word Walter dumbfounded him by remarking, "Jerry'll send yuh a cheque, soon as you tell her how much."

Fagner said nothing, but moved off quickly in search of a telephone. His smile reassured the crowd, who began to see now that this was business after all. They gazed at Walter solemnly, for business is no joking matter.

At the other end of the telephone Jerry assured the skipper that the option on his new yacht was being taken up seriously. He came hurriedly back.

"You really mean to take me up, Walter?" he asked.

"Sure; unless you've changed your mind?"

Walter stopped fumbling with his sailor knots and straightened up. The crowd looked on expectantly.

"Oh, no!" Fagner laughed. "I'm game! I said I'd do it, and I will! But," he added half to himself, "this is certainly one on me." Aloud he asked, "Are you sure you don't want the *Moodiks*?"

"Nope," said Walter, bending to his rope again.

"Well, let me tow you down with my motor?"

"Nope," said Walter. "I'll tow her myself."

In a few minutes more the little "cat" was heading down the Lake with the new yacht in tow.

"What's the matter?" someone asked Fagner. "You look as if you'd lost something."

"Oh, no," laughed Fagner. "I've only just been 'called' with four mixed diamonds and one black card."

"Didn't you want to sell to the boy?" asked one of his workmen, a good old fellow to whom one could be confidential.

"What!" cried Fagner. "Want to sell that?" He pointed to the beautiful fragile craft which a moment or two before had been his. It was following the "cat" as if it had no weight at all. "Absolutely not! That little beauty is the fastest sailing boat in America. Do you see the way she glides? That boat slips over the water like a skimming stone. But she'll have to be skippered," he smiled grimly. "After he loses a few races I'll buy her back. I agreed to sell him either boat, provided he would skipper it himself, and provided also that he would give me an option on a resell. I think I'm safe—although I feel just now like a kid that has had his candy snatched out of his hand."

Jerry, in the meantime, was busy with the documents piled up on the library table. There had been order about them once, but it took time to discover which were out of date and which still operative. Careful memoranda on slips of cardboard were helpful here and there, but it would require reading packets of correspondence before all the matters could be cleared up; and George Alexander would have to be interviewed. George Alexander had had complete charge of the house and farm end of things during the trip abroad.

This left Richard to his own devices. For a time he made quick friends with "Count"—pointers are not very discriminating. Then with the dog "heeling" beautifully, he marched down the hill to take a swim. Phœbe Norris was sewing on her water-front porch.

"I came down for a swim if I——"

"Prevaricator!" she remarked pleasantly.

"Jove! You're right," he exclaimed. "It's you I'm after comin' to see! There's heaps I want to tell you."

"Sit down," she jabbed a needle at a chair, "and get it off your chest."

He told her about Walter from the time of his first acquaintance with him in the smoker of the *Victoria*—omitting, of course, the real facts about his own change of name—up to the latest incident of the refusal of his daily "nip." Then he related the astonishing transformation in Mrs. Wells, her sudden taking on of the privileges of age, ending with her placing Jerry in charge of the Wells finances.

"The Wells seem prosperous," he half inquired.

"They are," Phœbe answered; "they have six hundred acres, mostly under cultivation. The vineyards are especially profitable. The negroes under George Alexander manage the place excellently. Besides, they have a lot of money invested in mortgages and wine stocks. It's a perfectly safe investment, young man. Don't be afraid to commit yourself."

Phœbe Norris was notoriously direct, but the point seemed to slip by Richard.

"Then there's all the more reason for Jerry to get legal control."

"And why, pray?"

He explained the danger that might suddenly loom up with the transfer of the property to Walter.

"You are tremendously interested in Walter. You're not thinking of marryin' Walter, are you?"

"Jove, no! I'm not thinking of marrying anybody. What has that to do with the case?"

"You seem to be sensible enough," she looked at him critically. "But," she sighed, "you never can tell. Lots of times you would have sworn, now, that Seth was as whole-minded as that sleepin' pup." "Count" had flopped at Richard's feet. "But all the while he was probably undecided whether to try the axe on me or the bread knife."

"I give up," Richard cried, as a child might at a hard riddle, "what's the answer?"

"Of course," she nodded towards the log hut in the garden, "there's always the 'pen' as a last resort. I'll keep it open for you. But not bein' married to you I promise to knock you on the head if you grow violent."

He must have missed the point of some remark, he thought. Or could long association with a madman have given her an unsteady turn herself? He wondered.

"You see, can't you," he began again, "that Mrs. Wells might put it in Walter's power to— —"

"Oh, yes! yes!" she interrupted impatiently. "I'm not a bat. I see that. Go on with the next instalment." And she went on with her sewing.

"So I suggested that Jerry have the mother give her a 'power of attorney' to manage the estate."

Phœbe dropped her sewing in her lap. "And what would a girl like Jerry be doing with all that business to look after?"

"She could do it. She'd like that sort of thing."

"Is Mrs. Wells out of her mind completely?"

"No. But she's losing her grip more than you'd believe. You should see her. Her very face has changed. We don't want her— —"

"*We* don't—who's 'we'?"

"Jerry and I—we both feel that the whole thing will be safer if Jerry has legal rights. Of course, if the boy were fit, there would not be the slightest objection to turning over the management to him."

"There wouldn't?"

"No."

"You wouldn't object to that?"

"Not a particle—if he were capable."

Again Phœbe scrutinized the man before her.

"That 'power of attorney' is a very clever idea," she remarked. "Who thought that all out?"

"I did," he admitted. "I'm not sure if it will work— —"

"Oh, it'll work all right, young man; and you know it well enough. You're just modest, that's all."

He asked her abruptly what she meant. She replied, "I'm Irish and I'm also Scotch; so let me give you a Scotch answer, by asking you what *you* mean. You're not featherin' a soft nest for yourself, perhaps?" She flung a hand towards the Wells' house.

Richard looked out into the Lake, but made no answer at all. For the first time in many weeks Richard Richard became his old self, shy and silent. His ears glowed; he became uncomfortable and awkward, as self-conscious persons will; and the gates of his fluency closed. It had been pleasant, this new life of his, and his instinct told him it was good; but now another instinct warned him that it might not be wholly good. Phœbe's cold interrogations had given him first a vague uneasiness and then alarm. Her mind was distinctly not friendly. He felt it, or rather, the sensitive antennæ of his mind caught the vibrations and warned him that he had been out of his shell quite long enough.

Perhaps they sat for ten minutes in tableau, she sewing and he gazing out into the Lake. The dog, "Count," added to the picture by resting a rigid head on two outstretched paws.

"Smoke, if you want to," Phœbe suggested finally.

"Thanks," he said; but he did not smoke.

This man exhibited all the symptoms of guilt, but, somehow, he did not act the convincing villain. And yet had not everything pointed to the rôle? A casual visit to either Sampson's or Cornwell's moving-picture theatres would have convinced anyone: handsome man; no particular occupation; also no money; acquaintance made by accident; handsome girl; rich mother growing feeble and trusting. All the characters were here, including the clever Irish girl whose keen wit rescues the tottering family. "But, hang it all," thought Phœbe, "why do I feel so mean about it? I ought to feel heroic (or is it heroinic?) and flushed with righteousness. But I don't. I feel like a criminal myself."

Other minutes passed by, but Richard seemed not to note them. "I wish I could talk," he was saying to himself. "This infirmity of mine is like an epileptic fit where one knows all that is happening about him but can give no sign. And I thought I had got rid of it up in this fine country." But he said not a word.

"*Chills and fever!*" Phœbe suddenly stamped her foot and shook her red hair at him. "Aren't you ever goin' to speak again?"

"Count" leaped to his feet, yelped suddenly, and started about the room, his nose to the ground.

"Glory be!" laughed Phœbe. "He thought I was a gun flying off. The same I was. I couldn't keep still that long again without explodin'. You go take a bath, young man. You'll feel better. You'll find the same suit dried out and hangin' up in the room on the right. Go take a swim and then come up here, and we'll get things straightened out."

He rose and went towards the little room, but he said nothing. A nod of his head seemed to be enough, and a kindly smile expressed acquiescence.

"I wouldn't make a good lady detective," sighed Phœbe. If the villain was fine and good-looking, she thought, and gazed afar off across the water with mild, blue eyes—ach! she would be pounding away at his chains with a saw and a jimmy and inventing ways of escape from the lock-up. Her heart was too soft for that business. Well! she could keep her eye open, at any rate. Even if she had lived in the country all her life she knew a thing or two, the which Handsome Harrys might find out. What was the use of subscribing yearly to the *New York Times* if it wasn't to give you a vicarious experience of the ways of the world?

As Richard passed her he stooped for a moment to examine her sewing — something or other the largest ingredient of which seemed to be lace — looked straight into her face, gently, almost boyishly shy, and then without a word walked out to the end of the little dock. He dived immediately and struck out at a diagonal for the farther shore.

Occasionally Phœbe looked up to note the receding figure. When about the middle of the Lake she saw him turn and make straight out towards the main branch. It may be remembered that Lake Keuka is shaped like a mitten with a very large thumb. Mrs. Norris' cottage was at the tip-end of the thumb. Towards the rest of the "hand" Richard swam, a distance of over two miles. Soon he was not discernible, except through Phœbe's fine field-glass, wherein he could be observed swimming a long steady stroke.

"The villain escapes by swimming the Lake," Phœbe chuckled. "Sure it's a fine movie actor he'd make." She sewed on thoughtfully for a minute or two and then added, "Well, if he doesn't come back it's a good bargain I've made swapping Seth's cotton bathing togs for an all-wool Norfolk suit."

The cool refreshing water was as balm to the troubled "villain." As the world judged matters he knew he was a failure; but generally he was strong enough to ignore the world and live his individual life. Often, however, the constant pressure of inquiry or of accusation—the world will harry you if you do not conform, as all martyrs will testify—had their cumulative effect of inducing depression. It was only by vigorous open-air exercise or the summoning of all his will that he was able to stand erect and unshaken. The waters of Lake Keuka were tonic to the will. As he plied on, his spirits rose. He saw the law of his own life clearer; he resolved to be true to nothing but himself. His shyness waned and vanished, and strength came. "Resolve to be thyself," he quoted, "and know that he who finds himself loses his misery."

Bluff Point began to loom on his left as he passed out of the "thumb" and got out into the main branch, here over a mile wide. The Point was a sheer rise out of the water of almost a thousand feet, and it towered like a huge mountain. He turned about and faced north in order to get a better view of the Point, and became aware of a familiar cat-boat tacking across in front of him.

It had in tow a stately little yacht, looking without sails like the skeleton of a spectre sloop.

"Ahoy! Captain Wells, ahoy!" he called.

Walter saw him and came about. In a few minutes of manœuvering the two men were jabbering over the beauties of *Sago-ye-wat-ha*. Richard had found his voice again.

It was long after the noon hour when they tied up at Phœbe Norris' dock. Phœbe was not at home. She had found it impossible to sit and sew as she had planned. She could not decide whether she were suffering from a guilty conscience or a desire to gad; at any rate she concluded that Richard's silence had put a spell on her cabin for the afternoon. Gathering up the sewing material, she called to "Count," who was trying to stir up a rabbit among her cabbages, and plodded up the hill to the "Big House," as the negroes called the Wells' dwelling.

At the entrance to the drive she came upon a fattish young man, fairly well dressed—clean, at least, she said to herself—and evidently from the Big City.

He turned a broad Irish face upon her and opened a mouth which exposed large irregular teeth. Her father had such a face, she remembered distinctly, and just such great white teeth.

"Is it Mrs. Emma Wells I see before me?" He raised his hat and bowed like a Dublin ballad vender.

"As Mrs. Emma Wells is sixty years old," Phœbe retorted, "it's blind your eyes must be."

"Blinded by the glamour of the sun on your— —"

"Red head," she helped.

"On your saffron locks," he went on, "and by the charm of your sweet face."

"Blarney!" she retorted. "Who are you that's wantin' to see Mrs. Emma Wells?"

"Ah!" he put a long finger to the side of his nose. "I divulge nothing. I don't know who I am till I've seen my confederate, Mr. Dick."

"Where's your grip?" she asked suddenly.

"Grip?"

"Yes, grip—bag, carry-all, Gladstone, suitcase?—the thing you carry your sample books in. But you'd better be makin' off. Mrs. Wells has all the encyclopedias, handy books of information and guide books she'll need this side of Paradise."

"But it's a visit I'm making," said he.

"You wrote your own invitation, then," said she.

While they talked so tartly at each other they walked along up the drive and grinned with enjoyment. Only the Celt can understand that this sort of palaver is the salt of living.

"Wrote my own invitation? Indeed I did not," he insisted. "The lady of the house herself it was who sent me the invitation by my very dear friend, Mr. Dick. You don't know Mr. Dick?"

"No."

"Humph!" he ruminated. "I should think all the housemaids would be knowing him by this time. He's the handsome one! But perhaps with all your time taken up in the kitchen— —"

For that he received a sounding thwack on the side of the face.

"Holy Michael!" he started back. "If it isn't my mother's old fraternity grip you're giving me! Shake hands! I didn't know you were Irish till that minute. Shake hands with a compatriot, and forgive me for taking you for aught save a princess. Of course I knew who you were all the while. It's the handsome Miss Wells that Mr. Dick's so full of, the heiress; only he should have said a word about the glory of your hair. Never a word he said."

"Who is this Mr. Dick?" she asked as they walked up the steps.

"How can I know till I have a chat with him?" he returned. "Our stories must agree, you know."

"Are you sure his name is Dick?"

"Well, now," he stopped and pondered, "now that you've put the doubt in my head, I'm not so sure. I've lost the letter that tells me all about it. I think he said his name was Mr. Dick. Sure, it was. Dick? Of course it was Dick. What do you mean by confusing my mind over the name of my oldest and dearest friend?"

"And what might your name be?"

They had arrived at the house.

"'Jawn,'" he said.

"'Jawn' what?"

"I'll have to consider," he smiled knowingly. "No doubt Mr. Dick has arranged all that. I mustn't commit myself just yet. For the time being you may call me 'Jawn.'"

Phœbe darted suddenly to this side of the big porch and then to the other, looking carefully about the central pillars, "Non" and "Da," all to induce "Jawn" to inquire the reason, as he well knew.

"What's the game?" he asked. "Solitaire hide-and-seek?"

"I'm lookin' for the man with the box?" she said; "the one that grinds out the pictures. Maybe you don't know it, young man, but we're both of us in a moving-picture story. One villain has just escaped by swimming the Lake; another—that's you—comes up with an assumed name; mistakes me first for the cook and then for the heiress and is about to enter and make off with the family jewels. If a fillum man doesn't get this he's missin' a good story. But come in! And wipe your feet on that mat! Your heart may be black"—the two good-natured faces fairly beamed at each other, belying any literal meaning in the words—"but that's the Lord's business. At least I can see to it that your feet are clean."

These were two different types of American Irish. "Jawn" was the pure breed, one generation out of the peat-bogs, but speeded forward a thousand years by the magic of America; Phœbe was the refined gold of the Celt untarnished by a dozen strains of alien blood. But they were playboys, both of them. A fantastic attitude towards the world was to them more serious and important than all the workaday habits of smug other-peoples. They came of a race who have the saddest thoughts on the ineffectiveness of living, and present the gayest face to the whole dull business. And both were on a holiday, "Jawn" freed from the psychological clinic, and Phœbe fluttering with unaccustomed wings after ten years of captivity.

"Wait!" cried "Jawn," suspending operations on the mat. "I feel a limerick coming! It's a disease." He mumbled and rolled his eyes, then brightened up as the rhymes came out properly.

One glance at Phœbe's illuminated face would be convincing enough that she was enjoying hugely this bit of impromptu and apropos doggerel. But she shook her head dolorously and sighed.

"It is sure a disease," she said; "are you taken often with the fit?"

"It's the air," he explained as they entered the open door and walked through the entrance-hall and turned into the library. Jerry had taken her documents to her room, and Mrs. Wells was busy among the perennials. "I felt it coming on me the moment I got a sniff of the waters of Lake Keuka. It's like hay-fever, you know." They seated themselves in the library.

There have been waves of limericks in America, but it is questionable if the loping doggerel will ever go quite out of style. The Irish never tire of the monotonous rhythm. In the twilight summer evenings along the hedges, or in winter around the huge kitchen fire, the young Irish lad is for ever contributing impromptu limericks. The verses are usually of a low tone morally, and so local in their application that the stranger needs much explanation, but their popularity is perennial. Jawn had his gift straight from the father, but the son had raised them a tone or two to fit American taste.

Jawn's bad lines were covered by exquisite acting. The purse of the lip, the ecstatic roll of the eye, and the sudden flash of big teeth—these were enough to bring laughter to the face of his most superior critic. So Phœbe was compelled to break through a forced reserve and let her own laughter loose. And hers was of the vaulting kind.

"Go on with you, man!" she cried. "It's a movie actor you'd make with that face! And what was your next fit like?"

Mrs. Wells, with a great bunch of phlox, was entering the rear hall when "Jawn" began; she came to the door of the library in time to hear the conclusion.

Jawn was a good fellow and an expert psychologist, but, alas, his humour was not always refined. He took a huge interest in the rough side of life, wherein he was not only true to type but true to his early training on the West Side. The Celtic flavour saved the dish, however. And he never went beyond the bounds set by his instinctively good sense.

Phœbe, who secretly loved many of those proper coarse things of life on which a Puritan world has set a superstitious taboo, mingled her shrill peal with Jawn's heavy laughter when Mrs. Wells appeared.

It was the first time Phœbe had seen Mrs. Wells since her return from abroad, and although she had been prepared in advance she was not ready for the extraordinary physical transformation. Mrs. Wells was not only greyer, but she had grown puffy and weak; an amiable softness had settled in her eyes and in the lines about the mouth. But Phœbe covered her surprise in effusive greetings.

"Phœbe!" Mrs. Wells had exclaimed.

"Mother Wells!" Phœbe had shrilled, a pet name, the private privilege of Phœbe.

"Phœbe," thought Jawn; "it is the daughter's name; and I figured it was Geraldine. My memory is gone entirely."

The greetings over, Mrs. Wells waited patiently for some explanation of the smiling visitor. Evidently, from the uproarious conversation she had interrupted, these two were well-enough acquainted.

"Who is—your—uh——?" Mrs. Wells helped.

"He's not my anything," retorted Phœbe. "I haven't the least idea who he is; and he doesn't seem to have clear ideas on the subject himself."

"This is Mrs. Emma Wells?" Jawn was presenting a hand and his widest smile.

"Ye-s," Mrs. Wells admitted, on her guard instantly. "If you came about mortgages or business you'll have to see my daughter Geraldine. She is upstairs in her room. Shall I send for her?"

"Weren't you expecting me?" Jawn asked.

"No-o; I think not."

"But Mr. Dick said you had invited me to pay you a visit."

"Mr. Dick? I don't know any Mr. Dick, unless you mean Mr. Dickson? He lives across the Lake."

"Didn't anyone tell you to expect 'Jawn' Galloway?"

"No."

"He's forgot it!"

"Please let me send for Jerry," Mrs. Wells suggested nervously. "Please——"

"Oh, I have nothing to do with business." He waved a large palm. "I'm just a guest."

"Your name, you said——" Mrs. Wells tried to clear the mystery.

"No, I haven't said, have I?" he asked blandly.

Phœbe broke in. "You have; you just asked us if we weren't expecting a 'Jawn' Galloway?"

"I did," he nodded; "but by the same token that's not saying 'Jawn' Galloway's my name."

"I think," Phœbe remarked emphatically, "we had better 'phone for Casey—Casey is the police force, Mr. 'Jawn'—and have done with it."

Mrs. Wells told the visitor not to mind Mrs. Norris, and explained how she always said the opposite of what she really meant. But she was puzzled, and plainly showed it. Once or twice she started towards the door. It would be such a relief to turn the matter over to Geraldine. Meanwhile "Jawn" Galloway was carried away by the thought of getting rid of his plain Irish name. Evidently his good pal, "Mr. Dick"—if that was the name he had taken—had forgotten to mention "Jawn" Galloway at all. That was thoroughly characteristic of "Mr. Dick." Well, why not play his own game and adopt a fancy cognomen, too? Professor "Jawn" Galloway was getting too well known, anyway. He couldn't walk down the street without someone consulting him on some sort of mental upset. After an article of his in a popular magazine his friends had been calling him up of a morning to get his interpretation of their dreams of the night before. "Jawn" he would have to stick to, for he had admitted as much to this red-headed daughter, who had started out Geraldine and had turned into Phœbe and then into Mrs. Norris. Besides he never could get used to any other first name. "Dalrymple"—that sounded distinguished and upper-class or—ah! he had it—"De Lancey!"

"But if you would tell us your name," Mrs. Wells was saying gently, "I am sure we could then understand—ah! here's Geraldine!" Mrs. Wells was radiantly relieved.

In a word she put the mystery to Jerry, who understood immediately. It was "Jawn" Galloway, and she came forward with outstretched hand, intending to explain. But "Jawn" was on his feet and reaching out his own hand.

"Jerry!" he called. "I'm betting that this is the Jerry my good friend has been writing to me about. Only he didn't have ink vivid enough," he shook her hand warmly. "It is Jerry, is it not?"

"Yes."

"Well, I'm 'Jawn' De Lancey."

"De Lancey?" she looked puzzled.

"Didn't Mr. Dick tell you?"

"Mr. Dick. Do you mean Mr. Richard?"

He laughed, throwing back his head.

"We all call him Mr. Dick in New York. Of course, you would not know that. Mr. Richard! How stupid of me. Mr. Richard, of course."

Explanations followed, Jerry looming large as an explainer; but Phœbe was plainly unconvinced.

"I still insist," she was firm, "upon calling Casey. But first I would count the silver."

CHAPTER XV
THE LADY DETECTIVE

Any friend of Mr. Richard's was welcome to "Red Jacket," Mrs. Wells assured Jawn; and no questions asked; one could never tell when Phœbe Norris was joking and when she was serious; Phœbe Norris herself was never quite certain. When Mrs. Wells remonstrated mildly at her too inquisitive questions on Jawn's past, Phœbe puzzled Mrs. Wells still further by remarking, "But I must act up to me part of lady detective, mustn't I? It's a movie play we're in. The man with the box is concealed somewhere about, I'm sure. We'll see the whole thing some evening at Cornwall's Theatre, I'll warrant ye!"

"All the world's a movie," agreed Jawn, "and men and women merely——"

"Merely fillum," Phœbe shot in her interruption. "Some bein' hairbreadth horrors and some, like you, Jawn, bein' just 'comics.'"

"Wait!" cried Jawn, striking an attitude.

"He's got a limerick in him!" shouted Phœbe. "Hush!"

Mrs. Wells was disturbed. "He's got a what?" she asked.

"Limerick!" cried Phœbe; "it's kind of fit!"

"Shan't I get a glass of water?" Mrs. Wells rose timorously.

Phœbe's laughter pealed again. "No!" she said. "Would you quench the fire of divine doggerel?"

Jawn minded them not at all. His eye was fixed on distance and his hand waved gently and his lips moved.

Mrs. Wells was not quite assured of the humour of the lines, but she found herself laughing with the others at the droll face of the reciter. He seemed a pleasant sort of man, although his laugh was rather startling. But he was a friend of Richard's; that was enough to assure her; so he was invited to become a guest at "Red Jacket."

It was a relief to know that he had not called on business connected with the estate. Since the return from Europe Mrs. Wells had found it impossible to focus her mind upon the financial end of her household affairs. Never before had she realized how complicated everything was. Not that she had ever conceived her task to be easy; but she had always been able heretofore to summon her will to the problem, and like an almost impossible puzzle, the answer had come out eventually. One had only to persist, she always told herself. If interest on mortgages was due and the bank balance was needed to pay off the vineyard helpers, there was always a new loan on this or that stock; and if the bills for last year's grape baskets or this year's spraying and willow-wiring became too accumulative, one could hypothecate the wine stock or sell a parcel of orchard land or—many things that a resourceful business woman could think of.

Naturally her bookkeeping had assumed an Egyptian character; a private sign here and there, a subtraction indicated without a balance being drawn, a borrowing from this page not paid over to the other page—in short, a system that amounted to a code understood solely by Mrs. Wells. And not always to Mrs. Wells was the code instantly clear. There were days when she puzzled over the meaning of this or that entry; and sometimes surprising cheques were received on accounts which she had scored off as settled, and even more surprising bills were presented whose existence had faded from her memory. Concentration had always opened a way of at least temporary escape; but the mental lassitude which had seized her since her return from abroad had made concentration impossible. Even the thought of the figures was terrifying.

There had been strange visitors several times during the previous eight or ten years, men representing corporations with which she had had dealings on matters of mortgages and loans. They had been very pleasant fellows, just like Jawn, only not so boisterous and self-assured; and always she had needed her strength to meet all their exacting requirements. When certain recent polite letters had assured her that it was about time for one to appear, then it was that she had decided to surrender unconditionally and let her healthy grown-up daughter do the worrying.

When the luncheon-gong sounded Phœbe prepared to stay on without question. George Alexander always looked about him before he set the places, and the presence of Phœbe before a meal always meant a place for her. Besides, she announced that Jawn had to be watched.

Mr. Richard's non-appearance had been explained by Phœbe.

"I was talkin' nice and pretty to him," she said, "askin' him if he thought we'd ever have rain, and all of a sudden he gets displeased and wouldn't speak to me at all—just sulked, he did."

"That's—uh—that's Richard all right," said Jawn. "He's the champion sulker in New York city. I've known him to sit for six evenings in a row and never give anybody the gift of a word."

"On board the *Victoria* he was that way, too," Jerry corroborated.

"I never noticed it," said Mrs. Wells.

"I mean all day on the way from Genoa to Naples," Jerry hastened to explain.

"Why, child," Mrs. Wells remembered, "you did not meet him until the Captain introduced you at Naples!"

"Ha! ha!" cried Phœbe, "more conspiracies for the movie man! Before she met him she had met him all day long, and when he talked to her he didn't say a word! Doesn't that strike you as about the time to have another fit, Jawn? It ought to begin:

'There was a young lady from Naples——'"

"Wait!" Jawn raised a warning finger.

"Wait yourself!" retorted Phœbe, raising a finger, too. "'There was a young lady from Naples——' faples, saples, daples, raples, japles—ding it! There ain't no more rhymes for Naples!"

Jawn was not disturbed, although the evident intention was to clip his budding limerick. When she had quite finished he nodded his head and gave her a limerick with a sufficiency of proper rhymes for "Naples."

Jerry was not pressed for explanation of her statement concerning the habits of Richard before she had met him. Jawn's limericks drew attention away from her, and as the luncheon progressed Phœbe noted the far-off approach of the cat-boat with its yacht in tow. From the dining-room the Lake was in full view. And Jerry remembered her telephone communication with Fagner, and explained the purpose of the new yacht. But before luncheon was over Jerry managed to get Jawn to herself.

"Why do you confuse us by taking a strange name?" she asked. "You are really Professor John Galloway, aren't you?"

"It's all the style!" he told her. "Your Mr. Richard took a fancy name and he gave me the idea. What's wrong with John De Lancey? I'm enjoying it. Already I feel like an aristocrat. Your Richard writes me that the new name has made a complete change in his personality. As a psychologist that interests me, so I'm trying it out. I hope to get a new personality, too; you don't know how tired I am of the old one."

She had spent the morning upstairs in a fruitless endeavour to get some sense out of the tangle of domestic accounts. There were some worrisome entries in the books, and naturally she was not in the spirit to comprehend Jawn's humour to the full.

"I fear it will do harm if mother discovers we are all hoaxing her," she told him.

"She'll enjoy it," he insisted. The mother was laughing immoderately at some witticism from Phœbe Norris. "Trust me to clear everything up when the time comes. I'll study out some special limericks for the occasion. Anyone can see that she is a born lover of limericks. But tell me, how did Mr. Richard become Mr. Richard?"

She explained the beginnings of the incognito and let him understand that she was sorry the innocent lark had developed so far.

"Of course you know who he really is," he said.

"No."

"What?" he cried, and was about to explain, but she stopped him.

"Richard must make his own explanations," she declared. "It would seem like probing; and he is our guest, you know."

She tried to get him to talk about Walter, but he was very frank in saying that that was Richard's case.

"But he asked you to come here solely to consult you about Walter."

It might be, Jawn agreed; but he was on a vacation. It was all guess-work anyway, he assured her; and any man's guess was as good as another's. When Richard got going on a thing he could be guaranteed to put genius into it.

The young lady before him appealed more to his interest; and he was not slow in indicating as much. He quoted what he could remember of Richard's letter to prove that it was Jerry and not Walter that had induced him to come to "Red Jacket." There was enough chaffing in his tone to cover up the bluntness of his statements, but there was no doubt as to his meaning.

There are many ways to meet this sort of gallantry. Some women affect indifference and grow stupidly reserved—they are the ones hit hardest!—and some simper and pretend that they do not understand; but a wiser group admit everything and bring the game right out in the open, where it quickly perishes for lack of pursuit.

"That was quite right of Richard," Jerry returned. "Naturally he would recommend me first, but at that time, you know, he had not seen

Phœbe Norris." She explained Phœbe's widowhood and enlarged upon her qualities. "Phœbe will just suit you," she concluded, and her good-humoured tone turned all Jawn's blarneying back on him and made Jerry herself more reserved and unapproachable than ever.

Jawn made a wry face.

"Never!" he whispered, like a stage-aside. "There's nothing mysterious and romantic in Phœbe to me. We Irish understand one another too well. I know every twist in her head, and she's on to me, every curve of me. All my charms would be jokes to her; it would be carrying coals to Newcastle with a vengeance. No! the Irish get along best with aliens. In Ireland my father was a subservient peat digger; in America he became instantly an eccentric genius, a man of parts, a West Side statesman and diplomat. The big-wigs in politics consult him now, and his sayings are quoted by the newspaper 'columnists'; in Ireland he was just like thousands of others. No! Phœbe and I suspect each other already. The feud is on."

"She seemed to enjoy your verses."

"Pure bluff to put me off my guard," he averred. "We're like a pair of beggars knocking at the same gate."

"How so?"

She was amused at his obvious humour, and interested; proving his point, he told her, that the alien would love him better than the native.

"How so?" he repeated. "Well, she was the clever, unusual one before I came. Isn't it true? I see it is. Now I'm proving how easy is all that so-called Irish wit."

"I'm listenin', Jawn de Lancey Gallagher," Phœbe leaned her red head far over the table. "But don't tempt me to punish you."

"Maybe I might," said he, "if I knew the penalty."

"Well," she considered, "fight fair, or I may be tempted to go to extremes."

"And what'd that be?"

"Marry you," she said.

"Mother of John!" he cried. "Not in America, lass! It's forbid by the Constitution."

"How's that?"

"It's the law of the land that prohibits cruel and unjust punishments."

"That's true," she recovered quickly, "but for the minute I wasn't thinkin' of myself."

"Oh! oh!" he cried, acknowledging the hit.

"It *would* be a kind of slow female suicide, now wouldn't it, Jerry?"

"That's not a bad definition of marriage," commented Jerry thoughtfully; "at least in the majority of cases that we see about us."

"What's a good definition of marriage?" inquired Jawn.

"A kind of slow female suicide."

"Help! Help!" cried Jawn. "They're both against me! I'm in the lair of the professional man-hater. Which leads me to ask a connundrum——"

"Do you think this is a children's party, Jawn de Lancey McGinnis?" snapped Phœbe.

"Well, isn't it?" he stared about him. "Sure we're all kids here. Look at Mrs. Wells." Mrs. Wells was ready to laugh before the connundrum was even proposed, and that sudden touch sent her off. "And look at that grey-haired old kid over there!" Black George Alexander, hovering at the door, broke into African cackles. Jawn's huge face had the native comedian power; wherever he turned it laughter sprang, except in one quarter. Phœbe Norris looked straight at him with face set and cold.

"Go on with your connundrum, man," she commanded icily.

"Well," he said, evidently shifting his original plan, "why is Mrs. Phœbe Norris' face like—like—like the Tombs of the Pharaohs?"

Phœbe's face, in turn, became the instigator to mirth. If it had been stony before, it grew steadily now into a veritable sphinx. Comment and inquiry could not dislodge her external claim.

"Why?" inquired Mrs. Wells; she was rather fond of connundrums, intelligent ones like this one, which brought in one's knowledge of ancient history. "Why is Phœbe's face like the Tombs of the Pharaohs?"

"The Lord only knows why," said John solemnly; "but like the Tombs of the Pharaohs it is."

A crinkle came to Phœbe's eyes, and her mouth quivered.

"I'm not laughin'," she insisted. "My face slipped."

"And is there no other answer?" inquired Mrs. Wells.

"His wit has run dry," Phœbe explained. "He opened the sluice too wide at first."

"Oh, yes," assented Jawn. "Her face is like the Tombs of the Pharaohs because there's more wisdom within than the deepest archæologist can ever translate; because the best part of her is hieroglyphic; because it's worth travelling ten thousand miles to see her; because she is built fit for a king; because no man knows the mystery of her creation, yet all wonder at the marvel of it; because—do you want any more?"

"I just wished to bring you out, Jawn," Phœbe apologized. "I didn't want the reputation of the race to languish. And thank you for the compliments. I'm so glad you didn't say—because it looks so derned life-like and everybody knows it's a dead one. But that would be a mummy, wouldn't it, and not the Tomb of the Pharaohs?"

"If it had been a mummy," said Jawn, "I might have said, because in spite of years of married life she is still so well preserved; or because— —"

"That's enough," said Phœbe; "in a minute more you'll be sayin' somethin' you'll be ashamed of. Don't forget, Jawn, that the Wells' are very refined."

"I was only going to say— —" the light of deviltry was in Jawn's eyes, warning enough to this country woman.

"I'm goin'!" she cried, and started from the room. "The boys have docked, I see, and they'll be wantin' food. It's a word of warnin' I'm tellin' you, Jawn de Lancey Maguire—save all your piggy sayin's for me who understands them, and don't go makin' me ashamed of you before the quality."

She courtesied to Jerry and Mrs. Wells, threw a kiss to Jawn, and slipped away.

"It's a sprite she is," said Jawn, "a red-headed Irish fay."

"She is a very great joy to us," said Mrs. Wells deliberately. "And who would think she was ten years married and a widow! Phœbe hasn't changed a mite since she was twenty."

"She'll never be old," said Jawn. "I can hardly keep my eyes off her hair— it's so brilliant and fascinating." He was about to say something equally complimentary when he caught her shadow at the long front windows. Mrs. Wells had seen her, too, peeping behind a curtain, and showed the knowledge in her face. "Fascinating?" he continued, "yes. And charming? Not a doubt. She'll be that way when she's eighty—I've known many of her kind—having all the young boys dancing about her—unless she takes cold and dies from poking her dainty head in at draughty windows!"

"Jawn de Lancey O'Rourke," she poked her dainty head further in, "you'll force me to marry you yet in self-defence."

This time she was really gone. Down the road she walked briskly, a fine glow on her face. It was such an unusual joy for her to meet a mind as absurd as her own. What good is a sense of the ridiculous, a kinship with the Comic Spirit, if folks about you are for ever taking you seriously? It simply means offence when you had meant none; and scandal where none was dreamed. The Wells were the right sort, because they took nothing seriously from Phœbe, which was a good thing in many ways: it gave Phœbe an outlet for some real heavy matters that weighed on her soul, and she never need fear too much sympathy. And it gave her a chance to say the most literal truths about her neighbours, to let loose her satire on their shortcomings, and never to be suspected of wisdom.

The Wells, notwithstanding, were hardly more than appreciative audience; Jawn, now, was a "pardner"—to use the technical term of comedians. He stirred her mind, provoked it, as none of the others did. And every ripple of his own she felt akin to. It would be glorious fun to fight quip with quip; even though he were a rascal.

Of course he was a rascal. The pair of them were. About Richard she might have had doubts, but about Jawn—never! She knew an Irish villain when she saw one. He was a rascal, but she was not sure that she would be against him in the final reckoning. After all, life was a game of matching wits; and if this Wells Virginia-English strain was stupid should it not pay the penalty? But that explanation of her partnership was discarded before she got half-way down the hill. The Irish rascal was a rascal for high philosophic reasons: it was because he placed so little value upon the world's goods that he concerned himself even less about the matter of precise ownership.—"I am taking your watch," he might say kindly, "about which you should not grieve too much; for consider, when you come to your last dozen breaths, how little value this watch will have in your eyes, and how quickly you'd give it for another year of living."

That's what made the Irish villain so captivating a character in picturesque romances. He cracked his little joke at the world; if he got off with it, he laughed; if he got caught he laughed. The whole business of having and losing is so trivial when life itself is trivial.

In some such ways she defended Jawn, but resolved to watch him, nevertheless. If for no other reason than to get the joy of the play of his mind, she would watch him. And it was delightful to see how easily the good Wells were taken in. Their idea of a swindler was of a sneaking, Uriah Heepish, Sing-Singish cut-throat. They had not the wit to conceive of an honest blarneying lad who went straight at his task, open and above-board.

And what, in the name of pity, had happened to the mistress of the house? The most imposing creature in Jerusalem township had actually shrunk into a timid, smiling—it was as if the Red Queen ("Off with his head!") had suddenly become the White Queen ("Pat her on the head and see how pleased she'll be"). We all know how age creeps on us, but this time, thought Phœbe, it had pounced! Mrs. Wells had lost her rigidly erect bearing, her face had given up the fixed effort of concentration, she was aimlessly drifting. "A little kindness—and putting her hair in papers— would do wonders with her!" Phœbe laughed at this picture of the helpless White Queen, but the laugh soon died away. The reality was not at all comic.

But no one would have guessed that back of Phœbe's public mirth and jollity was even a serious observation of the change in Mother Wells. A fine sense of consideration had kept even the glance of curiosity out of her eyes. She was not the sort to greet a lady friend with, "Goodness! Aren't you getting a little stouter?"

She would not let even her own thoughts dwell too long on her friend's misfortune. The villains were summoned again before her. Of course, Phœbe agreed before she reached "Lombardy," her cottage, that she would keep an open mind about these mysterious gentlemen with changeable names. They might in the end turn out to be respectable. Very well. Her plan was to stand guard and never be suspected. And the way never to be suspected is to tell all your plans to the enemy. They won't believe you, which is exactly what you want. "I'll tell them they're a set of rascals," she chuckled, "and that I'm watchin' every move of them, and they'll laugh their heads off and never be disturbed by my little joke."

Richard and Walter were quite ready for Phœbe's impromptu luncheon, which she managed in the quickest possible time and set for them on her porch. She listened to their story of the lucky arrival of the yacht, heard its name, *Sago-ye-wat-ha*, and listened to its virtues extolled, but kept aloof from their enthusiasm.

‾ Walter was the first to notice her silence. "You tol' me to get it," he said; "an'—I got it."

"Well! well!" said Richard. "Are you at the bottom of this, too?"

Richard had found his voice again.

"I always said if he owned his own boat he could do wonders on this Lake."

"You are very keen," he smiled at her.

"Oh, I know my tables," she replied cheerily; "and I know a good sailor when I see one; and I know your fellow-conspirator, Mr. De Lancey."

Richard looked up from a sandwich, but said nothing.

"I hope you're not going to go into the sulks again?" she asked. "There'll be no fun in houndin' you to earth and layin' bare your nefarious plots if every time I get you in a corner you play deaf and dumb."

He laughed good-naturedly. All the kinks were out of his mind now; he felt vigorous and alert, and knew—he was thankful—that Phœbe had ceased to depress him into speechlessness. And following consistently his tried theory, he knew that all was well between them.

"I was rude, wasn't I?" he admitted. "That's an infirmity of mine, like an epileptic fit— —"

"Oh, your friend De Lancey has fits, too. You are a pair, all right."

"I give up," he said. "De Lancey is no friend of mine. Please explain."

"You don't know a John De Lancey?"

"Never heard of him."

"Well, he's up at the Big House this minute. You may not know him, but he knows you. To be sure he got twisted in your name—said it was Mr. Dick—until Jerry foolishly gave you away. Then he was sure it was Mr. Richard. He said he had forgotten for the moment what name you had agreed to travel on. You two had better get together and rehearse. You're both bad actors. I'll give you that much help, although I'm warnin' you," she smiled broadly as she spoke, "that I'm a lady detective in disguise. So look out!"

Walter looked on wisely as they talked. At first he thought he would tell Phœbe what he knew about assumed names; but decided later that she would find it out soon enough. It was not his affair. He had his boat, and he would go off and borrow old sails somewhere and try her out. But before he went he exacted from Phœbe the approval of his latest achievement.

"You said to get one," he repeated, "an' I got one."

"Good boy!" she nodded to him cheerily. "I knew you'd do it."

That was enough to start him off to the tender in great spirits.

Richard came back to the former topic.

"Really, Mrs. Norris— —"

"Don't Mrs. Norris me."

"Really, Phœbe, I don't know any De Lancey. What sort of man is he?"

"Well, to begin with he is the happiest liar, outside of your good self, that I've yet met. He's Irish, and he's chuck full of limericks and connund— —"

"Jove!" cried Richard. "It's Jawn!"

"Jawn it is; Jawn De Lancey."

"It's Jawn Galloway," he corrected. "It would be just like him to imitate me and take another name— —"

"Then Mr. Richard is not your name?" she broke in triumphantly.

"No," he smiled wryly. "But you mustn't tell Mrs. Wells. Jerry knows. And so does Walter. You may as well know too. In fact, I thought Jerry had told you. But think of Jawn Galloway taking on a—did you say De Lancey? Jack De Lancey! That is comic."

"Very comic," she mimicked. "You're doin' well. But as I'm goin' to get you both in the end you might as well light yourself a cigarette and confess everything. And I may let you off altogether if you flatter me a little. I'm very susceptible to kind words. There's your cue, man. Now, go on with your tale."

In a very straightforward manner he told her the whole story from the accidental meeting with Jerry on board the *Victoria* at Naples up to the complication made by Walter's outbreak.

As the story developed, Phœbe gradually lost her chipper attitude. There was something terribly convincing about the Walter episode. She knew all about that threat to do away with himself; it had been made to her, too, and it had taken all her diplomacy to put a right attitude in the boy and start him off on his trip with the mother freed from much of his unnatural antipathy. But secretly she had always believed that Walter's threats were idle boasts. The reality frightened her, for Richard made no attempt either to minimize or magnify the determined struggle of the boy to end his mixed-up life on the stern of the steamer.

"Well," she drew in a deep breath, "you may be featherin' your nest or not; all I say is you've earned the right to do what you please up at the Big House. As far as you are concerned, Mr. What-ever-your-name-is, I resign; but I'll keep my eye on your Jawn friend a little longer, if you don't mind."

Richard smoked away for a while in great contentment.

"Do you know, Phœbe," he turned to her chummily, "I really may be feathering my nest, as you call it; and without ever intending to perform that delicate operation."

"I guess you're old enough to know your way about." She busied herself clearing away the lunch dishes.

"Age doesn't help at that," he said, "it hinders. The older you grow the more sure you seem; but you fool yourself.... I'm sure I don't know why I do anything."

"You didn't come all the way to Penn Yan on a wild-goose chase. Don't tell me that."

"That's life exactly," he said, "a wild-goose chase."

"Humph!" she sniffed significantly. "You can't fool your grandmother! Every sensible person in this world is after something, and he knows mighty well what it is. It's all moonshine, this not knowin' why you do things. Now, own up; it wasn't an overpowering interest in Walter that brought you here; now, was it?"

"I don't believe it was," he admitted cheerfully.

"And it wasn't due to the overpowering attractions of Phœbe Norris?" she persisted in her cross-examination.

"It may have been," he looked at her calmly.

"What?" she cried. "You'd never heard of me."

"Well," he argued, "Adam had never heard of Eve, but God went on confidently making all the arrangements."

She mused over the thought.

"I forgot," she said finally. "I did invite you to lay on a little flattery. And you did it well. And, by the same token, though I know it's a lie, it gives one a mighty pleasin' sensation.... Go along with you, man!... Adam and Eve!... Pfut!... It's a scandalous picture you're after puttin' into my mind!"

CHAPTER XVI
TREMOR CORDIS

Richard showed no indication to leave his comfortable place on Phœbe Norris' porch. And Phœbe hummed about her work like a young healthy bee. When she felt particularly pleased she put little burbles of low laughter between her sentences; chuckles is not the exact word; they were suggestive rather of the cooing of pigeons. On the Lake the conversation could not be distinguished, but these interjectory ripples floated out clearly enough.

It was the first thing Walter heard when he had staggered down to the dock with an old mainsail and a tattered jib which he had resurrected from the top of a neighbouring oat stack. The music heartened him, though he was physically pretty well spent. It was all right, he said to himself; all right.

"Don't you think you had better be going to the rescue of your friend Jawn De Lancey Galloway O'Toole?" Phœbe remarked as she stood before Richard and polished a plate. "He'll be needin' you, I'm thinkin'."

"Jawn can take care of himself," Richard had rejoined.

"Ordinarily, yes," she agreed, "if he weren't gallivantin'. But when an Irishman like Jawn begins to gallivant, his tongue waggles at both ends."

"What's gallivanting?" inquired Richard lazily. "Comes from 'galli' to gallop—doesn't it?—and 'vanti,' vanity; 'The vanity of horsemanship.' The only thing Jawn can ride successfully is a subway express."

"You're wrong entirely on your etymology, young man," she nodded sagely. "The word 'gallivant' comes from the 'gal,' meaning 'woman,' and 'vanting,' meanin' 'wantin' 'em bad.' At the rate he was goin' when I left him," she chuckled—or burbled, or whatever name you choose for a yet unnamed accomplishment, "he's probably on the way to the priest-house by this time."

"Who's the woman?" Richard inquired.

"Well, *he* didn't begin by pretendin' it was the old lady!"

Richard considered that statement for several seconds, while Phœbe hummed about him.

"Let him!" he finally said.

"One of the first symptoms of insanity," Phœbe suggested judicially, although she knew exactly the train of unexpressed thought that led to the "Let him!" "one of the very first signs — and I should know what I am talking about — is sudden and unexpected jumps in the conversation. When I would remark to Seth that it was time to feed the chickens and he would reply, 'I wish I had a white rat,' I always knew it was time to hide the hammer and lock up the axe.... You're not feelin' a bit ferocious, are you?"

It was the joking over Richard's possible madness that led to the particular set of intimate "burbles" which caught Walter's attention suddenly, and made him stop in the midst of "bending on" the mainsail, and listen. He caught not a single word, but the *timbre*, if one may so describe it, of the conference was unmistakably friendly and affectionate. Just so she had laughed and joked with him to cheer him out of moodiness, and the lilt in her voice had been the only decent memory in his life. Somehow, he could not believe that she would ever offer it to anyone else — madmen and lovers have such notions — it was his private possession, he thought; but now she was hovering over another man and — —

Something Richard said — a bit of nonsense, no doubt — had brought a little shriek of delight from Phœbe, but the remainder of his speech she would not have. Quickly she had darted back of him and had placed a hand firmly over his mouth, cutting off a sentence in mid-air. But her low vibrating laughter showed that she had appreciated the humour of whatever had been said.

That act, trifling in itself and thoroughly characteristic of Phœbe Norris, inflamed Walter; it sent a shock through him that started the blood coursing and left him shaking violently with nervousness. He opened his mouth the better to breathe; spasms of trembling swept over him; he sat crouched up amid a swirl of sail-cloth and stared at the two happy persons before him.

An impartial judge would have decided that the relations between Mr. Richard and Mrs. Norris had not altered one thousandth of a millimetre from luncheon. Before Walter or behind Walter there had not been the slightest shadow of change in the outward attitude. The low laughter had been pulsating before; the jests had been passed and repassed; and even the friendly fillip had been exposed to view. But to Walter, seared with the burning iron of sudden jealousy, all these personal touches were born of the moment, staged now for the first time, as the bill-boards say. The data for that sort of thing has been worked over pretty thoroughly; see the case of Othello versus Desdemona, or Leontes, king of Sicilia, versus Hermione, his queen. Over an innocent public leave-taking, one remembers, — the guest,

Polixenes, is making his farewells to the hostess—Leontes cries, "I have tremor cordis on me! My heart dances, but not for joy! not joy!"

"Tremor cordis" it was, but Walter could make no pretty speeches about it. No word could have come from him. It was pitiful to see him struggling to get breath; pitiful unless one saw also the gleam of hate in his eye.

What should he do to rid himself of the suffering that possessed him? His first impulse was to burst in upon them and fight it out openly with whatever weapon appeared; but that impulse never got so far as a single movement: the big man, he knew, could fling him into the Lake, and the woman could pierce him with a glance and a score of scornful words. Craft whispered in his ear to bide his time and, above all, make sure. Jealousy demands evidence, concrete proof, specific torture to add to the mental anguish. Perhaps—Phœbe had gone off in a matter-of-fact way to see to her chickens, and Richard was coming down to the dock—perhaps there was nothing to it after all.

Almost as abruptly as it came the feeling of being dispossessed left him; all but the memory of it and a vague presentiment that he must be ever watchful. The exultant mood that followed took him to the other extreme. He laughed and seized the sail vigorously; and when Richard reached the dock he was humming a sort of a tune.

"Good boy!" Richard encouraged, when he saw the amount of work already done. "Here Phœbe and I have been fooling away the time while you have been working like a shoemaker. Why, we'll be able to try her out to-day; won't we?"

In spite of his feeling that all was well again Walter found it hard to control his speech.

"N-not t-to-day," he managed. "No w-wind."

What he meant to say was that he was too dog-tired to hoist sail and take the trial. It took all his strength to make the boat shipshape for the night.

"Oh, isn't there?" Richard squinted about the heavens. "Well then, if it's all the same to you, old chap, I'll just trot up to the house and see my friend Jawn. Jawn's a wild one when he's on his vacation, and the Lord only knows what I'll have to apologize for. So long!"

Walter watched him greedily to see if he really took the road that led to the Big House; and then, when his eyes had assured him, his suspicious brain suggested plots and stratagems. He stood up in the boat and craned his head to listen for sounds of Phœbe talking to her chickens. From the "chicken-runs" came not a single "cluck." Some of the former "tremor cordis" seized him again, but not so violently; he shot a leg into the tender, tilting it at a frightful angle, and luckily managed to pilot the skiff to shore successfully. There was ten feet of water at the end of the dock.

Phœbe was not among the chickens; nor could he see her in the orchard, nor in the vineyards tilted up in full view on the hill. They had gone off together! It was a ruse to fool him! Oaths slipped from him, as he dashed up the hill and then down through the orchard to Phœbe's house. He almost ran into her as she emerged suddenly from among the dahlias. She had a large bunch of deep purple flowers in her arm, which she almost dropped at his sudden excited appearance.

"Land o' Goshen!" she ejaculated. "If you start runnin' wild about here, I'll be forgettin' myself and takin' ye for Seth and lock you up for the night in the 'pen'!... What's the matter with you, boy? You're all of a shake."

A little tenderness softened her tone. She tried to take hold of his trembling hand, but he grinned and brought himself together.

"Jus' l-lookin' for y-you," he stammered foolishly.

"You're a funny boy," she laughed, with some of her native crooning in her voice. "A funny boy!... Come in and sit down and tell me all about the new boat. I'm all excited about the races. I see myself standin' on the dock at Alley's Inn with a pair of field-glasses screwed to me two eyes and rainin' curses on my good friends Tyler and Fagner."

"Goin' to beat 'em both;" Walter glowed under her loyal chatter.

"An' don't forget, boy," she told him gravely, "that if you don't win I'll be feelin' all the more sympathy for you. It'll be much better for you if you lose; for then I'll spend *all* my time thinkin' of you."

"If I don't win," he began savagely, "I'll—I'll——"

"You'll do nothin' of the kind," she calmed him firmly. "You'll just try again, like everybody else. There isn't a skipper on the Lake but what has lost a race some time or other."

After a long chat together—Walter could always talk to Phœbe Norris— Phœbe told him it was time to go home. He did not want to go. The lunch was fine, but there were too many at lunch. Why not have a little cosy supper together—just the two of them—on the porch, watching the sunset?

"You're goin' home, boy;" she was jocular but determined. "The breath of scandal has never yet tarnished me fair escutcheon. I don't know what an escutcheon is, my boy, or whether it's right and proper for a female to have one; but I know I'm not goin' to be entertainin' handsome young bachelors—meanin' you—all alone by meself at seducin' suppers. Go 'long with you."

And although she drove him off and he was very much disappointed, yet he walked up the hill delighted with himself. Phœbe always had that effect on him, and she was quite aware of it. She watched him like a mother as he stalked on, and waved a hand when he turned half-way up the hill and looked back.

"Well, he seems chipper enough now," she puzzled over him, "but he was rather wild at first.... I wonder what got into the lad."

Richard had not gone directly up to "Red Jacket." The vineyards took his eye. The rows and rows of dwarfed grape plants and their thick clusters of perfect grapes—now hard and green, of course—reminded him of similar vineyards in France and along the banks of the Rhine. A negro workman here and there was quite willing to stop and talk. There were two interests here for Richard—one was the methods used for keeping these vines free from the thousand and one enemies of the fruit, and the other was the curious bit of history represented by these descendants of a Virginia slave plantation transferred to the North and still working for the old family.

So it was growing upon dusk before he left the vineyard and strolled up to the Big House. "Tshoti," "Non," "Da" and "Waga"—the four huge porch columns—loomed tremendously in the half light. He caught a portion of their mystery and remembered Jerry's prediction that one night he should come upon them unexpectedly as they performed their sentinel guard, and that he would feel himself grow small in their presence.

Jawn was entertaining the Wells family when Richard arrived.

"Make a limerick on Phœbe Norris?" he was repeating a question, possibly to gain time. "Sure I can!" He rolled his eyes upward. "Sure I can! It's a simple matter, if you know how. Uh—let me see. 'There was a young lady named Phœbe.' No! That would never do. The only rhyme for Phœbe is 'Hebe,' the goddess of beer. U-m!... I have it! Well, how's this?"

Richard spoiled that limerick by asking:

"Won't someone introduce me to the poet?" and his hand went out eagerly to meet Jawn's.

Jawn, however, was not so receptive. With a jocularity that was understood by everyone but the watchful Walter, he protested that he couldn't be certain whether he ought to meet the gentleman for the first time or kiss him on either cheek as an old boyhood friend; he couldn't be certain until they got together secretly and connived a bit. A bit of conniving now and then, he assured everybody, was relished by the best of men—and the worst of women. He had come to "Red Jacket," he complained, with a perfectly good alias, and hardly had he been enjoying a high-class name for an hour when the daughter of the house saw through his verbal disguise and exposed him to the ridicule of the natives.

"Under the aristocratic name of Jawn Dalrymple—or was it Dalton?" he looked about him imploringly.

"It was De Lancey," helped Jerry.

"De Lancey, of course!——"

Mrs. Wells interrupted. "I beg pardon," she said, "I don't want to seem stupid, but I thought you said your name was De Lancey? Isn't that your name, Mr. De Lancey?"

Jerry explained carefully. "He was just joking us, mother. He is Mr. Richard's old friend Mr. Galloway, Professor John Galloway of Columbia University."

"The cat's out!" Jawn turned disconsolately to Richard; "so I might as well shake hands and own up. It was a great mistake. I see it now. I ought to have worn whiskers."

"But, really," Mrs. Wells seemed very much concerned, "I can't see why he should not have said Galloway from the beginning."

The attempt to make clear Jawn's reason for an incognito was not very successful, due to the fact that Richard's incognito could not be explained. Even Jawn saw that. Both Richard and Jerry gave him open signals that it would not be politic to try to clear up two incognitos in one evening—all of which was not lost on Walter—and Mrs. Wells' disturbed face was ample evidence that silence on that score was the best policy.

"I'll tell you how it is," Jawn jumped into the breach. "My real name is De Lancey, but when a lad I was adopted by a wealthy New York banker named Galloway. Well, he lost all his money and died leaving me nothing but the name. Naturally I sometimes forget and use the old one out of habit."

The romantic explanation pleased Mrs. Wells immensely. She grew tremendously interested in the rich banker and wanted to know many particulars. Jawn was never at a loss for details.

Walter was keenly interested in Jawn's talk but, he told himself, he was not at all taken in by it. A numbing remembrance of the afternoon's suspicions came into the background of his mind and settled there. It was a spectre at all his banquets of happiness: it darted its chill into his best re-visioning of even that latest chat with Phœbe when she called him a handsome young bachelor and hinted scandalous things. So it behoved him to prepare his defences against attack.

The situation was very clear to Walter. This "Mr. Richard" was some sort of a confidence man. He first attracted the ladies and then subtracted their purses, or borrowed huge sums from them on bad notes, or got them to invest in worthless stocks. He had heard about these fellows. The books were full of them—not only the paper-backs, either, but real books— meaning cloth-covers—like *Wallingford* and *Blacky Daw* and *Raffles*. Jawn, of course, was a detective on the trail of Richard. In spite of all his joking and laughing, anyone could see that he kept his eye on Richard. Did Richard know that he was being trailed? Walter suspected that he did not.

He wondered if it were criminal to use another man's name, a big man's name at that, one whose reputation was world-wide, whose millions of money earned as railroad and steamship owner, international banker and dealer in monopolies in general, had made his name known even to children. That was the name on the card tacked carelessly on "Mr. Richard's" door. He must be engaged in crime on a big scale to need to assume that name. And why had he changed it? And what was his real name? These were questions which Walter would like answered. Perhaps a little careful probing of Jerry would tell him something.

Later in the evening she was conscious of his following her about. In the tail of her eye she could see him sidling along the hall as she turned into a room, or standing afar off and watching strangely while she talked to someone. One got used to having a "queer" brother in the house, but these movements, stealthy and clumsy at once, were not usual.

"Want to see yuh," he said to her finally.

"All right, Walter," she agreed; "go out on the porch and sit beside 'Waga.'"

"Jes' y-you," he nodded; "n-nobody else."

"All right, Walter."

Between "Waga" and "Da" they sat and looked out upon the wide sheet of blue water, startlingly clear in the moonlight.

"H-he's gotta keep away from Phœbe," Walter managed to begin.

Jerry was too used to managing her brother to show astonishment at any remark. He was easily frightened off.

"What makes you think so?" she asked quietly.

"H-he's been hangin' 'round, laughin' and—lookin' at her."

"But everyone does, Walter," she said; "who can help it? She is wonderful, you know."

"She's all right," said he.

Walter seemed to have nothing further to add to that topic, and Jerry knew better than to try to force him to talk. She waited until he began again.

"Smart boy, he is." His speech became clearer as he grew in confidence, and his manner became more aggressive. "Talks a lot.... But he's a crook."

The "he," Jerry figured, must mean Jawn.

"Funny names, and all that," he explained.

After a moment he laughed derisively, almost vindictively. "Says his name's Richard! Huh! Richard Richard! Hah! Fools the women all right. But don't fool me.... Has 'nother name, too." He fumbled in his pocket and produced the card that Richard had ripped off his stateroom door. "But I cornered him. Tol' me 'at was a fake name, too. Found it on his things ... in his stateroom.... Big gun, he was tryin' to be.... Big gun."

Mechanically Jerry took the card. By the light from the window she could see the hold black characters. It was indeed a big gun, one of the Crœsuses of his age. It seemed less like the name of a person, as she studied it, than that of some heavily advertised merchandise.

Jerry was not a newspaper reader, but vaguely she was conscious of knowing something about that name. While Walter bragged of his cleverness in discovering this further act of imposture, she was searching over her memory. Suddenly it became clear that the man whose card she held in her hand had been dead several years; he had gone down at sea with his whole family; she was not sure, but she thought she remembered something about an accident to a sea-going yacht off the Newfoundland Banks.

"Where did you find this card?" she asked.

"On his door."

"His stateroom door?"

"Yes. That's the name he was goin' to use at first, but I scared him off. Tore it down, he did, when I came 'long."

"Perhaps somebody else put it there by mistake."

"Nope! He owned up all right, when I put it to him."

"Just how did he 'own up,' as you say?"

"Said——" Walter thought for a moment to get the words right, "—said he was sorry to use a fine name like that; said if I'd keep mum he'd stick by me."

"And so you are keeping mum."

"Well!" he flared. "Guess I c'n tell it to my own sister, can't I?... An' he ain't stickin' by me."

"Oh!" she recalled. "You think he is interested in Phœbe?"

"Well, he better not be."

No matter what Jerry may have privately thought she knew her duty at this moment, and that was to rid this boy's mind of the suspicions that had begun to darken it. She was startled by the revelation; she would have to get alone and think things together before she could make up her mind as to the meaning of the facts Walter had presented; particularly was she astonished at Walter's interest in protecting Phœbe Norris; but all that she cast aside and bent to the task of reassuring Walter of Richard's good faith. She reminded him of the scene at the back of the *Victoria*, and drew tactfully the picture of Richard's work in saving Walter from a terrible "accident"; she repeated Richard's constant expression of interest in Walter's welfare; but none of these seemed to affect the boy in the least.

Then she was driven out of the truth. "A fib in time saves nine," she remembered one of Richard's jokes. Prevarications had been piling up ever since that first deception. "Oh, what a tangled web we weave when first we practise to deceive!" One must keep in mind that in spite of Jerry's calm in Walter's presence she had always been afraid of him. He was absolutely heartless and, when he had the courage, brutal. In her own heart she believed he was a harmless lunatic who might any moment become violent. So she steadied herself for a final effort.

"You are quite wrong about Richard and Phœbe. They are simply good friends," she said.

"How do you know?" he cried. "I've seen 'em together and he talks soft to her an'——" He began to work himself into a dangerous mood.

"I know what I'm talking about, Walter," she increased the firmness of her tone. "Richard is not interested in Phœbe at all, in the way you mean."

"Got to show me," he muttered.

"I can prove it."

"Aw! He'd lie quick enough."

"Do you think I would lie to you, Walter?"

No; Walter did not think so. Jerry always spoke the truth. Jerry was all right.

"Well, then," she said, nerving herself for the statement, "Richard is not interested in Phœbe Norris; he—he is interested in me."

The effect upon Walter was all that she had expected. He softened up suddenly, grew exultant at the turn which his clogged mind had not guessed, but which, all at once, seemed perfectly apparent.

"Is that so!" he cried. "Did he ask you to marry him?"

"Richard and I understand each other," she replied evasively.

"Good girl!" he said, thinking only of his own luck.

After ruminating over the new situation for a while he rose to go. His laugh was almost pleasant.

"Clever boy, that Richard," he said; "clever boy, he is! Always said he was a clever boy. Smart, he is! Smart! I tol' him——" He chuckled at the thought.

"Yes?"

"I tol' him once 'at you had the tin——"

"Tin? Oh, yes; I understand. Go on."

"I tol' him you'd have a good share; and he seemed mighty pleased. Oh, he's smart, he is!"

"How is your boat, Walter?" she asked.

"Aw right.... Tol' me, he did, 'at he didn't believe in work. Pfut!" he spluttered out an ironic laugh; "no use workin' when you c'n jus' pick it up easy. Oh, he's a very smart, clever boy!"

It took all Jerry's will to control her instinctive desire to slap the boy's smirking face.

"Well," she smiled; "it's rather late for a skipper, isn't it? Early to bed nowadays if you want to have a chance in these races."

"Tha's right," he agreed and yawned prodigiously. "Guess I'll be goin' to bed." But the single idea was not easily dislodged from his mind. "Clever boy, he is! Clever and—smart!"

"Good-night, Walter." Jerry spoke very sweetly, a great tribute to her growing power of control over speech.

As Walter sauntered in the great central door she heard the voices of Jawn and Richard. Evidently they were coming out upon the porch.

"Where's Jerry?" she heard Richard ask.

While Walter was mumbling his reply—his tones were cheerful, she was glad to note—she slipped into the grounds at the side and made quickly off to the winding road at the back which leads up to the top of the ridge. Until she could collect her thoughts she did not want to see either man. In her perturbed condition Richard's mildness would have stirred her to quarrel, and Jawn's hearty volubility would have led to a blow. She was quite sure that if he had attempted another limerick she would have screamed.

The walk up the old familiar road was a soothing delight. She went on till she came to the hunter's hut wherein she had spent many a fine winter night. An old kitchen chair was waiting invitingly on its slender porch. There she sat and tried to get her mental bearings while the serene moon grew higher and higher in the sky.

Alone on the porch of the hunter's lodge with the dark valley before her and a patch of the white-blue Lake shining brilliantly in the moonlight, Jerry called herself to account. The quickly planned "fib" which she had just told to Walter was worrying her. To be sure, Richard of all persons would understand exactly the motive that led her to her supposed confession and he would see the necessity of it. That did not bother her half so much as the effect which the spoken words had had upon herself. The moment they were uttered she experienced a most uncomfortable feeling of joy and guilt. It was as if she had unwittingly expressed her very self.

Richard, no doubt, would explain it glibly with his theory of "subliminal self," which is always telling us the unknown truth. Why had that expedient come so pat to her tongue? She did not need to ask. Whether or not the questionable "subliminal" had spoken, she, the only self she really believed in, knew it to be the expression of her own wish.

Had she known this disturbing fact from the beginning? Lovers are prone to claim as much. Isn't it the time-honoured formula to ask. "When did you—ah—begin to care?" and to answer, "From the beginning." As she reviewed their days together from that long uncomfortable first day on the steamer when unknown to him she had lounged beside him in her steamer-chair and watched him repel each invader of his solitude, the design of her life began to appear; and she knew, then, that she had "cared from the beginning."

Predestination, Richard would call it. She smiled at the picture of his mild interested face as he would analyze the rare experience into terms of kismet. "The gods" would be blamed cheerfully.

Each incident was fitted into its mate to make the full design. She had watched the modern Gobelin weavers in Paris and noted how the meaningless splotches of colour here and there grew gradually into a meaningful pattern. Life was like that. Her suggestion that they go about Naples together; the intimacy caused by the incognito; her own insistence upon secrecy; the invitation to "Red Jacket"; even her indignation at his suggestion that she would eventually make eyes at him—all these were parts of the curious weaving.

And she had begun already to make eyes at him! Not in a literal sense, to be sure—she would die before she did that—but in confessing her hopes to Walter she had gone a considerable step toward making the first move.

Hers was the type of mind which cleared up one confused thought at a time. The important matter of her own relation to Richard having been settled, she permitted Walter's accusations to come in review. Was this impersonal friendly Richard a genteel bad man, after all? She could not decide. The actual card which Walter had found on his door looked like the practice of some sort of confidence man. She remembered that he had been most reluctant to give up the comfortable "Mr. Richard" which she had dubbed him. And his philosophy of drifting along, coupled with no occupation and a shocking state of low funds—all that seemed to fit in; along with his even more shocking lack of a sense of the culpability of all wrong-doers.

And she had been quite taken by his philosophy. A faithful Episcopalian—true to her Virginia traditions—she had never questioned religious matters. She had neither believed deeply nor troubled herself to disbelieve. Richard it was who constantly reminded her of the foundation principles of her own faith. "Neither do I condemn thee" had been one of his most striking quotations. "Judge not lest ye also be judged" was another; and "Father, forgive them; they know not what they do." And now she saw that this attitude would be consistent with the credo of a man who might choose to act against the moral code of those about him. According to Walter, Richard was after her "tin." "Well," she laughed, "he is welcome to it—what there is of it—so long as he is willing to take me, too."

But Walter had also hinted rather strongly—strange how this important thought had come last in review!—that Richard had been paying open court to Phœbe Norris. So far her mind had worked openly and frankly in the light. Now it began to deceive her; or rather, to put it in terms that Richard might have employed, the subliminal self did not lay all its cards on the table. It was a most uncomfortable thought that Richard and Phœbe Norris should be chatting and laughing together intimately—a most uncomfortable thought. But Jerry did not at all recognize the little wave of "tremor cordis" that made her "heart dance." She saw instead the evil that might come to Richard and to Phœbe if an innocent and proper relationship should be allowed to grow until Walter might be aroused to some vile deed. They must all be saved from that! She would warn them both. Oh, it was very necessary that they should be warned.

And with that decision a tranquil feeling possessed her, which assured her that she had decided exactly right; so tranquil and inspiriting that she rose and walked along the ridge for a mile or more until she came to the spot where she could see the main body of Lake Keuka spread out wondrously before her. Then she walked briskly home and went light-heartedly to bed.

CHAPTER XVII
LOVE LIMERICKS OF A LEFT-TENANT

The next morning the men were off early to inspect the new yacht and to assist Walter in "bending on" the last make-shift sail. Jawn, however, went reluctantly.

"It's a beautiful view from here," he objected lazily; "why go down into it and mess it up with us? We don't help the landscape much. We're not a set of Corot dancing wood-nymphs."

Richard tried to tell him that it was imperative to study Walter at first hand.

"Nymphs, now," Jawn went on, boldly disregarding all Richard's patter. "Nymphs, now, is a good suggestive word. It stimulates the rhyming sense. You see there a hard word and you say to yourself, Can it be done? And you reply, If it is the business of a man to do 't I'll do 't. U-m!..."

He waved a large forefinger, beating time to a story of "two pale gentleman nymphs" made ineffably fragile through the fact that their "forbears were lacking in lymphs."

Walter had gone on ahead. Richard and Jawn were following slowly.

"I had rather stay and add more kindling to my fire of devotion." Jawn turned in the road and flung a stage kiss at the Ionic columns.

"It is a fine old house," grinned Richard; "I don't wonder at your devotion to it."

"Humph!" Jawn grunted as he trudged down the hill. "Do you think I am attached to the architecture like a bit of indecent ivy? It's not a parasite, I am. I'm a—what's an amorite, friend Richard? Hasn't it something to do with the divine passion?"

"Amorite?" Richard studied. "That's the sexton, isn't it? The chap who marches ahead of the rector carrying a banner or something. You wouldn't do for that at all, Jawn."

"Ach! You're thinking of acolyte, you fool. You can't pass me on ecclesiastical forms; I was once a sweet cherub of an altar boy and know all about such matters. No," he sighed; "it's no leanings toward priesthood I have; but something entirely worldly and fleshly and devilly."

"How many does this make, Jawn?"

"How many?" he retorted. "I suppose you mean to imply that my devotion lacks in constancy?"

"Oh, you are constant enough!" Richard laughed. "You're always completely gone on some girl—always."

"It's a terrible infirmity."

"Did you bring your book with you?"

"Yes," snapped Jawn.

"Well, what number is this one?"

"Seventy-seven. But you needn't grin so sarcastic like; I'm feeling that this is the final number."

"How so?"

"I'm no astrologer," Jawn explained, "but I have eyes in my head. Now, anyone can see how mystical and sonorous is the number seventy-seven. If you multiply the first digit by the second digit you get forty-nine; and if you divide immediately by the second digit you get the golden number seven. If you add the first digit to the second digit you get fourteen, which divided by the number of digits, two you get back your golden number seven. And there you have four golden number sevens dancing before you like a bunch of four-leaf clover."

"And if you subtract the first digit from the second digit," Richard suggested, "you get nothing."

"Precisely!" cried Jawn. "And in the occult language of figurology any novice would read, 'Here endeth the list of heart-broken maidens; behold! there will be no more!'"

"Jawn," said Richard, "I think I know the reason why you always fail."

"Fail!" Jawn exploded. "I never fail. The sad part of the business is that I always succeed. Scattered over the eastern and middle-western United States are seventy-six forlorn women of all years who are now hopelessly married to men they must hate. For why? When Lazarus came back from the gates of Paradise do you suppose he ever again took delight in the left-overs from Dives' table? No more they. But what could I do? Unbidden the amorous passion came and swift and unbidden it went. So what could I do but write their names in a book, add the date of their amorous demise——"

"Which always corresponded to the date of their wedding!"

"Exactly. You wouldn't have me getting mixed up with the unwritten laws of the land, would you? I simply write their names and add a touching obituary limerick."

Richard suggested that the seventy-seventh limerick—since Jawn was so assured that it would be the last—should end the series, and that the collection be published.

"It would add to your fame as a poet," Richard argued, "immortalize the ladies in everlasting verse and bring you a financial heart-balm."

Jawn mused over the possible titles. "'The Seventy-seven Amours,'" he tried out one. "Sounds too much like a history of Chicago.... 'Love Limericks.' No. There's a female touch to that that I don't like.... Ah! I have it! 'Love Limericks of a Left-tenant.' It's thoroughly male and gives the proper Irish picture of a forcible eviction!"

"Have you written Jerry's yet?" Richard asked.

"What, man!" Jawn affected great disgust. "Would you write an obituary verse while the corpse is still sitting up and drinking beer with you? Have you no artistic sense? Of course not! Well, then, have you even common decency?"

"Well," Richard probed him. "I thought as this one was going to be the climax you would take a running start, as it were."

"Yes!" Jawn was derisive. "I know your sort. You're the kind who sample all the bottles before the wake begins, and start premature explosions which spoil the solemnity and gaiety of the rest of the mourners. Besides, there ain't going to be no corpse this time. Ergo, there won't be no limerick. It'll be an ode I'll write, a bursting prothalamium, a lyrical celebration of the joys of requited affection."

They were now coming in sight of Walter at work.

"No, it won't," said Richard. "It will be a limerick like all the others. You are doomed to failure, Jawn; and the reason is that you ply your amours too well. You are a professional. You are too perfect. There's not a flaw in your attack, and therefore you fail to attract. It's the perfect manufactured article versus the crude hand-made bit of craftsmanship. No; Jawn, I fear you'll die a Left-tenant."

"I fear so," admitted Jawn cheerfully. "I fear so; and I hope so! Lord love you! My memory is so full of delicious experiences that I'd feel like Bluebeard if I ever settled down to simple domestic servitude. And I wouldn't like it, I know. Ach! I'd rather be a left-tenant every day in the week than a major-domo for ever."

While they waited on the dock for Walter to row in with the tender, Richard asked Jawn what he thought of the boy.

"What do I think of him?" Jawn echoed. "Well, to speak in technical language which all the world understands, I think he's a damned young fool."

Richard pressed him to look at the case seriously.

"This is no case for me," said Jawn decisively. "He's got a screw loose. It's hardware he needs," Jawn tapped his head, "and I'm not in the business. Besides, I'm on my vacation. You doctor him. I'm too busy. I'm specializing on the sister."

Jawn was obstinately determined to enjoy his vacation. He was willing to psychologize all winter, he said, and in the Summer School when compelled by the Dean, but vacation means "to vacate," he protested; and that means to let your mind loaf, and be silly, and wallow in its uncultivated, native soil.

Jawn was a very modern type of American "professor" and corresponded not at all to the conventional conception. He was not beetle-eyed, nor ponderous, nor absent-minded, a picture we have borrowed from Europe where dignity is demanded of the professor, and all the pompous qualities of solemnity. The European sort exists in America, too—he was the original settler!—but side by side is a distinctive American variety. The American type came in in the late '80's and early '90's when college teachers were ceasing to be so stiffly clerical in physical and mental cut; he arrived just at the time, too, when mere opinions in a professor began to be suggestive of lazy charlatanism, a time when all this new cult of laboratory research, exact measuring, statistical proof, historical evidence from first-hand sources, was beginning to be demanded of the man who professed anything.

This new sort of professor is quite apt to look on the professional title as a joke, except in so far as it is a distinction that carries real difference in wages. We remember with what sturdy and solemn posing the professor of yester-year would wear his titles; how deftly he would correct the forgetful who lapsed into "Mr."! How he would announce himself as "Professor" with such simple faith in its power to awe the unrefined! Jawn was a perfect example of the newer school which, we fear, has gone to the other extreme: it lacks terribly in dignity; in fact, it suspects all dignity of a subtle attempt to counterfeit intelligence—which is often the case!—it is careless of mere external show, but it toils like an Edison. It works hard when it works, and it plays with the abandon of a nest of puppies; it smokes, it drinks, it sings the wildest songs at purely male meetings; it employs the colloquialisms of the street; it tosses ball with the boys on the town lot; and, to oblige a friend, it may stay up all night to play poker. And on a holiday—which may be a night off, or a week-end—it "cuts up" as if life were just beer and skittles.

This modern investigator-professor is the despair of his European confrères, for, we must admit it, he lacks culture. He knows so much of one thing that he elects to know nothing of anything else, and cheerfully owns up; indeed every other speech is a confession of some sort of ignorance. And he lacks, he woefully lacks polish; and often—although there are tailored dandies among them—he lacks simple brushing and scouring!

In his clinics Jawn Galloway tended his awkward flock of wayward children—the mentally twisted and the morally awry—with the dignity and the sweetness of a Roman cardinal. He was genial and sympathetic, but he was also strong and masterful. In the clinic no one thought of him with other feeling than that of respect for his wise mind, his deft hand, his atmosphere of confidence. Over twenty thousand cases of wrong-mindedness had come under his observation; he had held himself to a laboratory vigil of from twelve to fourteen hours a day for months at a time; and his "notes" had formulated a new theory and practice in dealing with the abnormal mind. In his clinics he was learned without pedantry, and wise without snobbishness; but off duty he was a perpetual sophomore—often, we fear, equally as irritating to mature persons. His boisterous laughter got on one's nerves; his persistent doggerel, his bubbling vivacity, his everlasting acting-a-part stirred many a less highly strung person to combativeness. "He a professor!" was the commonest remark voiced by fellow vacationists who did not know of his serious work. Of course they could not be aware that his perfected scale for measuring the intelligence of morons had brought him the approval of the most serious-minded men in Europe and America.

His friends had often to apologize for Jawn Galloway, for the type is not yet conventionalized. Our comic papers continue to make the professor a deep-browed simpleton, and our novels and our drama perpetuate the picture; but that sort is as obsolete as Ichabod Crane.

"All right," Richard nodded at Jawn's persistent flippancy. "I'll wait. You're resting—I know you! You're just skylarking to get your mind cleaned up. I'll wait. And one of these days Walter's case will seize you as it has me. You'll get fascinated. I know you! And then we'll get something out of this visit; you'll sing another song instead——"

"Instead of just Lewis-carrolling, eh?" Jawn laughed.

"All right," laughed Richard in turn. "I'll wait. But you'll work for your wittles yet, old boy!"

Any further talk was cut short by the approach of Walter.

"A left-tenant never made a good sailor," said Jawn, as he stepped on the yacht. "But here I am to serve as ordered and, if necessary, go down with the ship. Which is the saloon deck, and if this is it, where's the bar?"

The old sail lifted creakingly, the jib fluttered and filled, and the *Sago-ye-wat-ha* moved off smoothly for its maiden trip on the waters of Lake Keuka.

Jawn was instructed in managing the starboard sidestays. It was made clear to him that when the mainsail was swung over on the port side the strain was enough to split the mast unless he fastened the sustaining rope, or "stay," securely to the cleats before him. When she came about he was to loosen the "stay" on his side while Richard quickly secured the supporting port "stay."

"So I'm to loosen her stays, am I?" queried Jawn.

"Yes; and tighten them up, too, when we give you the word, or that stick will snap off like a tree on the path of a cyclone."

"And when you say the word," he repeated the orders, "I'm to lace 'em up again, eh?"

"That's not the technical phrase," laughed Richard, "but it will do."

"Another reason why a ship is called a she," said Jawn. "I think the minstrel troupes of the country have missed that one.... It's a strange thing, now," he mused, "for a modest young man like me to be squatting here in the bodice of the ship—I hope I'm using the proper language—sitting here in the bodice of the ship with life and death in the balance. Still, if I survive you, I'll put the thing in proper nautical language for the local papers: 'Suddenly on Friday last the good ship *What's-her-name* capsized in a sudden squall and was slowly strangled to death because no one was able to reach her in time to loosen her stays.'"

Walter was very well pleased with his boat. Out in the main body of water he tried her under all sorts of conditions and had little brushes with other yachts, one or two of which were "Class A scows," and it seemed always that the *Sago-ye-wat-ha* could overhaul anything either on short tack or long reach.

They tacked up the Lake under a stiff northeaster, which gave Jawn plenty of practice in attending properly to the "stays." When they prepared to put about and came back the wind dropped to a light breeze. So they slipped along leisurely, taking over an hour to round Bluff Point. During this time of lazy inactivity Jawn, relieved of his duties, found his voice. He sang songs, offered connundrums, stories and impromptu limericks. Several times during his chat he had forgotten himself and called Richard by another name. Walter became alert. When it had happened more than once, he spoke up.

"Tryin' to work me, are you?" he asked, "like you do the women?"

Jawn did not see the point and asked him what in the name of the seven devils he meant. Jawn Galloway could be a very belligerent fellow at times.

"Oh, nothin'; on'y them names don't fool me." Walter modified his tone discreetly; one could easily take the spirit out of him. "I know he ain't Richard, and I know he ain't the other one, either."

"But I am the 'other one,' Walter," Richard soothed him.

"Like hell y'are!"

"Hey!" cried Jawn, searching about for a weapon. "Drop that Billy Sunday talk or I'll lam you over the head with a——" he kicked about among several tools lying at his feet—"where the blazes do you keep your marlin-spikes? Have to have a marlin-spike. If I were on land, now, I'd knock you down with my fist or just kick you in the stomach, but the etiquette of the sea demands marlin-spikes. What sort of a ship do you call this?"

Walter did not know whether to be amused or scared. Jawn could roar like Bottom, the weaver. But he decided, finally, that the situation was not as perilous as it sounded.

"He's a big gun, he is—that fellow," he went on, with his thought on the name. "But you ain't."

"He has heard of my father, Jawn." Richard turned quickly. "You know I wrote you that he knew; he found one of my cards on the steamer. The name was familiar to him, naturally; but he did not know that father and I had the same names; and he did not know of father's death."

"Everyone knows about it," snapped Jawn.

"Of course, Walter," Richard explained, "when father died I was no longer a 'junior.' We have the same name. Naturally you had never heard of me. I have the distinguished name and have done nothing to earn it. That's why I am so contented with this nondescript Mr. Richard. You can't imagine how pleasant it is not to be questioned and stared at. It's a dreadful nuisance to have distinguished parents."

"Please don't be disrespectful to the father of my own offspring," Jawn objected. "I'm getting to be a notorious character, with my name in the print every time a bug gets loose in somebody's head. By the time my children come along I'll be as famous as Mr. Riley whom they speak of so highly; I mean Mr. Riley who keeps the hotel. Have you heard the song, Walter? Well, you will." And he sung it as only an Irishman can.

So they were going to keep up the bluff, act it out boldly; they were a daring lot, thought Walter; but they couldn't fool him.

"If he's the B-Big Gun," Walter persisted, "he'd be r-rich."

"No, Walter," Richard was very patient. "That was father's money, not mine. He made it, not I. Since I left college I have been making my own way. Money doesn't interest me, especially money I have never earned. I couldn't be happy with it; it would be just a refined sort of slavery, and I have always preferred to be free. Let's don't talk about it, if you don't mind."

"But I don't see — —" Walter began.

"Then shut up!" cried Jawn brutally.

"Jawn!" remonstrated Richard.

"By George, I'm forgetting myself!" Jawn showed all his big teeth in an expansive grin. "Listen at me shutting up the captain of the boat! It's mutiny they'll be charging me with, and be hanging me at the yardarm." He cocked an eye aloft. "Is that her yardarm, up there, sticking indecently out of the top of her stays?"

The laughter that followed reassured Walter, but he was careful not to bring up the topic of names again. These were dangerous fellows and he had best keep in with them. They could do what they pleased so long as they left his preserves alone. The comforting thought made him watch the shore carefully — they had turned Bluff Point and were tacking into the Branch; and after a time he was rewarded by a flutter of something white on Phœbe's porch. She had been watching for him, too; and was waving a welcome home. The breeze strengthened almost in answer to his own exultation, and shortly they were dropping sails before the Norris dock.

"Aye! aye! Captain Wells!" she called. "An' how is everything for'ard?"

"Aw right!" he grinned.

"What's your cargo — garden truck or cattle?" She pretended not to distinguish the men at first. "Ach! It's the two gentlemen pirates out of the movies! Ahoy, you two! What's the latest news of the police courts?"

Jawn put his hands together and megaphoned, "Woman arrested for speeding. Her tongue ran away with her head."

"That joke is in Genesis," she retorted. It is, no doubt, an aged masculine fling.

"Sure!" he called back as they stepped up on the dock. "If Eve had been deaf and dumb we'd *all* be in Paradise yet."

"Ye devil!" she answered.

"You flatter the ould Boy," said he.

"Ooh!" she shivered, "is he worse than you?"

"Much worse."

"Don't add to the terrors o' death, man, but come in and have a cup o' tea. I set it a-brewin' the moment I saw you."

Walter could not be persuaded to leave his boat until every sail was furled and stowed away properly. He took his time over it, too; for he knew instinctively that he could not shine before Phœbe in the presence of such glib gentlemen. They were shining gloriously when he appeared, and their free laughter set him a-grinning before he knew the cause.

"Walter," Phœbe called, "you're the jury. I'm puttin' these two good-lookin' gentlemen through a cross-examination. Up to this moment I've been the judge and the prosecuting attorney and the jury, too; but it's tryin' on the nerves. I'm glad you came in when you did. The prisoners were insultin' the Court with indecent flattery. I need a tipstave and a sheriff's posse, I do. Sit ye there, boy; and decide fair. The charge against these two malefactors— —"

"I object, your honour," interrupted Jawn. "We can't be malefactors until the charge is proved against us. You'll be prejudicing the jury against us before he has finished his cup of tea. And besides, I told the jury to shut up this afternoon, so we'll need all the close decisions."

"Who's tryin' this case?" demanded Phœbe. "The charge is gallivantin' with malice aforethought."

"Gallivanting with intent to kill," agreed Jawn. "We plead guilty."

"Is this your first offence?" asked the "judge."

"Good Lord!" ejaculated Jawn. "It's my seventy-seventh! Do you take me for a fledgling? I've got records to prove it. My dear lady, I shaved when I was eleven."

"May it please the Court," Richard spoke with the gravest deference, and told of the passions of Jawn as illustrated in his forthcoming book, "Love Limericks of a Left-tenant."

"Out with them, man; out with them!" demanded Phœbe.

"Some of them need expurgating badly," warned Richard.

"The Court must be entertained," said Phœbe, "even at the expense of a little vulgarity. Proceed, sir."

"The saddest case," Jawn searched his memory, "is that of a lady of my college days whose name I did not know, but who welcomed and nobly assisted my young aspirations; who, in short, taught me much."

Then he recited the "epitaph" of the lass who caught his heart during the early weeks of his Freshmanhood, who led him on outrageously, who looked the part of an under-grad in the high school, but who turned out to be the wife of the Dean!

"These college professors will often fool you," Jawn explained. "They marry the cutest little springers with the feathers still on their legs— —"

"Don't remind me of my Orpingtons!" cried Phœbe.

"—And with round little blushing peach-blow faces! It would fool anyone. You see, they are a shy lot all their young days, the professors are, the years when they should have been prancing about colt-like and finding out things. So they fly from the sight of women and sit in their cells and grow ogre-eyed and brainy. Then late in life they slide out in the twilight and grab a Young One. There ought to be a law against it."

The charge of "gallivantin'" was amply proved, at least against Jawn, by his own series of poetic confessions.

"And you say you've already had seventy-seven affairs with the ladies!" Phœbe expressed her incredulity.

"He's on his seventy-seventh now," corrected Richard.

"H-m!" Phœbe eyed him. "It's not me you're after makin' eyes at, is it?"

"I decline to commit myself," said Jawn solemnly. "I appeal to the legal decency of the jury that a man can't be compelled to bear testimony against himself."

The jury shifted about uneasily. The jury was obviously disturbed. Like many unhappy persons on this earth, Walter understood everything in the situation but the humour of it, and so missed its very salt.

"The jury will please mind its own business," the Court admonished; "I merely remind the prisoner that if he tries any gallivantin' with this Court he'll find himself muzzled and manacled in holy matrimony before he can think up a rhyme for 'God-help-me.' This Court finds the single state very depressing, and is gettin' entirely too old to miss a chance. All of which reminds me, Jawn, that you must have begun early. Have you any early records?"

Richard laughed appreciatively. He knew what was coming.

"Oh, a very good record," said Jawn. "It is the only one about whose ranking I feel positively sure. I call it 'My Firth,' for I was entirely too young to speak plainly. The official account goes this way,

> "To myself on the day of my birth
>
> I lisped, 'What a charming young nurth!'
>
> And then when she faced me
>
> And frankly embraced me,
>
> I remarked, 'Not tho bad, thith ol' Earth!'"

"Oh, beautiful! beautiful!" Phœbe clapped her hands. "I could love you for that one, Jawn."

"It is strikingly optimistic," commented Richard. "'Not tho bad, thith ol' Earth!' And it is absolutely characteristic of Jawn."

"I can believe it!" — this from Phœbe. "He was an imp of a lad from the cradle!"

"Jawn's the only specimen of pure lover left from the Middle Ages," said Richard, "for he believes with Dante, Petrarch and the rest that true love dies with marriage."

"Devil a bit!" Jawn remonstrated. "There's often a fine spark of it left — —"

"For some other fellow," Phœbe broke in quickly. "My own thought, exactly!" he added, and joined with Phœbe in good hearty Irish laughter.

"Order!" suddenly cried the Court, pounding her tea-cup on the table. "What d'ye mean by gettin' the Court to commit herself like that!"

After much more such give and take the Court arraigned the prisoners and charged the jury. She acknowledged that the evidence was all against them from the start, but that long acquaintance with a criminal world had made her soft; besides, they had drunk her tea and had laughed at her jokes, and no Irishman could ever hang a man he had once laughed with. So she would recommend them to the mercy of the jury.

The jury was absolutely non-committal. Whether it was surly, sleepy or speechless no one could say.

"Wan' 'o see you alone," it muttered to Phœbe; and nothing else would it admit.

"The jury can't come to a unanimous verdict," the Court announced; "so if the prisoners will kindly run out and play, we'll reason with the obstinate members."

"What's the trouble, boy?" she asked when they were alone.

In semi-incoherent language he poured forth his feelings about the two men whose cleverness with words had been hoodwinking everybody. With her mind alert to sift out all the evidence he could produce, she presented a laughing mocking face. But she could not joke him out of his convictions.

The "card," which he always carried about with him, was produced and partially explained. Richard's latest version, for some occult reason of his own, Walter did not tell.

"Glory be!" ejaculated Phœbe as she read the name. "The villain! Why, this man is dead; I read about it in the papers several years ago; he went down with his whole family in a shipwreck. What do you think it means, boy?"

"Dunno."

"Well," she assumed a cheerful tone, "perhaps it is only a lark. They are a great pair of boys. They would not stop at anything." The memory of their skylarking came back to brighten her face. "I haven't had such a good laugh since—since Seth got into the paint house."

She hummed about her little dining-room, putting away the tea-things, and considered the meaning of Mr. Richard's assumption of the name of a dead man. Some years ago a sleek-looking chap with no obvious occupation had rented a house on Main Street, made the acquaintance of important citizens and had continued for months to be unnaturally Christian. Everyone in the village had made a guess as to the exact sort of swindle he would eventually introduce, so that when he finally began to talk rubber trees in Madagascar the laugh was so hearty and universal that he left without offering to let anybody in on the ground floor.

Would it be rubber trees in Madagascar, or just a plain case of "worthless cheque"? Or would it be "power of attorney" with one or the other of them getting the "heiress"? Phœbe hoped it would be the latter. "I've handled a lunatic," she said to herself, "which makes me hanker after the intelligent even if they be criminal."

"Well, we'll keep our eyes open, boy," said Phœbe; "but whatever you do don't let on you suspect anything. Meet a confidence man with confidence. You'll spoil everything if you go about like you were this afternoon lookin' as glum as cold beeswax. Didn't you see how I was jollyin' 'em along? Did you think I meant half what I said? Of course I didn't. It was to make them feel easy. The devil was never yet fooled by a pious face."

Phœbe understood Walter better than anyone else. This theory of her hilarious enjoyment filled him with peace and sent him home with his head in the air.

CHAPTER XVIII
HARDY PERENNIALS

Jerry's long walk the previous evening had given her an excuse to have her coffee and rolls served in her room. She did not want to admit even to herself that she was nervously apprehensive of committing herself in the presence of Richard, but an undefined fear of him had quenched some of her natural Virginia boldness. With so many willing blacks about the place breakfast in one's room was an easy matter at "Red Jacket"; and it was too common a custom to create comment. She might avoid luncheon, too, but she knew that she could not hide indefinitely; so she came down.

Some of her indefinite fears became definite when she faced Richard at table. The men were full of their sail and of their good times at Phœbe Norris'. That permitted her to watch them unobserved. Occasionally, however, Richard glanced at her as if curious about her expressionless silence, but, she admitted ruefully, he was unconscious of his effect on her, as unconscious as a contented kitten. He was a terribly satisfied person! That was due, she supposed, to his frank egoism, but whatever the cause she felt helpless before it. Could nothing move this man? His peaceful blue eyes fronted the world too serenely for her comfort. "Sea blue imperturbable," she thought, purposely twisting Carlyle's phrase.

There was one way to move him, but that would move him out of the county on the next train—to make eyes at him. She would never do that; never! Her lips closed firmly and a snap came into her eyes at the very thought of it. Nevertheless, she felt cornered, and it almost angered her. Here was the tragic dilemma of sex: she must not make the slightest advance, and unless she did, this man would never be budged.

She thought of all her fine speeches to him about the joy of being treated not as a woman but as a human being, but she did not care to remember his enthusiastic reception of this point of view. Other men had fluttered and looked unutterable male things at her and she had been annoyed. Why was this calm gentleman built on such an unflutterable mould? Jawn, now, was flirting with her this very minute; Richard—the thought of Richard flirting with anyone was so preposterous that she unconsciously smiled.

The eager Jawn was quick to pounce on that smile. He took it to himself and ogled back.

"Huh!" he puffed; "I worked hard for that! I thought you were going to walk in your sleep during the whole meal. It took five exceptionally clever remarks, each guaranteed to raise a laugh, to bring one little smile. Do we owe for last week's board, or something? Or have you missed a solid silver spoon?"

"I beg your pardon," Jerry became a penitent hostess; "have you been talking to me? I haven't heard a word. I'm sorry."

The laugh went against Jawn.

"The seventy-seventh will be no madrigal," Richard told him; "it will be just one more limerick, Jawn."

"Please tell me about the madrigal?" Jerry asked politely.

Jawn pretended reluctance, but when urged confessed frankly his life-long hunt for a soul-mate, and of his belief that in Jerry he had found his El Dorado. It was ridiculous, of course, and Jawn could always be trusted to put his fun unequivocally. Mrs. Wells was delighted, especially with the Love Limericks; and Richard's joy in his friend's achievements was quite open; but Jerry, to her own astonishment, was annoyed. It was like joking at death in the presence of the bereaved.

And Richard's off-hand discussion of the possibility of Jerry's surrendering as a charitable means of putting an end to a flow of bad verse—that was unendurable. Fortunately, the inward perturbation was not outwardly disclosed; it was a simple matter to make a coldly apt comment, plead "business," and withdraw to her room.

Jawn stared after her.

"Did you see how cut up she was?" he cried. "Ah, lad, it's no joking matter. I've got a fine chance yet! A fine chance!"

Jerry had hardly crossed the threshold and heard him distinctly. She heard Richard's reply, too.

"Possibly, Jawn! Possibly! Undoubtedly something moved her—moved her off without her dessert. I never saw her quite so confused, but I'm afraid the elephantine character of your wooing frightened her off."

"Jealous!" cried Jawn.

"I envy you only that final limerick, Jawn. I know it's going to be a corker."

"Mrs. Wells, I appeal to you as a woman of experience," Jawn persisted. "Do you think I have a chance?"

Jerry did not wait to hear her mother's opinion. Although her more sensible self told her that it was childish to take offence at anything so obviously good-natured, the blinding anger that seized her drove her out of hearing quickly. The thought of staying a moment longer frightened her. She knew that she was on the verge of breaking down and spilling out a surprising torrent of invective against poor unoffending Jawn. And that, she had sense enough left to know, would be fatal. It would be worse than making eyes!

But if she had stayed a moment or two longer she would have been shocked into frigidity. To the innocent jesting Walter contributed a serious note.

While Mrs. Wells was assuring them that she would play no favourites, an interruption of Richard's had led Jawn to say:

"You keep out of this. I won't have any interference from big handsome men with romantic blue eyes and perfect teeth. What you need is a woman like Mrs. Norris to let you down a peg daily, to remind you of your grovelling insignificance. Go to the widow, thou sluggard."

"I've been," laughed Richard; "we quarrel beautifully!"

"Splendid! A fine sign! True love guaranteed!"

"'S not so!" blurted Walter; "Jerry and him's got it all f-fixed up."

George Alexander had caught Mrs. Wells' attention and at that moment was getting his directions for dinner. She had not been accustomed to attend very carefully to remarks from Walter, so the colloquy that followed was lost on her.

"What's this?" said Jawn quietly.

Richard looked on curiously.

"G-got it all fixed up, them two."

"They have, have they? How do you know?"

"Jerry told me."

"When was all this?"

"Last night. She said h-him and her, they were goin' to get married. Said they h-had it all f-fixed up."

"What!" cried Richard.

"Mebbe oughtn't t' have said nothin'," Walter was a little frightened at his own temerity. "But 'at's what she s-said, anyhow."

Jawn whistled.

"Here's a pretty mess!" said he; "here's a how d' you do! Let's get this straight, young man; do you mean to tell us that——"

"S-sh!" warned Richard.

Mrs. Wells had dismissed George Alexander, and was turning inquiringly upon the group.

"What's the matter?" she asked. The sudden silence had attracted her attention.

Richard stepped quickly into the breach. "Walter thinks he has the fastest boat on the Lake," he explained, and went into a voluble tribute to *Sago-ye-wat-ha*.

"Why, Richard!" Mrs. Wells interrupted. "How red your face is!"

"He's blushing for shame," said Jawn, "for shame at the thought of how easy it'll be to take the cup away from those other poor yachtsmen. And well you may, Richard! And well you may!"

Richard's blushes threatened to be permanent. Throughout the luncheon and several hours afterward he glowed like a burning sumac bush. While anything from Walter should be taken with something more than the proverbial grain of salt, yet he had succeeded in producing a most confusing mental state in Richard. Jawn's gentle raillery after luncheon did nothing to help matters, and all of Richard's many explanations of the possible twist in Walter's meaning merely added further confusion.

He sought an excuse early to be alone, and for an hour or two hovered about the house waiting for Jerry to appear. Some of his lost shyness came back to benumb him and prevent his sending for her outright. Indeed, once when he thought he heard her coming down the stairs he grew so fearful of meeting her that he slipped out of a rear door and fled into a path that led to the garden.

Walter was a fool, "a young damned fool," to use Jawn's technical expression. Why should one take seriously the act of an idiot? Why, indeed! She could not have possibly said anything of the sort, even in fun. At any angle that he looked at it such a conversation between Walter and Jerry was unbelievable. Thunderation! What an idea to put into a man's head!

But to one's own brother may not one make confessions? He had never been a sister, himself, so he could not guess their habits; but hadn't he read somewhere in books that sometimes, especially at night, they talk things out frankly with the brother? Which only shows how far his mind had swung out of its normal course. Who could fancy anyone of Jerry's independence making sentimental confessions to a half-witted brother?

"G' mawnin', Mr. Richard! G' mawnin'!"

George Alexander's white poll rose slowly out of a hydrangea bush wherein he seemed almost to have been hiding.

"Good-morning, George Alexander," Richard responded eagerly. He was glad of the chance to talk to someone not of the immediate family. "That hydrangea is a bigger plant than you are!"

"Tol'rable big, sir! Tol'rable big! But up on de hill yondah, we's got young gi-unts. Trees, I calls 'em—reg'lar hydranj'a trees!"

"You've been here all your life, haven't you, George?" Richard asked.

"All my life—so fah!" he laughed; "I was bo'n hyah an' I plum reckon 'at some day, when I gets tir'd idlin' 'round, I'll jess natchully die hyah."

"I don't see you idling around much. You're always busy at something. Do you have charge of the gardens, too?"

"Yassuh," he nodded his old white head sagely. "I'm de boss! De black boys do de easy workin' 'round, an' I do all de heavy lookin' *ovah*!" George Alexander's laugh was a low, cackling "Hyah! Hyah!" He punctuated his speeches with it, a notice in each instance of a humorous remark, a laugh exactly timed to give one a chance to "see the point." In these days George Alexander was a great curiosity, one of the very last specimens of the old-time "darkey," intelligent, nimble-witted, outspoken but diplomatic, loyal, an efficient manager, never servile but absolutely determined to be nothing more than a perfect servant.

"Do you run the vineyards, too?" Richard asked incredulously.

"Mistah Richud," George Alexander assumed an air of great seriousness, "I nevah could understand why *any*body would prefeh to *stan'* when dey could talk jess as well *settin'*! Hyah! Hyah!"

His solemn face broke forth into radiant lines as he pointed towards two excellent rustic benches facing each other.

"Yassuh!" he came back to Richard's question after he had spread himself comfortably on one of the seats. "Yassuh! I take charge of de grapes. An' I used to take charge of de apples, too; but Mrs. Wells, she done let dem apples all go. Dey ain't so much in de grapes as dey used to be, but apples—why, dem apples, Mistuh Richud, was all pure gold. I tol' her she make a big mistake to let 'em go. An' Mistah Buttuhwo'th tol' her. Mistah Buttuhwo'th's from Philadelphia, an' he knows all about apples. He loves apples so much he says it's a'mos' wicked to eat one. Hyah! Hyah! He knows apples well enough to call 'em by dar fus' names, Mistah Buttuhwo'th does; hyah! hyah!"

"Did you have any trouble with the apples, George?"

"Trouble?" George straightened up as much as his old back would allow. "Apples ain't no trouble, Mistah Richud. Jes' spray 'em propuhly, dat's all dey asks. Spray 'em to kill de fungus while de trees is still a-winterin', an' spray 'em to kill de Hosay scale befo' de blossom comes, an' spray 'em to kill de red-bug after de fruit is a-growin', an' spray 'em to kill de cuddlin' moth all de middle of de summer, an' spray 'em to kill de tent caterpillar when de fruit is mos' grown, an' spray 'em to kill de rest of 'em when de fruit is done. An' even den if yo' fin' youse'f restless at night an' can't git to sleep, you'd better git up an' spray 'em agin fo' luck! Hyah! Hyah! Trouble? Dey ain't no trouble 'bout growin' *apples*; dey jes' grows natcherel de way de Lawd intended; de on'y thing dat breaks yo' back is killin' dem consarned, evahlastin' *bugs*.... Hyah! Hyah!"

Richard paid his full tribute of applause and then asked, "Why did Mrs. Wells let the apples go? Didn't they pay?"

Richard inquired out of no thought to pry. The old man was so interesting that it was a temptation to start him going.

"Pay? Why in *co'se* dey paid! We was gittin' fo' thousand barrels o' puhfeck fruit after Mistah Buttuhwo'th come up hyah and tol' us how to do it. Used to be gittin' on'y about fi' hundud. An' Mistah Buttuhwo'th, he'd take 'em down to Philadelphia an' put 'em in his big ice-house and set back and wait till all de apples was eat up an' folks got a-hankerin' fo' one—Mistah Buttuhwo'th says dah's a lot o' Adam left in folks yit! Hyah! Hyah!—an' den when dey's ready to pay 'mos' anything for even a Ben Davis, he brings out our genuine Baldwins, an' *pow*! de price goes sky-*yutin*'!"

"Then why didn't you keep the orchards?"

"Dah yo' gits me, Mistah Richud." He shook his white head. "'Ca'se why? 'Ca'se you asks me to unraffle de hardest knot de good Lawd evah tie up. Does *any*body know, Mistah Richud, why a woman'd do *dis-heah*," he waved a hand dramatically, "rathe 'n *dat-dere*?" His hand moved between the two imaginary situations. "Mrs. Wells, she sez we was a-sprayin' too much. She sez we'd been a-killin' grubs for so many yeahs that dey'd done forget how to get borned, mebbe. In co'se I tol' her diff'rent, an' Mistah

Buttuhwo'th nearly get down an' prayed to her about it, but she 'lowed she'd give dem pore trees a rest. Dey wa'n't no 'jections, fah as I could observe, from de niggahs what had de sprayin' job! Hyah! Hyah! Pow'ful sympathizin' dey was to dem pore trees! Hyah! Hyah!... Well, Mistah Buttuhwo'th, he says de nex' crop would be all bug-ged, an' dey was all bug-ged; an' he says de nex' crop 'ud be buggeder an', sho' 'nuf, dey *was* buggeder!"

"But couldn't they be sprayed again and put into shape?"

"Puffekly! Puffekly! Dat's 'xactly what Mistah Hopkins did who bought 'em. But Mrs. Wells 'low'd dat after all her kindness she wouldn't have nothin' mo to do with trees what was as ongrateful as dem trees. An' don't yo' think yo'se'f, Mistah Richud, dat it was kind o' low-down *onery* o' dem trees? Hyah! Hyah!"

"But I suppose Mrs. Wells got a good price for the orchard." Richard tried to give George Alexander a chance to make up for his indirect criticism.

"Nuffin' to say, Mistah Richud," George Alexander assured him solemnly. "I's got a mudder an' a fahder an' a whole pa'sel progenitohs waitin' up dah," he pointed piously above, "an' dey see me gettin' near de point o' followin' along, an' meetin' up wid 'em; but, Mistah Richud, if I opens my mouth on de sale-price ob dat o'cha'd my talk would be so blasphemious dat I'd sho' have to dispoint dem people up dah!"

Richard thought he would be on safe ground to ask about the grapes.

"Po'rly, Mistah Richud, po'rly," George Alexander pulled a long face. "Not 'nuff blue-stone. A spray what's all water, I says, ain't no spray 'tall.... It's a mighty good thing us black folks is all rich."

There was a joke here, no doubt, thought Richard. George Alexander's expressionless face seemed to be waiting for the "interlocutor" to bring the end-man out.

"Well," asked Richard good-naturedly, "what's the answer, Mr. Bones?"

"Ya-as," George Alexander drew in a deep, satisfied breath, "*we's* all right. If anything ebber happens to de Wellses, *we's* fixed."

"Oh, you've all saved up money, have you?"

"When we's bo'n," explained George Alexander, "an' gits big 'nuff to work 'round, Mrs. Wells puts us on de pay-roll, an' as long as we stays with her we draws half and she keeps half for us. When she dies or when dis place breaks up we gits all our savin's back an' int'rest on 'em. We's all got our books to show how much. I's been on dat pay-roll fo' fifty yeahs, Mistah

Richud. I's a rich man if I stays on here, an' I guess I can leave my chillun' sumpin', 'case anything happens."

There were thirty negroes working here and there on the Wells' land, George Alexander told Richard; entirely too many, of course, but it had always been the custom of the Wells family to look out for its blacks. All this explained the absolute absence of "labour troubles" for so many generations. Any capable negro was assured of an easy livelihood, care in illness, and a safe pension.

"An' what mo' does anybody want in dis yeah world?" asked George Alexander. "I'd be mighty thankful, Mistah Richud, to be shu' o' dat much up *dah*! Hyah! Hyah!"

In his artless way George Alexander had thrown considerable light on Red Jacket under Mrs. Wells' management. Richard recalled one of Jerry's illustrations of her mother's obstinacy whereby the year's grape crop had been lost. No doubt unrecorded history had similar stories with similar losses. Evidently there were funds enough to cover these bad balances and keep the big place going; if not Jerry would soon discover what she got to the bottom of the documents placed in her charge.

Jerry would sift things to the bottom, he felt sure. There was a certain satisfaction in lingering on the thought of Jerry's substantial character. She had the mother's persistence and will, and, he smiled to himself, a little of the mother's obstinacy. How he had misjudged her at first! But there was nothing surprising in that to Richard. Having practised open-mindedness all his life he was aware of the commonness of mistaken judgments. It is only the bigoted and partisan who experience infallibility.

His pleasant musings were interrupted by George Alexander.

"But we's makin' a big go ob dem hahdy puh-ren-nials, Mistah Richud, a great go!" he was saying, with emphasis.

"Dey mus' be 'bout twenty ob dem black boys up dah now, a-workin' an' a-hoein' an' a-prunin'. We's su'ten'y got de prize crop o' phlox an' yaller daisy! Hyah! Hyah! Dey's a whole mountain o' snapdragon, blues an' yallers an' pinks an' whites. You don't know o' any localities, Mistah Richud, what's hungerin' now fo' a mess o' peonies, does yo'? 'Ca'se if yo' do, it'd be de Lawd's mercy to let 'em loose up on dat hill yondah. An' hollyhocks! Lawd! If we could on'y send hollyhocks down to Mistah Buttuhwo'th's big ice-house in Philadelphia, we'd no need o' no apple o'cha'd, Mistah Richud. Hyah! Hyah! But I's not seen many puhsens hyeah-'bouts fallin' ober demselves to buy up our hollyhock crop, Mistah Richud. Hyah! Hyah! Not so many, Mistah Richud!"

There was always money enough for spray and soil for the hardy perennials, George Alexander averred. And there was always a strong demand for labour to thin out this group here and transplant there, and prune and cultivate and graft. The seed-pods were collected as if they were gold-dust; and bulbs were dug up, wrapped and saved; and slips were cut and planted in fresh places; and paths were made, hedges constructed for background effect and natural stone walls built for trailing vines, and so on and so on.

No doubt it was magnificent. Mr. Richard could see for himself. The whole hillside had been turned into a garden which renewed itself each year and flowered from early May when the first yellow forsythia sprang forth until the last cosmos had died and the hydrangeas had bent their dark heads. From the Lake it waved its flaunting colours, and visitors had motored many miles for a sight of it.

But it buttered no parsnips, said George Alexander. Flowers were all right, but you couldn't barrel them and send them to Mr. Butterworth in Philadelphia. George Alexander loved beauty, but he had been trained in the practical business of grape and apple farming. Grapes and apples should come first, he thought, not hardy perennials.

Of course he had not meant to be critical; but he had lived with the Wells family all his life; it was his family as much as anybody's and therefore he was going to stick up for it even if the family did not.

Oh, Mrs. Wells knew how he felt. He had always been frank and straightforward on the business end of "Red Jacket." But the whole trouble was that she avoided him. He was her black conscience that always reminded her of her sins; so she cleverly got him off the subject, or sent him on business at the other end of things, or claimed to have a headache.

George Alexander laughed shrewdly.

And the reason he had taken Mr. Richard aside to tell him the story was to get a helper. He had noticed that Mrs. Wells thought very highly of Mr. Richard's judgment. Well, George Alexander considered that it wouldn't do any harm to strengthen that judgment with his own!

And all the while Richard had fancied that this garrulous old darkey was just talking aimlessly! The craft of the old fellow!

There were other reasons, George Alexander was saying, while he scratched his white poll thoughtfully; but—he hesitated—but he'd let them wait. Yet it seemed to him that if things kept drifting along the way he had observed them—he hesitated again and winked a jovial eye at Mr. Richard—

well, he'd better not pursue that topic, as it was none of his business, but—he hoped—well, he wouldn't just say what his hopes were.

The chuckles and "Hyah hyahs" of the old fellow were meant undoubtedly to be significant of something. Richard's ears burned at the thought of what he might be meaning, but he thrust it aside swiftly as too absurd. Meanwhile something had to be done to stop the criminal grin on that black face, so Richard rose hastily and claimed that he must go immediately and look at the hardy perennials.

"You'll like 'em, Mistah Richud," George Alexander straightened out his face; "they'll tickle yo' eye like rainbows on a soap-bubble; but jess yo' keep yo' head, Mistah Richud, an' every time yo' shout, 'Be-yut-i-ful!' jess yo' say to you'self 'Grapes fust! Grapes fust!' Hahdy puh-rennials is all right. I's got no 'jection to dem—in dere own propuh place; although I don't mind sayin' to yo', Mistah Richud, dat de on'y hahdy puh-rennials dat I see any use in is dem combs an' hahr brushes dat de Penn Yan drug stores brings out ob dere hidin'-places and puts conspicuous on de front counters ebry Christmas time. Hyah! Hyah! Dey su'ten'y am *hahdy*, an' dey shu' is puh-rennial!"

CHAPTER XIX
MICHAELMAS DAISY AND ROSE-BUGS

A great hedge, cut to resemble the old-fashioned pillar-and-ball entrance to a driveway, welcomed one into the beginning of the gardens. Beyond the hedge the path curved abruptly, and a six-foot wall with high terraces beyond filled the view. Blue masses of sentinel-like larkspur in mounting tiers gave the first greeting. Here was the evidence of an intelligent planning to capture the eye right at the beginning and make one eager to follow the curving path to see what would be beyond. Instinctively Richard stopped and uttered the prophesied word, "Beautiful!" The thought of "Grapes fust!" never intruded.

At the curve the walk widened into a little circle of violet phlox, walled-up on all sides except towards the sun and towards the narrow arched opening that led farther on. The walls were not high and were almost concealed by the climbing blue clematis; beyond them was slightly higher ground crowded with blue harebell, and farther back a battalion of Chinese larkspur. Blue snapdragon—giants, every one—sprang out here and there, and a bevy of smaller border flowers filled in the scheme—all blue. An old-fashioned hickory settle invited one to sit and enjoy; and near it had been planted nests of the more fragrant plants, and borders of blue campanula, Jacob's ladder and creeping phlox.

Richard sat on the settle and admired. "Beautiful!" he exclaimed again and again. It was a bower of blue—blue and purple and violet and lavender and red-blue; but nothing clashed or interfered with the dominant cerulean note; there was enough rich green to separate what would otherwise be jarring shades.

What a puzzling mute Jerry Wells could be when she chose! In all their chatty hours together there had been hardly a word about this; and undoubtedly here was but the vestibule of the gardens. "Red Jacket" should be discovered for oneself, she always said. Well, it was better so; half the delight in life is the unanticipated joys.

Green shrubs blocked the view through the arch, but one turn—the garden was a maze of turns—and behold, a diminutive bridge and a slender spring-fed rivulet, and beyond, in clumps and patches raised at various elevations by hidden walls, blooms of delicate pink: Canterbury bells, hollyhock, phlox, gladiolus, lupine, foxglove.

The pink bower was larger than the blue and was, therefore, not to be taken in at once. Curving paths appeared leading to a series of surprises, a sward of rest-harrow here and a bevy of tall canna there, but no alien colour had been permitted to spoil the general tone.

Just over a hedge Richard heard voices and the light-hearted laugh of negroes at work. Someone in authority was giving directions; it sounded like Jerry's voice, so he chanted the family song, the two musical notes, the fifth and the third of the scale, "Hel-lo!"

The song came back, softly wafted over the green barrier, "Hel-lo!" — the "lo" held until it diminished into a whisper.

Eagerly he sought a path, singing the call occasionally as he missed his way and getting the response every time. The path that he chose dropped down broad flagstone steps and then rose. He had completed a half-circle before he came upon a hillside of yellow blooms, gaillardia, black-eyed Susans, and dahlia. They fairly shouted at him, especially the yellow daisies, but he did not see them at all. "Hel-lo!" he sang in his flutest tones; and "Hel-lo!" came back almost at his feet. He found himself standing on a six-foot wall at the top of a set of narrow stone steps; below him Mrs. Wells was engaging the attention of several negroes with wheelbarrows, spades and a whole galaxy of garden tools.

"Hel-lo!" she sang up at him.

Richard was astonished at his own disappointment. Courage to face folks was not always ready at call, and at this precise hour he felt no terrifying shyness. He was not one to be courageous at a moment's notice; his ridiculous left-handedness had a habit of visiting him when he least desired it; it was a pity that Jerry was not present now when he felt so able.

But to Mrs. Wells he showed no sign either of surprise or disappointment.

"Hel-lo!" he sang cheerfully; and came down the steep irregular steps.

"I'll never be kind to a Michaelmas daisy again," she greeted him, trowel in hand.

"Are they ungrateful?" he asked and looked at the black-eyed Susans. "They seem very sweet and ingratiating to me."

"Oh, I don't mean the rudbeckia," she laughed. "They are just as bad, but— —"

"Pardon me," Richard interrupted. "Introduce me to this bad rude Becky; I don't know her at all."

"The black-eyed Susans!" she laughed at his ignorance. "You are staring at them. We gardeners call them rudbeckias. You just daren't let them go to seed; they'd run over the whole place. Just look how they have multiplied since I have been away! But they're not half so bad as the Michaelmas daisy, who have no right to be in the yellow garden at all."

"Why, pray?" Richard searched about for the offending member.

"Because they are blue."

"H-m! Blue!" he still looked about him. "Perhaps I'm growing blinded by all the beauty hereabouts, but I don't see anything blue."

She laughed again, delighted with his stupidity.

"If you look into those barrows," she pointed, "you'll see the blue truants. They belong in the blue beds, but they got loose somehow and cropped up all over the place. I've been spending my hours hunting them out. Don't you see where we have been digging?"

Then Richard saw the great gashes, and admitted his folly. Everything was so wonderful and colossal he had not been able to see the defects, he told her. By this time his eye was taking in the spreading expanse of yellow field.

"'And then my heart with rapture fills,'" he quoted, "'and dances with the——' I don't see any daffodils."

Even the negroes laughed at this.

"Have I said something stupid?" he asked. "Don't blame me; blame Wordsworth. I'm sure he said daffodils—but perhaps he only did it for the rhyme. If Jawn were here he'd make a limerick to fit black-eyed Susans.... But just why are daffodils so funny?"

"Daffodils are a spring flower, my dear Richard," Mrs. Wells began to explain.

"Of course they are!" Richard remembered. "Wretchedly stupid of me. But I never can keep pace with that kind of information. I never know when it is kite time or top time.... We'll have to bring Wordsworth up to the minute. How is this:

"And then with joy my heart goes crazy

And dances with the Michaelmas daisy?"

"Not mine!" Mrs. Wells shook her head and flourished the trowel.

"Oh," he corrected himself, "your version should be,

"And then with anger my mind goes crazy
And trowels away at the Michaelmas daisy!
"It isn't as smooth as one of Jawn's, but the idea is sound."

"Quite right," agreed Mrs. Wells. "Michaelmas daisies are decent enough, like some of these black boys, when they know their proper places."

The black boys "hyah-hyahed" at this tribute to their ambitious proclivities. "Saul there," she went on, "is a black Michaelmas daisy"—Saul exploded with appreciative laughter—"he goes right into my refrigerator without so much as by-your-leave and helps himself to the best muskmelons. Some day I'll have to take my trowel to him and let you boys wheel him off to the weed-fire."

The darkies enjoyed this amiable attack on Saul's weakness for muskmelon, but none more than the black culprit. The Virginia give and take between master and servant was strangely at home in these northern hills. Evidently, thought Richard, the transplanting of a hundred years ago had been done with expert skill; none of the southern flavour had been lost.

"Trowel won't nebber do, M's Wells," cried Saul between choking guffaws; "reckon you-all'll hab to git a pickaxe! Yass'm—sho' hab to git a pickaxe."

Interested as Richard was in the plantation setting and in the glorious richness of the floral display his heart was not dancing like Wordsworth's for either daffodils or black-eyed Susans. The first eager thought that he might find Jerry alone in the gardens had left a strong desire to go to her. There was much that he had to say to that young lady. It had better be done now. "Do it now" was not his favourite motto; it smacked too much of commerce; but doing it now seemed suddenly to acquire appropriateness. With this idea in mind he turned towards the ladder of stones and began to mount.

"As we go up the steps and turn to the left," Mrs. Wells remarked as she followed, "you'll come upon something I very much wish you to admire. Jerry said I mustn't guide-book you about, so I'll say nothing about what you'll find; but I'm very proud of my—well, never mind what."

She was going with him! Well, he would take a look and then be off. Of course, the gardens were wonderful, but they would keep, and——

Suddenly he found himself saying, "Beautiful!" again, exactly as George Alexander had predicted. Through a dense mass of shrubbery they had picked their way until abruptly the hollyhocks broke upon them, thousands of them! It was like a magnificent western cornfield, tilted to the sun. Walks of snapdragon and lupine and hardy pinks wound their way among the giant flowers. And no particular colour had been allowed to grow in very large masses; the foxglove and the larkspur and the gladiolus came back, like the *leitmotiv* of a German opera, and all joined in a monster symphonic design, whose design was not apparent at all. It was the climax, the *finale*, of the piece, the full orchestra wherein the little bowers of blue and pink and yellow had been solos, unaccompanied flute and clarionet and French horn.

But even here there were turns of the path, hummocks of hardy shrubs, unexpected beflowered walls, and finally, at the top of the hill, in the early stage of light-green bloom, a veritable grove of hydrangeas. "*Gi*-unts, they is, reg-u-lar hydrang'a *gi*-unts!" George Alexander had called them. Through the myriad straight slender trunks the blue sky beyond the hill formed a perfect background; and with the massive clustered heads, seemingly clipped out into symmetrical designs, the scene had all the effect of a gigantic Maxfield Parrish poster.

For the first time Richard neglected to say "Beautiful!" Instead, he looked on in thoughtful wonder, turned about and took in the sweep of acres below him crowded with perennials, masses of deep red and old rose and white which he had not seen before. Then he began to understand the enormous effort of the thing, and the cost in money, time and labour. So he did not say "Beautiful," but he thought of George Alexander and said to himself, "Grapes fust!"

But he did not follow George Alexander's directions and say it aloud. The beauty of the scene before him was too rare an experience; and grapes, after all, were simply something for sale. It was not expected that George Alexander's mind could get above the rise and fall of the market. Beauty was an emotional experience, not something to be sold for a penny; and emotional experiences were the essence of living. Better a dinner of herbs where beauty is than many profitable baskets of grapes.

So he turned to the expectant woman beside him and praised and praised. These gardens were a revelation of her mind, he told her, a cross-section of her soul. Unconsciously he began to batter down George Alexander's arguments against thrift and close buying and selling and all the other despicable acts of trade.

The penniless are the most eloquent abusers of wealth! What is money, he asked her derisively, compared with the wealth before them! "Let the millioned-dollared ride! Barefoot trudging at his side" hath what wealth cannot purchase. Thrift? Economy? Profit? He repudiated them all and apostrophized the work before him, and crowned with rhetoric the Workwoman.

The Workwoman glowed and applauded; and for payment she let him into the secrets of her craft; her fight against mullein and sorrel, grubs, and cut-worms; the mysteries of mulch; the struggle to keep a steady Christian colour in sweet-williams, hollyhocks and columbines; the everlasting effort to lift the cup of cold water to the lips of the ever-thirsty gladiolus; the war against the onrush of Michaelmas daisy, Bouncing Bet and hawkbit; the constant necessity of nipping helianthus, phlox and golden glow, which otherwise grow rank and ungainly; the multifarious uses of sprays for killing everything from larkspur blight to rose-bugs. And she confessed her private theories of soils and her views on seed propagation and root splitting; on fertilizers; on cold frames; and on continuous bloom throughout the year.

"Helen Albee tells me that no one can get a continuous blue," she warmed up enthusiastically, "but I did it one year." And then she started a technical avalanche of names. "Who is Helen Albee? She is a fellow-conspirator among us hardy perennialists. I give her credit for all this—she and Lena Walker—I was nowhere until I met those two."

There was no false egotism about this artist. Richard was astonished at the change in her. Her old self had almost come back, and something moved him to tell her so. They had been sitting for some time in the shadow of the hydrangeas and were facing out towards the Lake.

"No;" she closed her lips firmly; "I am not myself yet.... I am not well. Ever since — —"

Abruptly she stopped speaking and with caution pressed a hand to her heart, almost furtively. It was there that Walter had struck her, but she would not have admitted it. The blow had been something more than mental; it had left a physical bruise which declined to heal; and she was conscious of occasional inward pain which she tried to tell herself would soon pass away. But Richard, who saw the quiver pass over her face, did not observe the motion of her hand, and he could not have suspected its cause. And even if he had guessed, this weak old woman would have straightened up valiantly and would have lied about it with deceiving outward cheerfulness. The Virginia plantation of the early nineteenth century had been moved north with all its characteristic virtues intact!

But she had begun to confess once more to this dutiful squire. "No; I am not well," she said.

"I am sorry," Richard said feelingly.

"I know you are," she nodded her head several times thoughtfully; "I feel your sincerity. That's why I tell you so much that I conceal from others. Let me tell you some more.... You are as good as a priest," she smiled at him. "It is only in my gardens that I feel my old self. I am not strong any more—no! you need not try to encourage me; I know. But up here among my flowers I fool myself—I act as if I were in control of things; I boss the black boys about and boss even the flowers and the rose-bugs. I'm happy up here; I have nothing to worry me."

She stopped, evidently at the preamble of her confession. Walter was on Richard's mind, and on that score he was preparing himself to infuse self-confidence into her; but her mind was leagues from Walter.

Richard laughed to dispel the effect of her gloomy tone and asked what on earth she had to worry about.

"'Red Jacket' is mortgaged to the limit, and the interest is long overdue; I have been borrowing for twenty years, and I don't know how many thousands I owe," she remarked simply, as casually as if she had invited him to enjoy the view.

The unexpected information shocked him, although certainly George Alexander had given him ample clues. He began a speech about the uselessness of money—one of his favourite poetic theories—but it did not ring true. For the first time in his life he found that Thoreauean point of view distasteful.

"Does Jerry know?" he interrupted himself.

"She'll know if she can ever make head or tail out of the books," she answered serenely. "Well!" she gave a tremendous sigh of relief and actually smiled. "I'm glad I don't have to do the juggling any longer. I've thrown it all on Jerry now. She's young and able, I guess. She'll find a way out, never fear."

And so she talked complacently, meanwhile with every other sentence giving ugly details which showed plainly enough, even to Richard's non-commercial experience, that Jerry would have to be a financial magician to find any way out except via bankruptcy. He tried to quiz her, but she put him off with the plea that the business of managing the estate was no longer her affair. She was too happy with her perennials to spoil it all with figures that would not come out right. She joked about it, too; showing all too clearly that if bossing things in the gardens had given her the appearance of her old masterful self, it was an appearance only. A bit of her mind, seemingly, had become atrophied without in the least harming the remainder. Heretofore she had been both a dominating manager of a complicated estate and a clever gardener; at present the dominating manager had vanished, leaving only the clever gardener.

Richard rose precipitately. He must see Jerry at once. She had seemed particularly worried lately; and he remembered with a pang that he and Jawn had been trying to joke her into good spirits. With this calamity hanging over her—already she must have got an inkling of the state of affairs—they had been unforgivably cruel. He must go to her instantly.

"Who is your lawyer?" he asked Mrs. Wells; his tone was almost crisp.

"My lawyer?" she inquired in turn. "I never had any."

"You speak of mortgages and bonds and transfers of property," he followed up quickly. "Whom do you consult about such matters?"

"Oh," she smiled sweetly; "you mean Mitchell Lear, I suppose. Of course, he's a lawyer; but I never go to him about law matters—only as a friend."

"Does he know about your affairs?"

She thought carefully. "Ye-es," she admitted. "He knows; not that I ever told him much, but he always guessed, I reckon. I fibbed to him about everything," she laughed at the remembrance, "but you can't fool Mitchell Lear. Words aren't anything to him; he just looks on quietly through your eyes and into the very privacy of your soul. Once I told him a long story about deciding to buy more orchard land—buy, you understand—and after I was quite done, he nodded his wise head and remarked, 'I'm sorry you've made up your mind to sell!' 'But I said "buy,"' said I. 'I heard you,' said he; 'and I say that you are making a mistake to sell.'"

Mrs. Wells laughed quietly and contentedly at the remembrance. "And the funny part of it was," she told Richard, "I had just sold all the orchard we possessed; and it *was* a mistake, too," she added, "just as he knew it would be.... Oh, well! I mustn't think of those things any more; they make me too unhappy."

Mrs. Wells was sorry to see Richard go—there were many more things to show him, but he would have none of them. With a faintly troubled face she watched him stride down a path and disappear behind a grove of hollyhocks. But in a moment or two she had forgotten about him and was calling her blacks about her. The imperative duty of the hour was rose-bugs.

CHAPTER XX
SETH'S WHIP

Richard's best singing of the "Hel-lo" call failed to bring a response from Jerry.

"Mrs." George Alexander, who, as "Sukie," presided over the kitchen, reckoned that Miss Geraldine had gone down to visit Mrs. Phœbe Norris. That's what she "reckoned," but she "'lowed" that Miss Geraldine might go even farther. One of the Wheelen boys was with her.

"When one o' dem Wheelen boys comes 'long," Sukie explained, "nobody c'd tell *whar* M's Geraldine 'ud lan' up. Ef she jes' tuck it in her head to go plum down dat Lake to Hammonspo't, plum down dat Lake she'd go! When M's Geraldine gits in dem canoes she jes' na'chully do' know when to git outen 'em!"

Off on a canoe trip! That did not sound like bankruptcy; although it corresponded surprisingly to the mother's free and easy Southern manner of handling high finance.

But perhaps Sukie's "reckoning" was more nearly correct than her "'lowing." He would investigate further at the Norris cottage.

"Too late, young man," cried Phœbe before he could state his errand. "Anyone could see by the rush you made down that hill and by the glitter in your eye that you are tryin' to overtake a woman. Jerry is gone. The other man has her, and my tip is that you had better bring matters to a point quickly—or you'll lose nest and feathers too."

His rapid-fire questions exhibited Phœbe in the light of a perfect mind-reader. But she had no help for him. They had gone off in Wheelen's canoe; there was no telling when they would be back.

"I'll wait," said Richard firmly, and sat down upon one of her comfortable porch chairs.

"I'm thinkin' of putting up a sign," remarked Phœbe. Richard gazed down the Lake and made no answer. "Only I'm not sure whether to make it 'Beware the dog,' or 'Trespassing forbidden.'... Perhaps I'll make it 'Huntin' not allowed on this land'—meanin' by that, 'girl huntin''—or mebbe I'll just have it read, 'The Norris Inn; Meals Furnished Free.'"

"Eh?" he came out of his fixed stare. "Did you say something about eating? I'm really quite hungry."

"Of course you would be!" she said. "Feed a stray dog an' he'll always come back. It was a mistake ever to give you two anything. Your friend Jawn was here for two-o'clock tea. What'll you have, sir?" She flung a bit of sewing over her left arm and impersonated an ingratiating waiter. "We recommend our toasted muffins and tea."

"Great!" he agreed politely. "I'd be delighted."

But anyone could see that his mind was not on food. Down the Lake he squinted with wrinkling brows as if he were trying to read the name on a far-distant steamer.

"As a rule canoes don't travel in the middle of the Lake," said Phœbe.

"Eh?" he looked up absently.

"They hug the shore," she said.

"Oh! Do they?... Why?"

"Canoeing is said to be a dangerous sport." Phœbe talked through the window as she prepared the muffins. "And it is. Although, for myself, I'm thinkin' there's less danger out in the middle of the Lake where everybody can see you with field-glasses than goin' in and out among the bushes and gettin' out ever so often to sit down under a tree and rest."

"I don't get that," said Richard.

"You wouldn't," commented Phœbe dryly. "I believe I once called you a clever rascal. I apologize and withdraw the 'clever.' You are not clever."

"Very good! Very good!" With an effort Richard had caught the point of her satire and applauded politely. But his mind was elsewhere, as evidenced by his sudden remark, "You told me the Wells' were prosperous."

"Well, aren't they?"

"No. They're in bad straits financially. Perhaps you have known; at any rate my instinct tells me that it will do no harm to tell you."

Phœbe left her muffins toasting and came out to him.

"Who's been puttin' that into your head?" she inquired seriously.

"Mrs. Wells."

For a moment Phœbe stared at him soberly; then she broke into merriment.

"It's no joke," he said solemnly. "She has sold off the land that paid the best income—the apples—and she has been borrowing and not paying back for twenty years."

Phœbe sat down weakly.

"You're tryin' to frighten me," she said.

"It's the truth. Furthermore——"

Richard ceased speaking and fumbled for cigarette paper.

"Furthermore what?" Phœbe demanded impatiently.

"Your muffins are burning."

"Let 'em! What's this furthermore business?"

"I'm very sensitive to odours."

"And I'm very sensitive to furthermores. Furthermore what?"

Richard puffed slowly.

"Well, it is only a fear I have that Mrs. Wells may have used money that was not, strictly speaking, her own."

"Take that back!"

Phœbe jumped to her feet, reached up deftly and unhooked the stout whip that had done duty for some years as a protector from Seth. "Take it back, I say!" she cried as she swung the lash, "or I'll make you take it back."

She was trembling with anger, and she looked murderous.

"All right," Richard puffed away quietly. "I'll take it back, although I think you should attend to those muffins before you cart-whip me. I'd rather have my muffins in the mouth than in the nose, if you don't mind."

Phœbe struggled a moment with her quivering anger and then put back her whip and strode to the rescue of the muffins.

Nearly a half-hour slipped away before she returned. Richard was only a desultory smoker, but he had time to roll a number of cigarettes before she appeared finally with a tray of fresh muffins, some jam and a pot of hot tea. All trace of her anger was gone, too.

"There is only one thing I hate worse than a lie," she began the conversation as she poured the tea, "and that is the truth."

"You are quite right," he agreed as he spread a hot muffin. "Truth is the nastiest dose in the pharmacopœia. Perhaps I came at you too strong, but I think I made no mistake in thinking you can stand a lot. I have always been frank with you, Phœbe, and my instinct tells me——"

"Your instinct had better be careful," she warned, flushing a little; "it nearly got you a welt across the face."

"And I am very glad," he replied calmly. "If you would flame up like that for your friends you would do a lot more to help them out of their troubles. I fear they'll need all the help you can give them."

"Perhaps you had better tell me what you know. You take your own risk, of course"—she was regaining her normal cheerfulness—"if I don't like what you know, you may get this pot of hot tea in your face.... Go on; I'm listenin'—carefully."

He related the confession which Mrs. Wells had made to him under the hydrangeas, but for prudential reasons he did not divulge the ground of his belief that some of Mrs. Wells' business transactions may not have been entirely business-like.

To Richard's surprise, Phœbe broke into nervous laughter.

"What a fool I've been," said she, "ever to get stirred up by all that! Can't you see that the old lady was just tryin' you out?"

"No; I don't see anything of the sort."

"You believe all she said?"

"Don't you?"

"I asked you first."

"Yes; I do believe it. If they were sold out to-morrow, the debts would overwhelm them."

"Then I suppose the jig's up?"

Phœbe was still intent on her moving-picture film of a pair of New York villains attempting to marry money; but Richard understood her differently.

"I fear the jig is up, as you say. Of course," he added, "I'll have to see Jerry first to make sure."

"Yes," agreed Phœbe, "you had better make sure. But I'm sorry for one thing——"

"Which is?"

"That I didn't give you that welt with the whip."

He laughed, not at all taking her seriously.

"But you may get it yet," she laughed in turn.... "*Walter told me your other name!*" She shot the information at him suddenly.

"Oh," he remarked casually; "he did, did he?"

"Rather a sporty name to be gallivantin' under, eh?"

"I never liked it."

"Why?"

"It made me too conspicuous.... And people asked such impertinent questions."

"They would!"

"Yes; Richard Richard is much better.... Don't tell Jerry about the other name yet, will you?"

She agreed. Somehow she felt sorry for the man. According to her theory he had played for high stakes and lost. About that she cared little. But his coolness and good nature pleased her; and he had courage, for he had never so much as flinched when she flung the big whip. No doubt he would have taken her blow without even lifting his guard. He had merely looked up at her with his mild blue eye, scrutinizing her with an almost disinterested curiosity. Seth had always dropped on all fours at the very sight of the whip; this man was built on a more courageous mould, and she admired him immensely for it.

"You're a good sport," she summed him up, "even if you are a bad lot."

"Thanks.... Where is Walter?" he asked.

"He and Jawn are sailing the new boat." She laughed at some memory of their setting forth. That laugh was a brave attempt to conceal her worry over the Wells' affairs. "Jawn's a bright lad, he is; but he—he ought to have the whip, too."

"I believe you," Richard assented. "Was he nice and vulgar to you to-day? Jawn loves to be vulgar."

"I'm no judge of such things," she parried; "it takes all my time just to enjoy them."

"Young woman," he told her in his smiling superior way, "that's a mighty fine formula to go through life on. Why be always judging and valuing? One needs all the time just to enjoy."

Silence fell between them. Hovering over the pleasant tea-table was the memory of the recent ugly scene and beyond that the fate of the Wells family.

"I believe you would!" Phœbe remarked in answer to one of her own thoughts.

"Perhaps." He sipped his tea contentedly, looked down the Lake and waited.

"If the Big House should go to smash," she explained finally, "I believe you would loaf about enjoyin' yourself with what was left in the refrigerator and then tramp off without caring a — —"

She left the sentence unfinished.

"Say it," he suggested. "'Damn' is no longer a bad word. It has been taken up by the best people."

"I believe you would!" she iterated.

"I would enjoy myself," he agreed; "and quite possibly I would tap the refrigerator, if it were hungry time; and even more possibly I would loaf; and maybe I would tramp off. Ye-es," he figured the matter over carefully, "I am sure I should enjoy it, too—immensely. Do you know, I am rather hoping the Big House will go to smash—although it's a point of view I never suspected I should hold. In fact, I'm getting more delight out of the thought every minute.... My whole life is turning right over like a turtle that has been on his back for thirty years.... You can't imagine how excited I am."

"No," she snapped; "praise be, I can't. I'm—I'm— —" a wave of emotion swept her—"dang it all, man, how can you sit there and grin with all this happenin' to Jerry!"

"All what?" he asked with a fine affectation of innocence.

"All what!" she exploded. "They've lived in the Big House ever since there was a Big House, and even before that in the log-cabins where the negroes are now. Of course I've always known something like this would happen— —"

"Ah! ha!" said the man, "you knew it, did you?"

"I have ears, man!" she snapped. "I hear without listenin' at keyholes. Everybody in Jerusalem township knows the Big House is mortgaged, but mortgages are respectable enough. We always thought she preferred to invest her money in better paying stocks and things.... What has she done with it all? That's what I should like to know."

"She has over thirty negroes on the pay-roll," he suggested without much concern, although he did not miss Phœbe's agitation. "That should mean at least five thousand a year in wages; and from what I know of the Wells' bounty, those negroes and their families get practically everything they need free. The gardens cost a couple of thousand a year. The accumulation of small wastage would amount to considerable; and then, you know, the income has been impaired mightily through the sale of the orchards, and the failure to get the most out of the grapes. They've been spending more than they earned—considerably more, I should judge—and they have tried the old expedient of making up the deficit each year by borrowing."

He said not a word about the possible breach of trust as to the negroes. Phœbe would have given much to be able to ask him; but, somehow, she could not get the question out. She feared the truth.

"They're about at the end of their rope," he went on. "The fiddler will have to be paid, that's all."

"That's *all!*" she echoed indignantly. "Isn't it enough? The money's nothin' and the food's nothin'," she went on excitedly. "I have plenty to keep both families alive and free from the necessity of doing a stroke the rest of their lives. It isn't that, man. The Wells family have been used to living on a big scale. They have been surrounded by negroes who fetch and carry for them, and they have been the 'big family' in this part of the country for a century or more. They could never come down. Don't you see it, man? It would kill them. They could never pig it along the way you and I could do. Don't sit there and grin at me, you blitherin' fool! What I want to know is what we're goin' to do about it?"

He puffed away deliberately and watched her animated face as if he enjoyed her dramatics. Then he said:

"We're going to pay off the debts, liquidate the mortgage and set the Wells family on its feet—bail 'em out, in short."

"We are, are we?" she tossed her head. "And with what?"

"Money."

"Whose money? I've got none; at least none that would count."

"My money."

"Talk sense, man," she stood up and sat down nervously. "It'll take thousands to— —"

"Easily that," he figured. "I'm counting on about sixty thousand. The place is mortgaged for forty-two thousand dollars, thirty thousand on a first mortgage and twelve thousand on a second. She has notes out amounting to about eight thousand more. That's fifty thousand. She owes the negroes about ten thousand more— —"

"What!" cried Phœbe, "the negroes. Where'd they get ten thou— —"

She stopped, aghast at the thought that had crossed her mind. She knew all about the Wells' scheme of keeping back half of the wages into a savings fund; and she knew that it was something more than a charity. A contract guaranteeing those savings had been drawn up for each employee on the

Wells estate. Such money belonged to the negroes, and Mrs. Wells was nothing more than a legal trustee of the funds. If that had been touched, Phœbe with her natural business experience knew that something more than the mild procedure of bankruptcy might be in store for Jerry's mother.

"Did she say she had used that money, too?" Phœbe asked breathlessly.

"I fear so," he told her kindly. "But don't worry, my dear girl. As soon as I have talked with Jerry—I want to see those documents—I'll get in touch with New York and fix the whole business up."

"You're not foolin' me, are you?" she asked plaintively.

"No."

"I thought you had no money."

"I hadn't until a few hours ago."

"How much have you got?"

"I don't know, Phœbe," he laughed excitedly like a boy. "Heaps of it. Barrels of it. Millions, I think."

"If I find you're jokin' with me, young man, I'll—I'll——"

Tears dropped from her eyes. She dashed them off with her hand in order the better to glare at him.

"Didn't Walter tell you who I am?" he asked soothingly.

"But you're not that man." She stamped her foot. "He died years ago—in a yacht—I read about it."

"That was my father; we had the same name."

With a word here and there he managed to calm her agitation. Slowly she became convinced that this easy-going young man was a financial aristocrat, a wizard come in time to save her friends.

He had been a sickly boy, he told her; so the family had let him grow up a recluse. It was not until he had arrived at college years that he began to develop physically, but by that time, although he had grown into a stalwart frame of a man, he was hopelessly bookish and "queer." The father was one of the dominant big men of his time, but he was kind and sympathetic with the boy, so "Richard" had gone his own way and was allowed peacefully to ply his individualism.

"After college," he told her, "I decided that I could not live the dependent life any longer. I talked it over with father and he told me to try things out for myself. He offered me money, but that did not seem like playing fair; so I told him that I'd feel much happier if I went it 'on my own,' as the English say. He said it wouldn't be a bad idea to knock about a bit and discover what I was best fitted to do. And so I drifted here and there, sometimes having things easy and sometimes not so easy, but you can't imagine how contented I was. I have an enormous curiosity about life—I'm perfectly greedy to know why things are the way they are.... Then I fell in with Jawn's group over on the West Side and met the 'Widow' Knowles, who gives me enough tutoring to do to keep me in food and raiment, and I lived—well, like the lilies of the field."

"But is it true that your father was— —" But she found she could not say it; it seemed too heartless to ask him.

"Quite true," he answered her unfinished question.

"It's a brute I am to ask you."

"Oh, not at all," he replied pleasantly. "Death is lying in wait for all of us.... The thing preyed on my mind for many months, but it taught me much in the end.... I think now I shall face my own death all the better."

"Please!" she covered her eyes. "Don't talk about it. Death is horrible."

"Death is only the end of the great adventure," he assured her; "and perhaps—who knows—the beginning of a more glorious one. I have a keen sense of the shortness of life, but that does not horrify me; it makes me all the more appreciative of each hour of it, and it makes me kinder to all men. That's why I refuse to make a frantic struggle out of it."

Richard's calm was very consoling to Phœbe; unconsciously she partook of it and lost some of her dolefulness. For several minutes their talk lapsed. Finally he asked, "Do I look scared?"

"What are you scared of? It's me that ought to be scared; and I am— scared that it's a big lie you're tellin' me. Millions! Huh! It's a hard dose to swallow."

"Just the same I'm frightened. It'll mean work— —"

"Ah!" Phœbe exulted. "So it's work you're scared at. There's a man for you!"

"It will mean work," he went on soberly, "and slavery."

"Go 'long with you, man! Slavery? It'll be the chauffeurs and the butler and the cooks and the landscape gardeners who'll be the slaves. What'll you need to slave at?"

"It will mean giving up this blessed freedom. All my life I have fled from responsibilities and burdens; now I am going straight out to seek them. Others will depend upon me. If I make mistakes, I'll suffer because others will suffer. That's why I'm scared. I'm like the soldier in an ugly bayonet fight; it's a sickening job, but it's his job and he must do it. I hope I'm not a coward——"

"Faith," chirped the practical Phœbe, "you can afford to be anything if you've got money."

"I remember my father"—something in his tone stopped her raillery.

"Tell me about your father," she interrupted quietly.

"He was a very sensitive man, and the world was very hard upon him. They called him a money-grabber. The cartoonist pictured him with an eternal dollar-mark on his forehead. Any comedian could raise a laugh by merely mentioning his name. Even in serious plays they made fun of him. Yet he never worked for himself. During the big panics he hardly slept. We have a private letter from a president of the United States, written in his own hand, praising father for his work in stopping a national disaster, yet that very president begged him not to disclose the fact that he had written. It would be misunderstood, he wrote; it would damage the government if the people knew.... My father treasured that letter, although it hurt him. But he never complained. He gave even more of his hours to the service of others.... I have seen the brooding anxiety in his eyes.... When he was ill he dare not let it be known—the market would feel it. He could not take holidays like other folks; he could not even be friendly; and he hungered for public appreciation.

"The world tore at his character during muck-raking days, and even struck at his family. Cameras snapped at us wherever we went. I used to hate to look at a newspaper. The boys in school jibed me until I grew positively mute. I think they were envious—some of them—of my public fame. Envy! Merciful heavens!... Father asked only to be let alone, and they gave him ugly notoriety. Even his tragic death was made the subject of horrible jokes.... And I am going to take up the work.... I'm scared, but only because I feel that I may not be worthy."

"Then what do you do it for?" asked Phœbe. "Come up on the Lake and let the world go to pot. What they say about you in the columns of the *Express* or the *Chronicle* won't keep you awake o' nights. Why do you mux your life up with finance and all that if you don't like it? I believe you do like it."

Some of the brooding anxiety of his father had come into his eyes.

"No," he spoke thoughtfully, "I think I never shall like it. But I must go forward just the same."

"Why?"

For a moment he did not answer. He seemed not to have heard her question. Finally he spoke.

"Some persons would call it Duty. That isn't what I call it. But I know exactly what it is. It is a force in you that will not be diverted. It points you to your job, whether it be loafing or playing or sweating labour. You may cry out against it, but you go on just the same. It keeps men—and women too—at the grubbiest of tasks. Without it civilization would not be.... My job is clear. I thought I never would do it, but now I know that I shall; and I know, too, that I always intended to. My wander-years were all preparing me for this—and I never suspected it until now. I have been standing aloof and watching life pass by, and now I am tumbled into the torrent.... It is part of the great plan.... But," he added wistfully, "the watching days were good—and they were necessary."

A chirp or two came into Phœbe's voice, but the brooding sense of disaster still lingered. Finally she said, "But I don't see how you can help them," meaning Mrs. Wells and Jerry.

"Father left his affairs in the hands of a trusted group of his friends," he explained. "They are to carry on the estate until such time as I shall make up my mind to take charge.... I thought that time was postponed for ever. Now," he stood up and cried exultantly, "now I'm eager for it!"

"And so you're not a villain after all."

"I'm afraid not, Phœbe."

"Humph!" She began to assert her old self. "Then Jawn is."

"Wrong again."

"Very well," she shook her head. "I'll watch him just the same. And I'll keep an eye on you, too, sonny. It's a nice story you've been tellin' me. Mebbe it's all true; but, I warn you, the moment either of you tries to sell me stock in rubber trees in Madagascar, I'll put the whip to you."

To help him out she told him of the meek gentleman who tried to hoodwink the village.

"I may own stock in that concern for all I know," he laughed. "Would you believe it, child, I'm crazy to find out what I do own!... But, remember, Jerry must know nothing until I tell her myself. Promise me you won't let the cat out of the bag."

"Tell her?" quoth she. "Is it garrulous as well as stupid you think I am? If Jerry knew the truth about you she'd die rather than accept a penny."

"Really?" He was genuinely concerned.

"You've got a hard job before you, young man!" She enjoyed his discomfiture. "I don't know which is the harder, to get sixty thousand dollars out of 'Red Jacket' or to get sixty thousand into it. The Wells' would rather go to the poorhouse than take an unearned penny from anybody. Tell her? You don't suppose I want to commit financial suicide, do you? Pfist!" She raised a warning finger. "They're comin' round the bend; they're almost on us. I wish you luck, 'Mr. Richard,'" she chuckled, "and, faith, you'll need it."

Around the bend they came, Jerry at the prow of a long birch canoe, the Wheelen boy at the stern. Slowly and silently she swung the slender paddle as Seneca maidens had done on those waters for hundreds of years; and with her brown conventional bathing suit and her braided brown hair she looked the part of aboriginal.

"Hel-lo!" he sang.

"Hel-lo!" came back across the water. There was not a sign of weakness or fear in the long-drawn "lo!" Evidently she was still ignorant of the meaning of all those cryptic entries in her mother's books.

CHAPTER XXI
POET

Within a dozen yards of the shore Jerry stopped paddling and held up her right hand, two fingers extended like a papal benediction. Anyone brought up in the country knows that silent code. It suggests willows and spring-boards and "sandy bottoms"; and translated into the vernacular it means, "Let's go swimmin'!"

But Richard Richard had never had a boyhood. Perhaps one of the things that made him so eager to look the world in the face was the fact that nurses and governesses and private tutors had been his portion, and what summers his sickly life had permitted were spent with other sheltered youth in the south of France or in the Swiss Alps.

"Are you giving me a Tshoti-non-da-waga blessing?" he asked when she stepped on the shore.

"Don't you know the sign?" she asked incredulously.

"No; what does it mean?"

"Really?" She stood before him looking at him curiously. "Where have you been brung up! It means, 'Let's go swimmin'.' Every country boy knows that."

"I wish I had been a country boy." He spoke with a touch of regret.

"Don't tell me you spent your summers in New York City."

"Even that would have been something," said he ruefully. "Those kids over on the West Side have lots of fun."

"Well," she smiled, "if you were neither a country boy nor a city boy, what were you?"

Phœbe joined them. The Wheelen boy had made his farewells and had piloted his canoe around the bend.

"I'll tell you," said Phœbe. "He was sent up to the Reform School at an early age and then transferred to Matteawan. He's just out of the crazy house. I know; I'm an expert. Besides, he's just been tellin' me all about it."

"That's just about the size of it," Richard admitted. "I was be-governessed and be-tutored all my young days. I was a frail lad, you know. You wouldn't believe it to see me now. I'm like Theodore Roosevelt in that respect. You know he was a discard in his young days, but he built himself into the prize-fighter class. That's what they did with me.... I got so used to being out of things which other boys were doing that, somehow, I didn't miss them. I was almost seventeen before I began to put on weight."

"Didn't you ever go swimming and orchard robbing and nutting with the 'gang'?" Jerry asked.

"Never."

"You poor boy!"

"Poor!" ejaculated Phœbe, then slapped a hand over her mouth and retreated into the house. "How ever am I going to keep my mouth shut?" she asked herself. "The only thing for me to do is to go out and dig garden until they go away."

The signal to go swimming was given again.

"Sure!" Richard assented with alacrity. "What's the way to answer that?"

"Two fingers of the left hand for 'All right,' and one finger for 'Can't.'"

He waved his two fingers and darted into the house.

When he came out he found her in the water at the head of the dock. Certainly as she moved about with exquisite grace in the transparent water she looked like some lithe aquatic animal.

"I don't like to be watched," she spoke quietly. "Come in."

He understood, and plunged immediately.

"That brown costume matches you so well," he explained, "you looked like a sleek otter, or like young Mowgli out of the *Jungle Book*, only you don't kick your legs like a frog."

"Of course not." They were moving very, very leisurely out into the Lake. "You would soon tire with that frog kick."

The day he had looked out of the window in Phœbe's house and had seen her swim by he had noticed — Keuka water is as clear as an aquarium — that she "walked" as she swam, one leg drawn after the other, the sign of the long-distance swimmer.

"Where shall we go?" he asked after a few moments of silent swimming. "I like to have something to aim at."

"Let's cross."

"Very well."

"That bushy clump of trees which come down to the water's edge; straight ahead now."

"I see them."

It was a diagonal cut, probably a mile and a half across, but the water was delicious, and they were in no haste. At times they spoke a sentence or two, but for the most part they moved on rhythmically without a word. Each seemed to know instinctively when to stop and "tread" or when to float and rest. It was the essence of tranquillity which speech would have spoiled.

Several times they faced each other for long, steady minutes. He could observe the easy swing of the arm, the coiled brown hair, the wet eyelashes and the silk insignia of the French swimming club on the edge of her garment; and she could note his natural ease in the water, but particularly his face of many lines. She would have liked to examine it furrow by furrow, but his scrutinizing blue eye kept too watchful a guard. And she was not quite certain if he had not begun to "make eyes at her"; so she would turn away and use a stroke that left him to study the coil on coil of braided hair. And then, safely turned away, she would permit her face to smile in quiet enjoyment of the catastrophe that would occur—panic, indeed!—if he could know what racing thoughts were hers!

And all the while he was thinking of the phenomena of communication: how each mind was busy on its own affairs with only a yard or two of space between, yet neither able to enter the privacy of the other. He conjectured that the documents which Mrs. Wells had given her to study had not yet told their story of disaster. Or else she was an incredible actor. And while he planned carefully how to settle the difficulties of the estate without giving her pride a chance to object, he was thankful for the miracle that separated their minds so absolutely.

He was thankful for other reasons. While he watched her face he wondered why she had told Walter that Richard and she had "fixed it up." Walter had been explicit; he insisted that Jerry had owned that she and Richard were agreed on marriage. Walter may have been mistaken, but Richard could not shake off the air of probability about Walter's assertion. If she had made such a statement—nothing in the calm face beside him remotely suggested such a thing—there was some good reason back of it. So much he assured himself, but, puzzle as he could, he found no satisfying explanation.

The swim was not fatiguing because they were experienced swimmers and knew how to make journeys of that sort; but, nevertheless, on reaching the other side, they lay down on the grass and took the precaution of a good rest.

"How goes the bookkeeping, Lady Manager?" he asked.

She did not reply at first.

"Not at all," she admitted at length. "But I fear I have not been putting my mind to it the way I should."

"Let me help."

She thought about that for several seconds before replying.

"I am not sure whether I want you to know," she spoke finally. "There are more entries about mortgages and notes than I care to expose.... Mother seems to have been borrowing like sixty for a great many years, and I haven't been able to discover yet what she has done with the proceeds.... I am beginning to fear that we are not so well off as I always believed."

"Would you care much?"

"I don't know," she reflected. "I've never had to think about money matters. It's like gravity or the weight of the atmosphere; I don't suppose we'd miss either unless they should suddenly leave us.... That swim was mighty close to it, though; wasn't it?" She had shifted the subject adroitly.

"Great!" he lolled at length. "It's a species of gravity-less universe we were floating in.... Great!"

She had not discovered the state of affairs yet, he thought, although she was "getting warm." So both were willing to drop the subject, but neither was inclined to bring up another. A minute or two slipped by, then five minutes, then twenty-five. Crickets droned lazily; near by a catbird called, and far off a pack of noisy crows quarrelled and fluttered about the top of a dead tree.

Speech would have kept these two young persons politely apart, but the silence was quivering with intimacies. And so, when Jerry sat up and raised two fingers mischievously, he flashed back the response and walked with her to the water without the necessity of a disturbing word.

Not until they reached the home shore did they speak. Then he said:

"You will let me help you on the books, won't you? I know a lot about such things"—in reality he knew nothing—"and I know a pack of big finance fellows in New York who will patch up anything in the shape of a note or mortgage or interest due. Do let me help?"

"You really want to?"

"Really."

"All right," she agreed. "If you are not too tired we can work over a few hard places before dinner. We have an hour."

This eager, plausible young man had better know exactly what he might expect out of "Red Jacket," and the earlier the better. The documents were not such an enigma to her as she had pretended, and she was not so young as not to be aware that men—and mothers—had often speculated on her desirability as a moneyed "catch." Not that she believed Walter's theory about Richard. He was no "bad man." Her half-suspicions of Richard had faded almost as quickly as they had come. The night's sleep had banished them. One might as well not have eyes and a mind if the guileless man before her were ever guilty of anything except kindness and improvidence. But improvidence he could be guilty of, and on a colossal scale. Besides, he was so different from other men that it would be just like him to rest satisfied at "Red Jacket." He would take it with no more shame than those sparrows were taking Phœbe's oats. So she would lead him straight to the documents and exhibit the accounts.

When Phœbe heard their voices at the dock she fled to the garden and seized a hoe. Reticence was not one of her virtues, and she had the sense to know it. "It's awful to have the gift of oratory," she chuckled as she dived in back of the corn. "An' it's never myself that thought I would be runnin' away from a chance to show it off!" Nevertheless she stayed out of sight until they dressed and had left the cottage.

They took the steep hill leisurely, stopping occasionally to rest and look back on the view; but they found speech as unessential here as on the long swim together. And, besides, the delicious fatigue had left little inclination for conversation.

They crossed the single trolley track that led from Penn Yan to Branchport and walked slowly up the lawn.

"Is there any better sensation than honest weariness?" he asked.

"None in the world," she agreed, although she mentally made note of several better ones.

"Do you really feel like figures?" he asked temptingly.

"Not in the least," she laughed, and noted his eager look towards the little open summer-house before them.

"Let's!" he suggested.

"All right," she agreed.

There they lounged and looked down upon the Lake.

"Whose boat is that?" He pointed towards a "Class A" yacht tacking across the Lake, evidently aiming for Phœbe's dock. "I believe it is Walter's boat with the new sails!"

They watched it for some time. As it drew nearer they could make out two figures, evidently Walter and Jawn. No doubt they had sailed up to Penn Yan to get the new canvas. The *Sago-ye-wat-ha* looked splendid in her new suit and seemed almost self-conscious. The races would begin next week, Jerry told him. They speculated on the chances of success, and grew loyally confident of "their" boat.

Neither of them wished to talk about Walter. The subject brought up uncomfortable memories. Several times she nerved herself to the point of telling him the ruse she had employed to check Walter's dangerous suspicions, but each time she swerved off. Throbbing blood-vessels warned her that she would not perform with her accustomed calm. She was too tired, she told herself. After she had fully recovered from the long swim, she assured herself, she would make the matter clear.

And several times he was on the point of letting her know that he knew. She must be told soon; one could never be sure of Jawn's indelicate humour. But his old shyness would seize him at the critical moment. So unwillingly their talk drifted to Mrs. Wells and the accounts.

"Have you still your five dollars?" she asked.

"Yes," he laughed and produced his wallet. "This is a fine place to live; there's no way to spend money. I think I'll frame this bill as a souvenir."

"You had better let me give you enough to pay for a ticket to New York— —"

"Oh, I have no intention of going yet!" said he.

"We may all have to go sooner than any of us suspect," she met his gaiety with calm seriousness.

He waited for her to explain.

"If mother's accounts are half-way right, I couldn't stay in Yates county," she explained.

"Oh, they're not so bad as you think," he encouraged. "You just let me get at them. I'm a crackerjack on accounts."

She smiled. "I should think you would be!"

Her smile reassured him. If she knew the truth, he argued, she would not be able to maintain that calm assurance, showing once more that he did not know the Virginia strain. So he found speech to prove what a financial wonder he was. "There are friends of mine in New York," he said, "who could make any account come out straight. There are thousands of ways of fixing up money troubles. My friends are past-masters in the art They have to be—that's their business."

"Can you stand a shock?" she asked quietly.

"If it is an interesting shock," he answered.

"It is far from interesting," she went on.... "We owe nearly eighty thousand dollars. We haven't even been paying the interest on our loans, and it is more than our income; and our yearly expenses are enormous. It looks to me as if the Wells family would have to quit."

It was indeed a shock. And she had known this for days! That accounted for her preoccupied air and the abrupt leaving of the luncheon table! But what could account for her serene spirit? He asked her bluntly.

She replied with a question. "Isn't it your own philosophy," she asked, "to take events as you find them?"

"Jerry," he turned to her abruptly, "will you marry me?"

She moved her head away. Even the Virginia strain is susceptible to some shocks!

"What a poet you are, Richard," she said.

"This is business," he pursued the subject vehemently. "Will you?"

"What a business man you are not!"

"Will you?"

He caught her shoulder and tried to turn her about so that she would face him.

She remained rigid, remarking, "That's my most sunburned shoulder, if you don't mind."

"Look at me!" he commanded.

She moved about slowly and faced him. The smile on her face was almost mournful. "It is still my most sunburned shoulder," she repeated, but did not flinch at his heavy grasp.

"Will you?"

"You are a funny boy," she remarked quietly. It was less trouble to look into his earnest face than she had thought. For a moment or two she forgot his question and busied herself with exploring the lines and furrows and wondering how this young man ever got so gnarled. Then she remembered and answered him.

"I like your poetry very much," she said. "Very much indeed. It is so like you.... It almost makes me want to cry.... That's because I'm tired.... But, Richard dear, it is also very, very comic." He was staring at her with the fiercest of frowns. "Especially when you wrinkle your forehead like that.... You are the most chivalrous man I know. The Wells family are about to go into the mire, and you rush to the rescue with," the smile on her face grew tender, "with your little Sir Walter Raleigh coat of a five-dollar bill. It is beautiful, Richard dear, and poetic, and just like your generous self, but, alas, it would not work."

The summer-house was a most public affair. Either from the porch of "Red Jacket" or from the road anyone could have observed every movement. The publicity had its effect, no doubt, but that was not his reason for inaction. The poise of the woman shook his resolution. He did not know that inwardly she was shaken with agitation. In this stage every inexperienced man is deceived. If he had taken her in his arms boldly she would have gone without resistance, even the passing of the Branchport trolley car might not have interfered; but, instead, he talked earnestly of his turbulent desire; and she met him with the sex defence of beautiful calmness.

Then instead of taking him seriously, she twitted him about his individualism and about his philosophy of egoism.

"I've thrown that all overboard," he insisted. "I've been waiting for this moment all my life," he cried enthusiastically. "You don't know how I have looked curiously at this woman and at that woman wondering if I were normal like other men, and if here or there was the one who would stir the fires in me. I see now what the trouble was; I was too self-conscious. 'Happiness to be got must be forgot,' George Palmer used to tell us. And it has come on when I wasn't looking for it. But I played the game square. I drifted on and had faith that this life is planned by Intelligence. It's no hit or miss. It's as mapped out as a liner's chart."

She was stirred by his vehemence and by the sudden note of seriousness which she caught in his speech. If he had chivalrously offered to marry her when she seemed helpless and dependent she would have had none of it. But chivalry does not make a man's voice shake or cause the tips of his fingers to burn like hot coals as they touch one's shoulder. She turned eagerly to ask him—for she would make sure.

"When did you know this?"

"To-day at luncheon," he drove on, "after you left. Walter said that you had told him last night— —"

"What!" She almost rose from her place beside him. "Did he— —"

"Yes," he went on clumsily, "he said that you had told him that you and I had fixed things up and that— —"

"Before the whole table?" she asked with deceiving coolness.

"Yes," he said. "That is, to Jawn and me. Your mother— —"

"Oh!" she interrupted quietly, but with no concealment of her irony, "just to you and Jawn! That is some comfort. Jawn is such an uncommunicative soul!"

"Oh, but don't you see," he tried to make it clear, "that's how I found out? I— —"

"I presume he has written a limerick on the subject by this time," she laughed, but without mirth. "That's how you found out? Found out what, pray?"

She had moved several inches away deliberately and settled herself against one of the corners. She seemed very self-possessed.

"Then I found out why I came here," he persisted. "If Walter had not spoken I might not have known. But that minute I knew. You seemed to be talking to me through him. I was never so stirred in my life; the thing shot through me like a galvanic shock. I went out into the gardens to try and get rid of the thought. But it clung to me, followed me about, danced in my brain and before my eyes all afternoon. And when I saw you step out of that canoe—I knew."

She lowered her head slightly and studied him for several uncomfortable minutes. As the seconds ticked by and her comic smile did not disappear his hopes oozed, and left him face to face with harsh reality.

"And so I made eyes at you, after all," she remarked bitterly, although the set smile did not leave her. She moved back further, threw her feet up on the bench, clasped her knees and looked at him through half-closed lids, as one might gaze at a likeable bad boy. "I made eyes at you via Walter, did I? And you did not run away as you promised."

He protested as a man might in such circumstances, but she continued to gaze at him satirically until he was compelled to halt.

"I suppose my younger brother's statements are all to be taken as gospel," she said.

"Well, of course— —" he began.

She went on firmly. "He was so exquisitely truthful about the trunks at Naples, and we've told you of other instances. Naturally he is to be believed."

"Then you didn't say — —"

"*Absolutely not!*" she cried.

After all, she was in a way telling the truth. She had not made an intentional sentimental confession to Walter. She had told him what she had believed to be a necessary invention, and learned only later that it was in reality the truth.

Everything she had said to Walter had been done with the lightest of motives; and this clumsy man before her was making her action shameful. The thing he suggested, *that* she had not said — absolutely not!

Tears glistened in her eyes, tears of vexation and anger. She rose and started to go.

"Stop!" he cried and detained her by force. He would not have her go that way. When she would not sit down he in turn grew angry. His eyes shot fire and his speech was most unnaturally rough. If she could not stand misunderstanding, neither could he! She had not heard his whole story, but by the lord Harry, she should! And this time he made himself clear.

"I believe you had told Walter exactly what he repeated to us, and when you consider that the boy is a half-idiot — —"

"Thank you," she said, but he heeded her interruption not at all.

"—I could easily understand that you had some good reason for telling him that or any other story that would come into your head. I did not say I believed you meant it. Woman, do you think I'm a complete fool? I thought perhaps you had lied to him, as I would do if it were necessary; maybe he was violent, I thought, and you had to say something to keep him quiet! The point is—this much I thought you would have the wit to understand— the point is that the suggestion overpowered me, made me conscious of what had been true from the moment I followed you here, but what I did not know until that moment, that—oh, well," he tried to calm his violence, "what's the use? You either feel the same as I do, or you don't; and nothing can force you.... Only I'm sorry.... Sorry."

"I really believe you were angry."

"I still am."

"Did I hurt you?"

"Good Lord!"

"It is so interesting to discover that you can be insulted after all, you who were so insult-proof."

"I was never so hurt in my life."

"Well," she was very deliberate, "it is a good lesson for you. You'll have much more sympathy for sensitive folks hereafter."

The turbulence subsided. It had been rather noisy for a moment or two—both voices had risen—all of which made the ensuing silence rather awkward. Jerry seemingly had remained serene throughout; but the man was naturally shaken—he had exhibited quite a new variety of Richard. But even he gradually got control of himself.

"Suppose," he began the conversation. "Suppose I am able to fix up the accounts," he ventured; "will you let me have a try at it?"

"What would you do?" she asked. But before he could answer she said, "I don't want you to think that I am not terribly concerned about 'Red Jacket.' I may not show it, but I feel those debts, especially the money we owe to the——" she could not tell him that disgrace, but he knew she was about to say "to the negroes"—"especially some of the debts," she corrected herself; "I feel the whole thing so keenly that nothing else matters.... I am not likely to show a thing like that.... There are many things I am not likely to show.... It's pride, I suppose; but we Virginians—oh, I'm a Virginian!— are proud of our pride; it is the one possession we have been taught to hold to.... When we sell out or borrow on that! well, we're done for!... It is a great wrench to tell you even this much, but you have misunderstood me more than once——"

"Forgive me, Jerry," he asked so sincerely that for a moment she hardly dared go on.

"Let's go home," she spoke abruptly and rose.

At the porch he asked her again to let him help with the finances.

"Someone must do it," she said; "it might as well be you. It's like the business of hiring an undertaker," she smiled squarely at him, gamely, "and you might as well get the job. I'll turn the papers over to you to-night, and the quicker you get at it the better. No," she changed her mind. "Don't do anything until after the races next week. And don't be surprised, Richard dear," she reverted to the phrase she had used at the top of the hill back of Naples, "if you find me quite careless and birdlike for the next few days. We own 'Red Jacket' until it is sold out from under us. I'll not let that sale begin in my mind until it begins in fact."

"Ah!" he joked, "don't you be too sure that it will be sold at all! Remember that I'm the financial manager now! I'm on the job, and don't you forget it!"

"Poet!" she tapped him ever so gently on the arm, "dear, good, kind, blue-eyed, impractical poet!"

He followed her to the stairs and watched her go slowly up to her room. At the turn in the landing she stopped and looked down upon him. If he had been a bolder man he would have known that now at last she was deliberately "making eyes at him," but when she shook her head with comic dolefulness and murmured, "Poet!" he saw only a beautiful sympathy for an unrequited affection!

CHAPTER XXII
THE COUNCIL FIRE

Mrs. Wells' "books" were not arranged to facilitate the work of an auditor, but her correspondence was of considerable help. With the aid of Jerry's notes and the letters Richard was able to get his clues. At occasional intervals Mitchell Lear's brief notes would come along, each such invariable good sense that Richard began to have a liking for the man before he had seen him. Evidently Lear had been consulted before each disastrous transaction, and his advice was always to refrain from doing what events proved should have not been done. His terse opinions were worded with almost humorous sameness: "As I advised you in our talk on Wednesday, you will do well not to dispose of the orchards" or "not to try out experiments in grape spraying," and so on. Mr. Lear was evidently a friend and a man of sound judgment; and in compensation for his long failure to have his advice followed he was a good man to consult now.

Mitchell Lear was engaged in bowing a client out of the office when Richard appeared.

"It is the sort of case I never touch," Mr. Lear was saying. There was a note of firm indignation in his voice, which his nervous, eager client seemed to miss.

"But your reputation at the bar would help us so— —"

"My reputation at the bar is not for sale!" Mr. Lear interrupted ominously. "I am busy. Good-day, sir."

"But if you could only see your way— —"

"Good-day, sir!"

Some of the indignation still lingered in Mr. Lear's keen eyes as he confronted Richard. The lawyer had the judicial rather than the legal face, and at this moment it was that of the righteous judge in the act of sentencing a deserving criminal.

"I am Mr. Richard," he held out a hand.

"Yes, I know," Mr. Lear took the hand firmly. "You are staying with the Wells' at 'Red Jacket.' There was a note of the fact in the local papers," he added by way of explanation. "Sit down. Excuse me if I seemed ruffled. That little rat was just about to—well, we won't talk about it."

His face remained stern as he looked expectantly towards Richard.

"You are Mrs. Wells' lawyer, I believe," Richard began.

The penetrating gaze of the lawyer was somewhat disconcerting; but at Richard's question the immovable features relaxed into the most genial of smiles and the eyes broke into abrupt laughter.

"Not that I know it," Mr. Lear chuckled. "I am simply her good friend. As such I give advice free. She always comes to me when she wants help in a bit of wrongdoing."

The words seemed out of character with the man who had just dismissed a client who, no doubt, had been suggesting a shady legal partnership; but the face shone with delight in the paradoxical situation.

"When Mrs. Wells wishes to do something which she knows is quite unwise," Mr. Lear explained, "something which her conscience tells her she should never do, she comes to me to get her will strengthened. She knows beforehand that I will decide against her and give her advice which she doesn't want to take, but without opposition she is weak and vacillating. I am the man she selects to arouse her combativeness. The more clearly I prove the folly of her proposed undertaking the stronger grows her resolution to undertake it. She usually comes into my office in a mood of guilty indecision, but she always goes out righteously obstinate and determined to do exactly the opposite of everything I suggest."

Richard knew that she would act exactly in that way, and he told Mr. Lear so; he told him also of the change that had come over her and the reason for it; and, as well, of Jerry's assumption of command. Then he sorted out the papers and the notes on the correspondence. There was a name here and there of a note-holder, a generous note-holder it seemed, who seemed to take the non-payment of interest as a sort of lark.

Mr. Lear knew him; he was a distant relative of the Wells'—Uncle John they called him, although he was no uncle—and a man whose name should be Great-heart. But Mr. Lear did not know of the shocking financial state of "Red Jacket." The smile left his face as he ran down the summary which Richard had prepared. Uncle John was generous, but it was not likely that he would be willing to underwrite so large a deficit, especially as the present income from the estate showed no chance of catching up with the expenses.

"She has too many negroes," Mr. Lear pointed out. "They eat up all the profits. She will not get rid of them; but, at least, she ought to employ them properly."

"How could she do that?" Richard asked.

"Buy back the orchards she sold Hoskins," he answered promptly. "Hoskins will sell, at a profit, of course. Then she should get Holloday's orchards and Fennill's and go into the business on a big scale. I shouldn't advise more grape land, although I would most strongly suggest letting George Alexander manage the sprays in his own way; she interferes with absolutely original theories—all wrong, of course—and she drags off his negroes to fool with her gardens."

Richard was taking rapid notes.

"Will you get an option on Hoskins' apples for us," he looked up eagerly, "and on Fennill's and the other fellow's, too?"

"I am no real-estate operator," Mitchell Lear assumed his most judicial expression.

How proud everyone was in Yates county, Richard thought; but he said genially, "But as a friend — —"

"Oh!" Lear laughed at the touch. "That is different. As a friend I would get an option on the Lake-side cemetery!"

"Good!" cried Richard. "And can you get those notes from—Uncle John, I believe you said; I mean if we raise the money?... As a friend!"

"As a friend," Lear entered into the scheme, "I will try to get the notes without the interest! Uncle John ought to be glad to get the principal! But how are you going to find all that money?"

"May I use your telephone?" Richard asked politely, as if he merely intended to talk to "Red Jacket."

"That's what it is for," said Mr. Lear. He was engaged seriously in checking off the accounts, but he raised his head in astonishment when he heard Richard ask for the name of one of the best known banking houses in New York city.

"I want Mr. Davis Clarkson," Richard told the operator. "No; no one else will do.... What? Oh! You can't get them right away? When? In about ten minutes.... Oh!... I am to do what? Hang what? Oh, yes; I see. I am to hang up the receiver until you get Mr. Clarkson for me.... Yes.... I understand. Thank you very much—very much indeed."

"I hope you don't intend to hold a very long conversation with Mr. Clarkson," Mr. Lear remarked grimly. "I forget whether it is one dollar or two dollars a minute to talk to New York. But I'm relieved to find you didn't open up Chicago or Denver!"

"Clarkson will pay," Richard assured him. "Clarkson has heaps of money."

"You are not very used to the long-distance telephone," the lawyer remarked shrewdly.

"No," Richard admitted. "I have rarely talked on any telephone. No; I don't believe I ever tried before to talk over any great distance. How did you know that?"

Mr. Lear laughed.

"Never mind," he said. "You do it very daintily, and you talk to the operator as if she were about to do you a personal favour. There goes the bell. That means you, I judge. Politeness pays; you've opened up New York city in record time."

"Is that you, Dave?" Richard applied himself eagerly.... "Sure it is! The very same! I've been at Penn Yan, New York. Put it down. Yes. Red Jacket, Penn Yan. Can you take a vacation and come up?... Well, listen and you'll change your mind, for I've changed mine.... Yes.... That's it. I've come over, just as you said I would; and now I want money.... About a hundred and fifty thousand.... Can't you bring it along with you?... Very well; any way you choose. I'm buying vineyards and apple orchards up here.... Yes; great spec.... Millions in it.... And wait!" He glanced at his notes. "Look up Noble, French and Company, and buy the mortgage to 'Red Jacket.'... Mrs. Emma Wells.... Yates county.... Well, that will do, only I'd much rather have you by me to see that everything is O.K.... Wait.... Make that cheque out to Mitchell Lear.... Certified? Oh, all right, if that's the proper way to do it.... No; I'd prefer to have it made out to Mitchell Lear." He spelled the name carefully. "He'll give me what I want. Yes, Mitchell Lear, Penn Yan, New York.... Yes, a hundred and fifty thousand will be quite enough, thank you, Dave.... Good-bye, old Dave!"

Richard turned quietly to the astonished lawyer. "Did you catch the conversation with Clarkson? He's going to send you a cheque, certified cheque, for $150,000. I don't want to be known in this, so I'll draw on you when I want funds. You see we just have to fix up the Wells' business, and what's the use of having money if you can't have some fun with it! I bet you are enjoying the prospect almost as much as I am. But we've got to do this with great cunning and delicacy; you know how proud everybody is in these parts!"

Lear was not only struck in a heap by the nonchalant attitude of the young man towards this rather large sum of money, but he was correspondingly elevated at the splendid trust imposed in him. It was startling to have a stranger exhibit such faith. Further evidence of that stranger's faith was forthcoming. Mr. Richard Richard laid off his incognito and he made clear his desires in settling up the troubles of the Wells estate; all of which Mr. Mitchell Lear was to perform as legal adviser, real-estate operator and friend, but shrouded, of course, in deepest secrecy.

"Will you conspire with me?" Richard asked.

"Will I?" echoed Mitchell Lear. "You won't find a more willing conspirator in twenty counties."

"Remember," Richard told him, "this is strictly business. You are to get your proper fees and all that sort of thing."

"Young man," the elder man rose and fastened him with his steel-grey eyes. "Young man, go to the devil!"

"But at least the telephone call— —"

"Young man," Mitchell Lear grew eloquent, "*go to the devil!*"

"Well," said Richard as he wrung his hand in parting, "I'll get even."

The young man went down Main Street with a springy step. His life had suddenly flopped over, like a turtle, as he had said, and he was as eager to follow up the new experience as the said turtle to try out his unused legs. Sam Fybush's neat tailoring establishment caught his eye; he went in and had himself measured for clothes, giving Mitchell Lear's name as reference; and he walked in Hopkin's jewellery store and began buying an assortment of rings, but stopped when he realized that his funds would not arrive for a day or two. He never before had such a flurry to spend; he was like a child with birthday money. "Lord!" he thought, "I'd be dangerous to let loose in Tiffany's just now!"

To Richard Richard there was nothing inconsistent in his sudden consuming desire to take up his inheritance. So long as one was honest with his desires nothing could be inconsistent to this young man. One might as well be disturbed over an eclipse of the moon. The law of his individual life was operating without flaw, he assured himself; and he was glad that he had never tried to impose artificially upon the perfect mechanism. Yesterday he was a communist; to-day he was a champion of property. Very well; and to-morrow he might be a Buddhist—it was all in the hands of the gods.

For that reason, perhaps, or for reasons deeper than he knew, he felt only the slightest undercurrent of disappointment over his failure in the conquest of Jerry. It would come out all right, was the burden of his faith. He would wait and try, in this as in other high matters, to accept cheerfully the predestined course of things.

The week slipped by more smoothly than either Richard or Jerry had expected. Richard was busy with his new interest, the financial rehabilitation of "Red Jacket," and Jerry threw herself into the arrangement of a lawn dinner-party which should signalize, as she thought, her farewell to Jerusalem township. With characteristic singleness of mind she could launch all the preparations without a thought as to what she should do after the curtain had been rung down. In many respects she was true to the traditions of her family: they had always lived in the immediate present. It is interesting to note that difference between Massachusetts and Virginia, even more noticeable if one contrasts Maine and Georgia: the North has looked ever towards the future, while the South has lived. The one has grown thrifty and has paid the penalty of prosperity, while the other has paid many times over the penalty of unpreparedness.

Mitchell Lear was Northern in his sense of future values. He had a long head, as we say, meaning that he did not deceive himself as to the eventual outcome of things; and, as well, that he knew the game of bargaining. Hoskins sold eagerly; he had bought the Wells' apple land because it was offered at a low figure; his main object was to sell at a profit. Fennill and Holloday sold because they were in need of cash, and because they had no knowledge of the real value of orchards properly cared for. To this lot was added a valuable tract of young trees not yet bearing which a wealthy summer visitor had started in the frenzy of a sudden interest and which he had grown tired of with equal suddenness.

On the day before the first yacht race—it took three wins to achieve the Lake cup—Richard sought Jerry out to present her with a summary of operations.

He explained that a friend of his in New York, Davis Clarkson, had bought in the mortgage and the notes and was willing to give unlimited time. In addition his friend had lent money for the purchase of apple lands in order that the estate might employ all the negroes and offer some chance for a return. These lands were held in Clarkson's name and not charged against the estate at all—not very business-like, but friendship will do wonders at times. Richard was not so clear in his explanations, but his summary was understandable.

Debts

Mortgages, Notes and other debts	$86,000	
New apple lands	15,000	
Total Indebtedness		$101,000

Income

Grapes (with G. A. in charge)	$8,000	
Apples—		
Hoskins' tract	6,000	
Fennill & Holloday	10,000	
New orchards (in 2 yrs.)	4,000	
Total Income		$28,000

Annual Payments

Interest	$5,050	
Wages, Taxes and up-keep of "Red Jacket"	10,000	
Sinking Fund (running 20 yrs.)	5,000	
Total		$20,050

Summary

Total Income	$28,000	
Annual out-go	20,050	
Yearly Balance		$7,950

"The sinking fund, you see," he explained, "will pay off the whole indebtedness in much less than twenty years, because every year the interest will grow less. And we have nearly $8,000 a year above all expenses—to provide for accidents and pin-money! Mitchell Lear says that George Alexander and young Bolivar should be given four times their present wages and put absolutely in charge of the orchards and the grapes. Those two men know fruit by instinct, but even at that you ought to be willing to pay out about two thousand a year for expert advice on soils and spray mixture. We're calculating, you see, on getting every cent out of those lands."

Jerry studied the report for a long time. She was searching for some act of charity, the tiniest morsel of which would have meant repudiation of the whole scheme.

"That means," she spoke at last, "that we keep 'Red Jacket,' and make the attempt to pay off the debt against it?"

"Exactly."

"I thought of that many times," she remarked quietly, as if she were trying to hold back some pent-up emotion, "but the best figures I could make showed income always less than out-go. And I could not dismiss the negroes, not ... not after ... not after I had seen what we...."

She could not put it into words. There are some things which the spirit rebels against saying aloud.

"But the new orchard lands!" Richard broke in. "They do the trick. Everything depends upon getting use out of the labour you have."

"Wait." She pondered over the figures before her, seeking some sign of philanthropy.

"What does your friend Clarkson get out of it?" she asked.

"He's a banker; don't you see? He is protected by interest on loans. And he holds the mortgage and the title to the new lands. Oh, it's absolutely business, every bit of it."

So it seemed, but she was still suspicious.

"You give only $15,000 for land which almost pays for itself in one year. How can that be done?" she asked.

"You've struck the one flaw in the statement," he laughed. "I've just put things in round figures and, of course, everything is not there. It will take several years to get the full income out of that land, but when it does come it will be greater even than the figure we give—that figure is just an average over a number of years. Oh! I know my lesson well; Mitchell Lear is a fine teacher!"

She was not satisfied.

"Why, then," she asked, "doesn't this Clarkson man work the land himself and not let us have all this profit? It looks to me like a gift."

"It is," said Richard.

"What!" she bristled.

"It is an outright gift of Mitchell Lear's wise brain. You might ask why Lear doesn't take the thing up as a personal speculation. The reason is that he is a lawyer by natural selection. He is a genius at making money, too; he told me a dozen ways to turn over cash right in this neighbourhood, but he's a lawyer first, last and all the time. Or you might ask why Fennill and Holloday and Hoskins don't go into the apple business properly. The answer is simple, they couldn't if they wanted to; they haven't the brains, Lear says. He says that some of those fellows haven't brains enough to raise dandelions! No; you've got to take off your hat to Mitchell Lear. He's as loyal to this family as George Alexander."

"I would not accept a cent as a gift," said Jerry firmly, "but I would take much in the name of loyalty."

To cover any possible misunderstanding of her last remark she asked quickly, "Suppose the income does not reach your expectations?"

"It's a risk," he admitted, "like all living. But I am trusting Mitchell Lear on those figures. He knows what is being done by careful grape and apple farmers hereabouts—the most scientific fellows—and he knows what 'Red Jacket' used to get before the spray experiment began, and he claims that he has made no over-statements. The biggest asset 'Red Jacket' has, he says, is its loyal labour, and the fortunate possession among the negroes of a half-dozen men like George Alexander and Bolivar, who have an uncanny knowledge of all this new tree and vine lore; and a still more uncanny knowledge of how to make those negroes work! It looks to me like good business," he examined the sheet proudly; "and you haven't said a word about my magnificent financial engineering."

She reached forward and patted him on the arm.

"It is magnificent!" she said. "Wonderful! I thought you were an impractical dreamer, and here you present me with a magician's wand.... I did not realize—no, I really did not—what 'Red Jacket' meant to me.... And it is fortunate that I didn't. I felt so cold and ... benumbed, because of the whole ugly business that I believe I should have walked out of that door and down the path without a tear, without even once looking back at old 'Tshoti' and 'Da' and 'Waga.'... You are a very wonderful, practical man, Richard-my-dear, but ... I liked you just as well as poet."

"Aye," he said, "there's the rub. 'Just as well!' Do you remember Mark Twain's statement that he could speak seven languages 'equally well'?... But, forgive me. I am not going to bother you again."

She looked straight at him, her head bent slightly and her eyes glancing up through half-closed lids. It was a mask of a face she presented, absolutely poised, with all expression removed save a flirting gleam about the eyes and the faintest suggestion of a smile on the lips. The steady gaze was too much for him; somehow it shamed him and made the blood slowly rise to his face. His ear-tips had begun to burn when he arose abruptly and asked:

"Will you do me a favour for all my hard work?"

It would depend; she was also business-like and did not make impossible promises. But he did not want much; he asked merely for the key to "Grandfather's Room" where the relics of Chief Red Jacket were kept.

She would do more than give him the key; she would personally conduct him.

"But it must be done with ancient ceremonies," she detained him a moment at the door. "Wait here until I give you the sign. Enter not," she raised her hand in mock seriousness, "enter not, paleface, until you are summoned to the council!"

She went off, presumably for the key, while he waited before the door of "Grandfather's Room." Many minutes slipped by but he was not conscious of them; his mind was elsewhere. Suddenly the door opened from within and an Indian maiden stood before him.

"Welcome, paleface," she said.

The paleface took one step within the big room, and looked about him with the keenest curiosity. He was gazing on an Indian village. There were wigwams, birch cabins, totem poles, and a score of Indian figures carved rudely out of wood. The latter were posed about in characteristic attitudes: making arrows, grinding corn on rounded stones, pounding at skins. There were squaws carrying babies and, far off among the rushes, a set of warriors in full regalia were sweeping forward in a war canoe. In the centre of the room the sachems squatted about a council fire.

She took him from group to group, showed him the beads, the belts, wampum; the hides, the arrows and the primitive knives and weapons, the pottery and a-hundred-and-one other things. About the wall were scores of documents, framed evidently in more modern times and protected by glass. These were descriptions in Great-grandfather Wells' hand—he had the spirit of an antiquary—descriptions of this and that native occupation, but, more important, many transcripts at first hand of the sayings of the famous Seneca orator, "Red Jacket."

"Jove!" Richard cried. "This is more important than grapes and apples!"

He did not specify what exactly was more important than grapes and apples, but she knew that he meant "Red Jacket" and its treasures made by generations of right living. Here were memories and traditions that could not be bought in the market, nor could they be moved about or transplanted.

Deep family roots were here, and he knew that some of the fine flower of that family would fade and wither were it forced to seek other ground.

"Of course it is," she replied in thorough understanding.

"And I'm more glad than ever that I bought up 'Red Jacket' for you. You couldn't have walked out, woman, and left all this!"

He waved his hand about excitedly.

She caught only the latter part of his speech.

"I know I couldn't," she replied.

"Wasn't it wonderful," he turned to her, "that just at this moment in your life the Great Spirit should have sent me to you?"

"I believe He sent you," she told him gravely.

Her low tone thrilled him. He bent over eagerly.

"Thank God I have money!" he half whispered. "Millions of it! Millions of it to spend on you! To buy you a thousand Big Houses, if you want them. You knew all along, didn't you?"

He reached out a nervous hand and lightly touched her.

"Knew what?"

She asked the question, but she was conscious only of the electric nearness of the man.

"Hasn't Walter told you? He had my card. I thought he had told. When — — "

"Yes," she said quietly. "But you are not — — "

"I am," he smiled grimly. "Does it make me less repulsive?"

"But that name! It — it can't he. He is — ⸗ "

"My father is dead, yes. We had the same name." In rapid sentences he sketched his history. As he talked she moved a step away from him and stood rigid.

"And you bought up 'Red Jacket' and presented it to me?" she asked, her face aflame.

He nodded, totally unprepared for the outburst that followed.

"Oh, how could you? How could you?" she cried. "I can't take it!" She stamped her foot. With every energetic protestation the three royal plumes in her head-dress quivered in sympathetic response. "I *won't* take it!" Her anger grew. "Why did you keep this from me? Why didn't you tell me before who you were?" In bitter speeches she upbraided him for his calm, smiling, superior secrecy.

He tried to explain that the secrecy was largely her own doing, but she would not have it that way. He had been playing with her, having his premeditated joke and then in the end had offered—*alms*! Very well! Very well! Tears were raining down her cheek, her speech was almost hysteric. Very well! She would leave as she had planned; but not until she got good and ready. "Red Jacket" was her home until she left it for good. "Oh! Richard Richard!" she exclaimed bitterly as she brushed past him, "this was a low trick to play on me!"

The door was slammed in his face or he might have followed her; and as it locked of itself in some mysterious manner he was compelled to tread his way back among the silent Indians and through a series of adjacent rooms to the main hall.

Once more an Indian council fire had broken up in a declaration of war!

CHAPTER XXIII
THE RACE

By the day of the first boat race Professor Jawn Galloway had become a perfect tender of "stays," and an enthusiastic champion of *Sago-ye-wat-ha* against the world. Richard was mustered in as the other "stay tender," and the Wheelen boy volunteered for jib and spinnaker. There was no questioning, of course, of Walter's position; the captain is always the helmsman and in complete charge of the yacht.

During the morning the crew tried out their various "tricks" and at noon dropped anchor before Alley's Inn, which since the days of the old Keuka Yacht Club had been the starting point of the Lake races. The distance was approximately twelve miles, three times around a triangular course, beginning at Alley's Inn, thence across the Lake to Willow Grove and up to the North Buoy and back.

At noon the wind dropped to a light breeze which faded into nothingness by one o'clock. At two, however, the Lake was white with racing "caps." A characteristic sudden southwester had sprung out of the hills and was sweeping up the Lake. In the cove before Alley's Inn the boats were securely sheltered, but once beyond the little headlands the fragile yachts felt the full sweep of the gale and bent over perilously and tugged at their side stays.

Automobiles were parking on the lawn, the trolley line was running extra cars, and motor-boats were chugging over from every part of the Lake. There was great curiosity to see the trial of the new yacht, but greater to see the erratic Walter Wells in the rôle of skipper. Alley's Inn was doing a big business. Luncheon tables overflowed to the wide porches and even on to the lawn.

Richard looked about him for Geraldine. He did not see her; but Phœbe was in evidence. Phœbe was at a table with Mrs. Wells and Walter. The boy was eating little, but he was obviously pleased at Phœbe's solicitous attention. She fluttered over him like a young hen, if a young hen could ever be gay, witty and encouraging, and could "burble" effervescently. After all, thought Richard, Walter was her "case." It was she who had suggested yachting; she had even named the boat. She was the only one with any practical influence over the boy.

Evidently Jerry did not intend to lunch at Alley's Inn. She had not appeared at breakfast. Sukie said she had gone off dressed in a walking gown—a short-skirted grey corduroy. Sukie said she went off just before sunrise and that she had taken "Count" with her.

Her reaction in "Grandfather's Room" had been exactly opposite of Richard's expectation. Her main anger, it seems, had been over the secrecy which she herself had originated, and which circumstances had prolonged. She had been a willing enough conspirator there, but, it appears, the conspirator had been conspired against. She believed that she was in the secret all along, and it turned out in the end that she had been completely out of it. The startling conclusion—rich man coming so pat to rescue the bankrupt heiress!—had been too much of a surprise; indeed, it seemed almost in the nature of a carefully-planned joke at her expense. That, no doubt, was part of the cause for her outburst, he reasoned.

Another cause, perhaps, was her pride in possession; she loved independence and hated dependence. How Virginia has always hated a tyrant! Her code would not permit her to be under permanent obligations to anyone. There must always be a chance to pay back, to make equal return; and what chance was here?—a bankrupt estate against millions.

There was another cause which Richard did not get—many others, indeed, but chief among them was the fact that Richard helpless and dependent upon her was a satisfactory situation, but Richard independent could fare his way whenever the so-called "spirit" should move him. His new rôle would make Jerry relatively the beggar-maid and Richard the opulent distributor of largess. She could not stand that. It was abhorrent. All her training was against succumbing to superiority.

Upon one phase of the case Richard knew his ground. He had noted the change in her the moment they had crossed the threshold of "Red Jacket." On board the steamer she had been a lively, intelligent, well-bred American, not to be distinguished from others of that delightful group; but the transfer to her own lands transformed her. In Europe she was one of many; at "Red Jacket" she was Somebody.

One time on the way home Mrs. Wells had confided to Richard that she would be glad to get home. "Europe is always wonderful, but I could not live there," she said. Richard confessed that he could live anywhere. But she shook her head, "In Europe I am one of a crowd; in Jerusalem township I am a Person with a capital P. There we have been the big family, for ever, it seems; and we have come to act and react like Persons. Out of Jerusalem township I always feel like a king without a country."

The big house and the grounds and the servants were necessary background to bring out Geraldine Wells. And she fitted into them naturally, not like someone presuming to be a Person, but as one manor-born.

While Richard cogitated these weighty personal matters he was standing on the high embankment overlooking the Lake and seemed to be watching Fagner as he manœuvred the *Moodiks* in the growing gale. Here Jawn joined him.

"Whoop-la!" Jawn cried. The *Moodiks* had flapped over suddenly. "She almost went over that time! It's a life-preserver I'll be needing if this blow keeps up. What's that? Thunder? Shiver-me-timbers, but it looks squally over to the sou' by sou'-sou'-sou'-west. Excuse me for the technical language, old hoss."

"Is 'old hoss' technical?" Richard inquired without turning around.

"No, you jackass," Jawn replied serenely. "I was referring to the nautical language. With white pants on I feel ridiculously nautical. Have you seen my white hat?"

"No."

"Well then, have you seen your own white hat?"

"Have I a white hat?"

"How in the blazes do you suppose you can tend 'stays' in a real yacht race for a silver cup unless you wear a white hat? You might as well seek an audience at Buckingham Palace in overalls and blickey; or play tennis in a dress-suit; or football in pyjamas; or—you're not listening at all."

"Eh?" Richard came out of his reverie. "Oh! So I have a hat, have I?"

Jawn sighed disconsolately.

"What's the use of the gift of speech," he groaned, "if nobody has the gift of listening to it?"

"Go on, Jawn," Richard turned pleasantly. "I'm listening. But I couldn't get my attention away from the *Moodiks*. Fagner'll have to take a reef in, don't you think? I don't believe he'll go over, but he'll waste so much time coming up into the wind; and that breeze is mighty gusty to-day."

"What do I care what happens to him?" Jawn asked. "The more time he takes the better we'll like it. We're going to win."

"How do you know?"

"Well," said Jawn, "I've timed the *Sago-ye-wat-ha* and she gets over ground better than the best records they have here. We did the whole course the other day in sixteen seconds less than the old *Tecumseh*, which holds the record. And besides I spent my good money on white sailor hats with blue bands on 'em. Wait till you see the blue bands with '*Sago-ye-wat-ha*' printed in gold! Yum! We'll look like regulars off a battleship. Walter's eyes nearly popped out of his head when I presented him with his."

Richard began to show interest.

"The boy has changed wonderfully, don't you think?"

Jawn dropped his bantering tone. Into his face came the serious gleam of the specialist; his holiday carelessness disappeared.

"You're quite right," he said. "The boy's got stuff in him. We've been chumming around a bit this past week. I thought he was a plain 'moron,' at first—not an idiot, but slightly off the normal, you know—but I've changed completely on that. I've been giving him all sorts of tests on the quiet. You were absolutely right in your first diagnosis. Drink is not his 'primary,' it's this yacht business. In some ways he's a fool, but not on board the *Sago-ye-wat-ha*! That's *his*, his very own. It's the first sensation of genuine ownership he's ever had, and it fills him so full of pride and self-glorification that his small brain hasn't room for anything else. The only thing I fear is that he won't be able to stand a loss to-day. I've tried to prepare him for it, but he won't think of losing. I'm afraid we've got to win this race, if we have to make a short cut across one of the buoys and trust that the judges aren't looking."

Tyler, the skipper of the *Cohlosa*, came up at this juncture. The men had met before.

"My friend, the enemy!" cried Jawn, shaking hands vigorously. "Old *Sago-ye-wat-ha* is after your scalp to-day, Tyler. The *Cohlosa* had better hold on tight to her hair-ribbons and stand ready to yell police any minute."

"The *Cohlosa* is easily frightened," said Tyler genially. "We have run away from a number of fierce boats."

Phœbe saw the men together and slipped over to them. Walter had gone on board the *Sago-ye-wat-ha*.

"Don't quarrel, now," she said. "Try to keep your tempers, men. I know how you feel, but hide it. Pretend at least to be friends. I'm shakin' hands with you, Mr. Tyler, but I'm countin' my beads for *Sago-ye-wat-ha* and rainin' my last curses on the *Cohlosa*, bad cess to it!"

"Well, I'm sorry," smiled Tyler; "for they say that the prayer of the righteous availeth much."

"Now don't talk that way!" she protested. "I must keep all the fires of hatred goin', an' how can I hate you properly, man, when you blarney me so beautifully? I never was the one to stand out against a man who'd flattered me. Well, I hope you come in second, then, Mr. Tyler, but don't tell me any more pretty lies or I'll be wishin' it a tie race. An' now, as man to woman, Mr. Tyler, give us a tip. Do you think we have a chance? An' is there any little thing you can suggest to help us beat you?"

"Votes for women!" cried Jawn. "Wait till they carry on a Presidential campaign, boys. We'll all be confessing to bribery and ballot-stuffing weeks before we start to do the crooked work. Own up, Tyler, that you've got a gasolene engine concealed under the rudder. Or perhaps you'll oblige a lady by boring a few auger holes in the bottom."

"Jawn Galloway!" Phœbe turned on him. "How can you have the nerve to go on talkin' an' in the same breath refer to *anything* bein' bored?"

Jawn surrendered and let Phœbe have the floor. Her bantering request to Tyler had a serious object back of it. This race was something more, as she well knew, than a test of skill; it was the test of a man. Walter's fate was more or less in the balance, and she wished to allay her painful anxiety by some encouraging word. Ordinarily she wouldn't have given a bundle of fiddle-strings to be the winner of a dozen Lake cups; but this race was not an ordinary race.

Somehow Tyler, a fine, sensitive man—sportsman every inch of him—caught the undercurrent of seriousness back of the laughing face.

"Fagner is always dangerous in a race," he said, "but this time we both have our eye on Walter. He's a fine, natural sailor, the best 'passenger' I ever had. He knows what I'm going to do before I do it and is ready to follow up the order without wasting valuable seconds. He has a splendid knowledge of local wind currents—almost unnatural. I've often asked his advice when I've been in a pinch. The only question is, has he the control to stand the strain of a long race? I'd like to see the boy win, Mrs. Norris——"

"You're a good lad!" Mrs. Norris broke in nervously. "Go on; tell me some more. It'll keep me from faintin' away. You're good as a drink, Mr. Tyler."

"I'd like to see him win," Tyler continued, "though, of course, I'm going to make him work. There's nothing more merciless in these parts than the yacht races, you know."

"Sure, we're not askin' for any gifts," chirped Phœbe, "but I thank you for the encouragin' word, just the same, Mr. Tyler."

It was close to three o'clock, the starting time, and Walter, with the help of Wheelen, was hoisting the mainsail. This was hint enough for Jawn and Richard to get on board. One searching glance around the grounds before Richard stepped from the dock into the *Sago-ye-wat-ha* gave no sign of Geraldine. As he took his place at the port-stays and coiled his ropes he wondered if she would come down, or if she were still marching away across the hills with "Count." Discouragement seized him, a rare mood of this optimistic man, and for several dismal minutes he lost his faith in "the gods" who held all things in their capacious laps.

When the "get ready" gun sounded the wind was half a gale and pointing almost directly up the Lake. The judges were questioning the wisdom of starting, but evidently decided to take a chance, for in a moment or two the starting gun went off and the *Pluma*, a small boat with a three-minute handicap, crossed the line, and the race was on. The *Aurora* followed a half-minute later and then came the anxious wait of two minutes while the *Cohlosa* and the *Moodiks* jockeyed along the edge of the starting line, each eager to get into the best position when their signal-gun should set them free. The *Cohlosa* and the *Moodiks* were boats of the same sail area, so their handicap was identical. *Sago-ye-wat-ha* carried a slightly larger mainsail, a matter of inches only, but it forced her to take the "scratch" position, a half-minute back of her two "Class A" rivals.

Both the *Cohlosa* and the *Moodiks* had taken the precaution of a single reef. Walter had not shown his hand until close to the starting minute. His mainsail was only half hoisted. But the moment the two "Class A" yachts nosed across the line—Fagner, as usual, getting the best position—he raised the sail and disclosed three reefs. It was a type of caution that the yachtsmen on shore did not expect of Walter Wells.

"Afraid of trouble?" Richard asked.

"No," said Walter. "Want speed. Can't get speed when she's half on keel."

So many exciting things were happening at once that hardly anyone noticed the *Sago-ye-wat-ha* as she struck the line with the gun. The *Pluma* had dropped her sail and her men were busy trying to keep it from ripping away. The *Aurora* had come right about into the wind. Her men were bailing like good fellows. Fagner and Tyler were beating over to the Willow Grove buoy bent nearly level with the water.

The *Sago-ye-wat-ha* stood up well and with her three reefs was able to steer a straight course. At Willow Grove the three boats seemed to be entangled. The judges were on tiptoe, glasses to face, watching for possible fouls, but no one was ready to see the *Sago-ye-wat-ha* move sedately around the buoy and fly off before the wind in the lead. In the first leg she had made up her half-minute handicap!

The strength of the wind was made instantly clear to the spectators on shore. By the recorded time Walter had nosed around the first buoy just six seconds ahead of Fagner, but while those six seconds were being ticked off he was speeding up the Lake with the gale behind him. As they all broke out in a line for the two-mile run north the gap between the first two boats seemed leagues.

Walter did not risk his spinnaker—any extra sail was perilous in that gale—but first Fagner and then Tyler flung their great balloon jibs out with the daring of veterans. It was a beautiful sight, that two-mile run; every inch of the race was in full view of the group on shore, although it took glasses to distinguish the yachts as they huddled together near the North Buoy.

Up to within a quarter of a mile of the North Buoy the yachts had maintained their distances, *Sago-ye-wat-ha* first, Fagner a hundred yards astern and Tyler a few feet in the rear. The *Pluma* and the *Aurora* had swamped and were towed ashore by ready motor-boats.

But within a quarter of a mile of the North Buoy the wind suddenly slackened. Then the spinnakers told. In the swift changes that occur in yacht races of this sort the positions seemed instantly to change. Again the three boats massed at the buoy, but this time the *Cohlosa* came about first, followed by the *Moodiks*. The *Sago-ye-wat-ha* was last.

Anyone can sail before the wind. The test of seamanship is in the cleverness of the tacking, and that test was now on. Tyler shot off to the east and, as everyone knew, Fagner did the opposite. Fagner's theory seemed to be that if you get an advantage of a slant of the wind it is better to have the other fellow in some other part of the Lake. Walter followed Tyler, but broke his tack early; so the three boats were soon in widely scattered portions of the Lake. As they crossed and recrossed each other's paths it was impossible to tell which was in the lead. The long beat down the Lake was therefore tremendously exciting to the partisans on shore, each group seeing its own the victor.

Characteristic of winds in this hilly country the breeze, still moderately stiff but no longer the fierce gale of the beginning, shifted to the southeast. Each skipper was thoroughly aware of the change, of course, but none, perhaps, were so mindful of the advantages of changing the original plans as Walter. In the middle of the Lake he suddenly let out his reefs and came about. He was now pointing almost directly to the cove at Electric Park just above Alley's Inn; and into this cove he slid until he was lost to the group on the high ground at the starting point. Fagner and Tyler were beating down to the starting buoy from the east, but it was soon obvious that each would have to take one more tack, although they "pointed" courageously; but as they put about reluctantly for one more try, the *Sago-ye-wat-ha* nosed along the shore and shot past Alley's Inn, crossed the starting line and swung out for a long tack to Willow Grove. Walter had been pointing straight into the southeast wind, seemingly an impossible feat. According to all the rules his mainsail and jib should have been flapping uselessly, but, instead, they had been comfortably filled. A back-current from the western hills had carried him forward.

It was three minutes before Fagner crossed the line and a minute more before Tyler finished the first leg. By that time Walter had rounded the Willow Grove buoy and was scudding up the Lake with the southeaster back of him. It was then that he flung out his spinnaker.

To the surprise of everyone he did not aim directly for the North Buoy, but crowded far to the east. In an uncanny way he had guessed that the freakish wind would soon shift to the east and then to the northeast. And so it did. He crossed the Lake with the wind still at his back and came about the North Buoy in time to get the new shift to northeast. His spinnaker was still ballooning beautifully as he came down to finish the second leg, while Fagner and Tyler were beating up in long tacks.

The wind had blown him up the Lake and obligingly had turned around to blow him down again. And while he had gone north in a straight line his competitors for the cup had been compelled to zigzag across the Lake, five times his distance.

Luck had been with Walter, of course, but at the same time he had been knowing enough to take advantage of his special knowledge of the ways of the wind. In his present position nothing short of a calm could have taken the race from him, and the northeaster that began to blow—it was the old storm, which had by this time veered to an opposite quarter—gave no signs of letting up.

The end came rapidly. When Walter crossed the finish line a winner of the first of the three races for the cup, the *Moodiks* and the *Cohlosa* had not yet reached the North Buoy on the final leg.

It was as the *Sago-ye-wat-ha* passed Alley's Inn a winner and sped on down the Lake towards Bluff Point and "home" that Richard caught sight of "Count" stretched out on the lawn and saw beside him a figure in grey standing silhouetted against the trees; then he knew that Jerry had been present to see at least the glorious finish. She had a pair of field-glasses to her eyes, and as he became conscious of the fact that she was following the fast retreating yacht his ears burned and the blood flushed his neck and forehead. It was fortunate at that moment that the *Sago-ye-wat-ha* had no urgent need of her "stay" tender!

Walter bore his victory very grimly. He smiled faintly towards the shore as the horns tooted and the motor whistles blew and he listened attentively to the chorus of exciting congratulations from his crew and from the crowd on the end of the dock and from unknown persons scooting by in motor-boats, but he said nothing. His eye was on Bluff Point and his mind seemed to be busy calculating if this sweeping northeaster would last long enough to carry him home.

The other members of the crew would have preferred to stay and bask in the victory. It would be pleasant to anchor off the Inn and watch the veterans, *Moodiks* and *Cohlosa*, fight it out for second place. But Walter said "No," and no one pressed him. The victory was his entirely, they realized, and in this happy hour the captain's wishes would be their law.

On his way home Richard spent his time watching the boy's face. In the past month Walter seemed to have grown several steps nearer to manhood; certainly as he held the tiller snug under his left arm and trimmed the mainsheet with his right hand he looked miles removed from the helpless creature of the S.S. *Victoria*. The "cure" had made great progress; so great, indeed, that Richard was quite puffed up with pride of this secret victory of his which outclassed the winning of a mere yacht race.

He wished to hear him talk, to see how he carried himself in this unique experience of having done something worthy of public commendation.

"If that wind-pocket is always off shore when a southeaster blows," he began, "how is it that the other skippers don't know of it?"

"'Tain't always there," said Walter; but he did not grin sheepishly, as he might have done several weeks ago.

"Oh!... Weren't you sure it was there to-day?"

"No, not sure; jes' took a chance. Things looked right."

"Suppose you had missed your guess?"

"We'd 'a' lost."

"Were you prepared to lose?"

"Sure! This ain't the on'y race! Best out o' five."

The races were scheduled one each week until one boat had taken three wins, but Richard knew that his work with Walter was over. There was no excuse he would offer to stay longer at "Red Jacket," for there would be volunteers a-plenty to tend port-stays, and, evidently, Walter had "found himself." Richard's feelings were a complex of disappointment and joy. The new life in New York was making a vigorous call upon him. His wander-years were over, and, as easily as season slips into season, he was turning directly about and facing with high curiosity the next stage when he would take up his father's work as man of many affairs.

Wheelen put off in his motor-boat, and Walter left as soon as everything was stowed away, but Jawn and Richard sat in the shade of the Lombardy poplars and enjoyed the fine August evening. Their talk was interrupted by a crash of some falling object in Phœbe's cottage. A trifling accident, probably. They had heard Phœbe's voice when Walter entered. Of course she had driven down with the Wells or probably had come down in the trolley and, naturally, would have made the distance in much less time than it took the yacht to round Bluff Point and beat up to the dock.

Voices in anger and another crash of furniture brought the two men to their feet. Before they had taken a dozen steps they saw Walter rush out and reach up to the little shelf where the whisky had rested untouched since early spring. Phœbe followed instantly; she was talking to him soothingly, although the men noticed that she had unhooked Seth's whip; but Walter was shrill and defiant. When Jerry, too, emerged from the house the men dropped into a walk and entered upon the scene with seeming calmness.

Jerry stood away from the boy, but Phœbe was not afraid of him.

"You said y'd marry me!" Walter shouted hoarsely and gripped the whisky. "You said — —"

"No, Walter," Phœbe pursued him calmly. "I said I would think about it. An' I *am* thinkin' about it, my boy."

"Y'r puttin' me off, an' puttin' me off!" he complained harshly. "An' I won't stan' it, d'ye hear? Won't stan' it! Gotta know some time 'r other. Gotta know *now!*"

"Listen to the lad!" Phœbe was purring cheerily. "He isn't satisfied to win a boat race, but he must win a woman all in the same day." Walter tossed his head defiantly and raised the bottle. "*If you so much as lift that stuff to your lips, young man,*" she cried suddenly, so suddenly as to upset a considerable portion of it on her porch; "*if ye even touch it,*" she cried, "I'll not only never marry you but I'll beat you with this whip till you cry for mercy!" Then when he dropped his arm she laughed softly—burbled, that is!—and coaxed him again. "How do I know I won't marry you, lad? You must give me time, now. It's a long while to be together as man an' wife—ah!" she sighed comically—"it's that sentimental I am I can't say the words without it sendin' me all a-flutter!... Come in, Walter; put that stuff up—no, don't throw it away! Put it back where you got it. I want you to have it right before you, to make sure you've got really done with it. An' by the same token, me lad, I'll just hang me little whip up here beside it, to keep it company like!" Her laugh took all the sting out of that remark, but it did not conceal the determination back of the words.

The men would have slipped off, but Phœbe invited them to stay. And she invited them also to help her prepare a fitting supper to celebrate the victory. In a few moments her chatter and laughter filled all the scene and blotted out the ugly episode. And every now and then she would give Walter little pats as she passed him—he made no effort to help with the "party"—and she would whisper startling little things in his ear and set him grinning in spite of himself.

And Jerry? She was still in her walking suit of grey corduroy, and her mood was somewhat of that sombre colour, but the victory of Walter's boat and the shock made by Walter's revelations of his relations with Phœbe had served to put a slight glow of warmth into her speech. To Richard she conversed frankly, but with an air of keeping something back.

Later in the evening when in the clatter of voices he managed to tell her that he would go to New York on the morrow, her eyes opened very wide, but she said nothing.

"It is for good," he tried to smile.

"What are you going to do there?" she asked indifferently.

"Take up my father's work, if I am able."

"That's rather inconsistent, isn't it?"

"Nothing that one does honestly is inconsistent," he replied firmly. "I never believed I could do it; but the inward voice calls very loud just now, and I am eager to try myself in this new experience."

"We shall miss you," she tried to tell him in a tone of polite sincerity, and she bravely declined to avoid looking at him. Their eyes met squarely. It was a dangerous moment, but she managed it with dramatic success; so much so that while his own eyes had the appearance of a pathetic dog waiting for his biscuit, hers resembled nothing so much as the round staring optics of those old-fashioned French dolls.

As abruptly as Phœbe had invited everyone to stay and sup with her, she invited everyone to leave. She wished to be alone, she said, to gather her scattered wits. Walter was expressly included in the notice of eviction, but he stubbornly remained behind.

Phœbe affected not to observe him as she cleared up briskly, humming as she went in and out doors, as she brushed crumbs, or moved chairs and benches about. Walter watched her hungrily, but his bravado was gone; he glanced at her now and then almost timidly, fearing, somehow, her very physical strength and the atmosphere she carried of confidence, determination, will—qualities he vaguely envied in her.

"Well, Walter," she turned to him at length, as if at last she had gathered those scattered wits and had them concentrated on a thing to do. "Well, Walter, we have a few matters to settle, haven't we?"

Walter tried to answer, but speech was not quite possible for him. He was keen enough to sense disaster in her tone, and knew not how to meet it with words.

"Did I ever say I would marry you?" she went at him with brisk directness.

"Yes," he answered doggedly.

"Think, boy," swiftly she softened her tone. "Wasn't it you who were always at me, and didn't I always tell you that I wouldn't even talk about it? Boy! Boy!" She came near him and mothered him with her smile. "Wasn't it always you? Always just you?"

"Yes," he managed huskily.

"I'm six years older than you——" she began, but he interrupted fiercely.

"That makes no difference!" he cried. "No difference at all!"

"If it were only that, boy," she continued. "But I am more than six years older, Walter; I am ages older. I have lived ... lived——" she stopped and let her eyes rove about the room. "Years! What are years!" She threw up her hands. "Twenty-eight? I'm nearer a hundred and twenty-eight! Life has burned me out, and all the faster because before the world I am too proud to own to it; in experience, boy, I am an old woman."

He stopped her and told her of her youth and her beauty and her compelling loveliness. His voice trembled, but he forced himself through a strong manly speech.

"Fine!" cried Phœbe. "Boy! Boy!" she crooned, "it's yourself you're comin' to now! Now you're talkin' like a man! Talkin' like a man, you are! And let me talk to you like a woman. Maybe I didn't say I would marry you, but I was ready to—if I was forced to it——"

"Forced!" he exclaimed. "What d' y' mean?"

"Just that—forced." Her voice was low now, and solemn. "If there had been no other way out, no other way to save you from yourself, I'd have done it. You and your mother and Jerry are all I have, and what would I not do for them? I would have done it; but it would have been like taking in some hunted creature that everybody had given up. And that is pity, Walter; just pity."

"Don't care what you call it," he said.

"Pity is all right for stray dogs, Walter. If you had been just a crippled little puppy—well, I could have shared everything with you. But to marry, to live together—I couldn't. I thought I could, but now I see that I never could. I am not big enough for that."

He stood up and began to summon his strength to combat her, but she waved him down.

"Listen," she said. "Listen until I finish.... Boy, it wouldn't work. We're not the mates for each other. No! No! We're not, I tell you."

Then he broke forth in speeches that were mixtures of strength and weakness. He demanded his rights; he begged her to be kind; he threatened; he pointed out the misery she was planning for him.

"And are you thinkin' of my misery?" she asked, so plaintively as to arrest him.

"You?"

"Yes—just me. Do you fancy for a moment that it wouldn't be misery for me? I pity you, and I care for you so much that my heart aches for you; I would give years of my life to see you grow into a strong dependable man, but I don't love you.... Don't speak yet; let me speak. I will tell you something that nobody else knows. In my bedroom is a tiny closet which nobody opens but me; and when it is opened it is an altar, with candles, and a sweet, old, crooked image of Saint Francis which belonged to my mother; Saint Francis who loved the birds and the souls of all dumb things. And I fool everybody, everybody but you; for I pray before my little altar—and I have oh! such faith! But nobody else knows that; nobody but you and me now. How I fool them all with my bad tongue!... And when I pray I pray for you. I pray that the good in you shall grow and grow and grow. And my prayer is answered daily! And I pray that the good Saint Francis shall spread out his arms and take you up and shield you from all bitterness and wrong thinking. 'Dear God,' I say, 'make my boy to see; reach out the hand to his stumbling feet; make my boy to see.'"

He tried to tell her something, but he could not speak. The pity in her voice, her swimming eyes, and the picture she conjured before him of the trustful suppliant bowed below her little candles—it was too much; it engulfed him.

Soon she went on. "I don't love you and you would find it out; and then—why, Walter, in the next ten years you will be still a youth, a youth demanding youth; while I will be forty and faded out. Oh, yes, I will! I know my kind. They are either very young or very old—no middle years at all. I will grow suddenly old—and it would come all the quicker if every day I should suffer."

He told her defiantly that she would not suffer.

"Oh, yes, I should," she nodded her head wisely. "For you, Walter, it might mean a little happiness, but for me it would be daily and hourly pain. I know. You look at the present, but I see the years and years ahead. No, boy; you must grow strong as you have been growing. You must throw off the evil that has gripped you. And then, some day when you have become a man among men, love will come to you, and you and she will ... will go off together ... as ... as once ... I thought I was going."

Softly she slipped into a chair and buried her face in her hands, and the quiet tears came.

After a painful moment or two Phœbe controlled her voice, but she did not look up as she spoke, nor take her hands away from her face.

"I haven't told you all, Walter," she said. "I have been trying not to say it ... but I must tell you. I have prayed that if it must be, I would take you and give my life to you.... And I will."

"You will?" he asked incredulously, and struggled to grasp the meaning of her startling suggestion.

"I will if it is God's will.... He will tell me.... Oh, I have great faith, boy. He will tell me in a very simple way. I offer all my life to you as I meant to do when you came here that night a year ago, and I got you on your feet and you promised to try. And you have tried, boy; I'm proud of the way you have tried!... I promised God then that if He willed it I would take you and save your soul.... He will tell me; it will be when you say again that you want me ... that you still want me to do it."

"When I say I— —" he began, but found no need to finish.

Walter saw all too clearly what she meant. She nodded, but did not remove her hands from her face. She seemed to be waiting tremulously for the verdict from on high.

If he still insisted that he wanted her, if his mind was blind to the sacrifice, then he would indeed need her; if he thought enough of her not to drag her down with him, then there was the spark of a man in him, and he would not need her. And as he spoke, so would God speak.

For an irresolute moment or two Walter stood watching her; then he swore a savage sort of oath and cried out that he would make her keep her word; and then he fled out of the house, as if fearful of himself. But the incoherencies had gone from his speech. He was a beaten man, but, Phœbe exulted as she dabbed at her eyes, he was a man! It was a bitter hour for him, but he was struggling now, not as a weakling, petulant and unreasonable, but as a man battling with grief. So in spite of her tears there was a smile on her face as she looked after him. She listened, and knew his step on the uneven planks of the dock. Then she heard the "plump" of his plunge into the tender, which gave her a horrid second of terror until the powerful strokes of oars creaking fainter and fainter told her that he was rowing out into the calm Lake.

She went to the window and watched his black silhouette. The moon was just beginning to mount.

"It's the Lake that we go to in our little troubles," she murmured. "The dear old mother of a Lake!"

CHAPTER XXIV
PROUD MISS PIDDIWIT

When the "party" broke up Jerry deliberately walked up the hill with Richard, and suggested, in the tone of the perfect hostess, that as this would be their last evening together for some time they might draw up chairs and sit under the spell of "Da" and "Waga."

"Tell me about your new work," she suggested. It was as an elderly lady might ask a very recent freshman about his studies in the new college. Nevertheless, he told her.

Somehow he felt himself on the defensive. The champion of egoism was about to shift square about and become altruist; for he made no attempt to conceal that his interest in taking up the complicated affairs of big business was prompted not by the wish of making a large fortune larger, but solely because of the conviction growing upon him that his responsibilities to others overshadowed the desires of self.

"Suddenly my need of others and their need of me has been made clear to me," he explained quietly. "I can no longer fare alone.... I used to be completely self-sustaining; I had no desires that I could not supply, for I was careful to keep my wants within my powers to satisfy them; I had need for no one, and therefore I never felt the call of co-operation. But the moment that a man finds his happiness gripped by another——" he hesitated, for it was a difficult matter to phrase—"the moment the needs of his spirit call to the spirit of another, then he sees how all are bound together, dependent one upon another.... I express the thought badly; I doubt if I can truly reason out the change that has come over me, but its results are clear—I go to my appointed task, a little late, to be sure, but at last with clear vision of what that appointed task is.... My caterpillar-views," he laughed softly, "look very odd now; perhaps I have broken my predestined chrysalis ... or perhaps it is the American father speaking in me at last. At any rate, my wander-years are over. I have been an English aristocrat, I find, in spite of my poverty— they are the greatest of natural loafers; 'barbarians,' somebody called them, and rightly. The English are most excellent loafers, exquisites at it. The American in me, I feel, is going to be no loafer; I can sense him pulling at me and driving me at service.... And I am still consistent with myself," he talked to fill in the empty spaces; she did not seem inclined to help much; "for I am still honest, and, you know, I never agreed to be more than that."

The night was pleasantly mild. A misshapen moon rose slowly over the Lake and began to light up hill and valley. No hint of the freakish weather of the afternoon was suggested by this warm summer evening; the old earth hummed with its crickets and frogs, and rustled its leaves lazily as if pretending that it had never been unruly in its life. It was too fine to go indoors, the two young persons agreed.

Topics of conversation grew uncomfortably scarce until Richard remembered Phœbe. What had she meant by her attitude towards Walter? Surely she did not intend to marry the boy, yet if ever mortal man was encouraged by woman that chap was Walter. And if she did not intend seriously to live up to her implied promise, wouldn't it be dangerous to lead him on?

Jerry sprang eagerly into the welcome topic. "I haven't had such a shock since— —" she could not think of a concrete comparison, at least none that she cared to mention in this company—"well, since ever so long. Isn't it unbelievable?"

"I think it is splendid!" he spoke warmly. "If she cares for him in the right way—and I have faith that she does—it will be one of the best arrangements that could be made."

"Cares for him?" repeated Jerry. "How could she!"

"It is just one more beautiful mystery," he said quietly. "Why do you insist upon thinking your own view-point is the whole truth?"

There was not the slightest suggestion of offence in his question. He seemed to be addressing not Jerry in particular, but the whole human species.

"But she doesn't really care for him," Jerry protested, "in the—the— way you mean, you know."

"How can you be sure?"

"Oh, she was very frank to me. She said she believed she was too strong-minded ever to be enslaved by a man. She made delicious fun of—of—love, and all that sort of nonsense. She said that what she wanted was devotion, deference—like du Barry and Madame Maintenon. She claims that if a woman wants nothing from a man she'll get everything she wants. Walter, she said, is the only man whom she can guarantee to stay devoted for life. Oh, she was very frank, and also very droll. I tried my best to be serious, but she had me laughing half the time."

Richard Richard | 263

"And so she fooled you, did she?" he asked.

Jerry protested, but he insisted that Phœbe was choosing her mate and that all her clever chatter was disguise.

"But she fooled me, too," he laughed. "She let me tell her all my theories about the reclamation of Walter. Jove! I thought climbing mastheads after fouled peak halyards was his trouble, but all the while it was a woman he was climbing after! A woman is his 'primary,' after all. Well! well! She is wonderful. I envy Walter."

The topic was a good one. It had made Jerry forget her stilted hostess manner. And after she had once thawed it was difficult, with that moon mounting gloriously, to freeze up again.

Richard was quick to follow up with another helpful topic—Jawn as a sailor lad. He retailed the palaver that Jawn had kept going throughout the whole race. He had made limericks on every part of the ship's tackle and on his rival yachtsmen, and he had punned almost to the limit of endurance. Some of the best ones Richard culled and repeated. They were too local to be of general interest, but that made their humour all the keener to a native. Again and again Jerry found herself limp with merriment, although deep within, something reproached her for unbending. But she was too weary to resist; she had spent a bad night and she had been tramping over the hills since sunrise.

Never mind! she told herself; let not the confident man before her plume himself on graciousness. A woman may smile and smile and be a—well, not exactly a villain, but as obstinate and unalterable as the best of villains. On that point she had no misgivings; the long meditations on the hills with "Count" had cleared her mind of every doubt and told her what she had to do. It would be silly—now that it was all decided for ever—to stand aloof like proud Miss Piddiwit.

"Proud Miss Piddiwit, there she goes.

What is she proud of? Nobody knows!"

Miss Piddiwit was an unfortunate figure of speech. Some imp of her mind, perhaps, some mischievous Puck of that unknown subliminal region it was who hoisted that forgotten picture of the old "Mother Goose" book up out of the mental depths and let it strut before her. Miss Piddiwit bore her head aloft at a perilous angle, and her little heels clicked on the pavement in staccato rhythm with the couplet, which the aforesaid subliminal imp took delight in chanting.

"Proud Miss Piddiwit, there she goes.

What is she proud of? Nobody knows!"

"Let's walk," she started up suddenly. "This night is too wonderful."

"Good!" he agreed.

They dropped down the lawn, passed the summer-house without seeming to notice it at all, and took the State Road which leads north to Penn Yan.

"You are your mother's daughter," he announced abruptly. He spoke as if it were the summing-up of a train of thinking.

"Naturally," she said.

They walked on for several seconds without speaking.

"You do not ask why," said Richard.

"Perhaps I know why."

The "imp" had been forcing her to keep step with the Piddiwit jingle.

"But it would help the conversation if you would ask questions."

"Is conversation necessary?"

"Ah!" he laughed. "What would distinguish us from the rest of the animal kingdom if we didn't talk! Yes," he went on, "conversation is necessary. Unless you run away I'm going to talk.... It may be our last conversation together—although I won't believe that——"

"How can you be sure, Mr. Richard?"

Into this question she tried to throw a satiric imitation of his question to her on the night of his arrival in Penn Yan, the night when she had protested that she at least would never make eyes at him; but, man-like, he had not the mind to catch such subtleties. Still, the remark gave her a little elation and put her in good spirits. She would show this young man!

"As you know," he replied, "I am sure of nothing. That discourages some people, but it makes me continually full of hope. Micawber, you know, was kept radiantly alive by it.... Yesterday I asked you to marry me——"

"Please!" she interrupted, and quickened her pace.

"Of course I won't speak if it worries you," he said contritely enough; "but it is a pity, I think, not to face every situation fairly. And I do so want to face this one."

She slowed up and thought the matter over carefully. Why shouldn't he talk if he cared to? The answer was, why, indeed!

"Very well," she summoned her most casual tones; "face it; only—don't expect me to help much."

"Oh," he broke in quickly, "I'm not so inexperienced as to believe anyone can argue away an emotion. Either you like me—in the way I mean, you know—or you don't. That's under neither your control nor mine. Words won't mend anything there. But words may help to clear up misunderstanding.... You are sure this won't worry you?"

"Why should it?"

"Quite so," he agreed grimly; "why should it?... Very well...." But he said nothing more.

She looked up at him quickly.

"Well?" he looked down earnestly.

"You have never been sulky with me," she explained. "Jawn says you go for weeks without speaking to anyone, and Phœbe said you went perfectly dumb on her porch one afternoon. I was just wondering if it were my turn at last."

"Oh, no! I don't feel that way at all! That's one of the signs that makes me sure that you—you are ... I can't get hold of the right words, that's all. And it isn't that, either. I've got the right words, bundles of them! But I'm afraid if I start in to pour them forth at you—if I start to tell you how much I—I—care about you—you'll take fright and also take this trolley home. So to make sure I'll wait till it passes. Thank goodness they run only two cars on this line—or is it the same one going frantically back and forth?"

They stepped aside to avoid the lights of the car. Somehow, both felt the necessity of keeping clear of publicity.

"I won't have you maligning the institutions of my country," she replied, with a touch of the old-time cheeriness. "We are not a restless people moving to and fro over the face of the earth and in subways seeking whom we may devour. Let me inform you, Mr. Richard Richard, that in the busy summer season we run *both* cars. If you were a woman you would not make the mistake of thinking them only one, for then you would have noticed that while each conductor is handsome, one is light and the other dark."

"Like beer," he joked.

"In these parts you should say, like port and champagne," she corrected. "This is a wine country, and we are famous for our champagne. But don't you think we should turn back? That is the last car down, and, as you suggest, I ought to keep within running distance of home. But I interrupted your beautiful speech. I'm sorry."

She was quite pleased with herself. At first she feared that she might not be able to carry off her part of the conversation without showing suspicious excitement; but here she was actually joking! She was proud of her control, was this Miss Piddiwit!

Lamely at first and then, as he ceased to pick his words, with surer touch Richard proceeded with his "beautiful speech." No smart retorts came to her aid; no retorts at all, indeed, for the man was sweeping her off her secured moorings—had she not spent half the night and the whole of the morning in steeling her will to oppose just this?—and he was driving her into a horrid state of weak nervousness. Richard Richard had studied frankness and soul analysis like a research student, and his speech carried with it an ozonic atmosphere of truth. Suddenly he came to an end.

Instead of crushing him with any of the carefully selected phrases which she had rehearsed in her morning tramp with "Count" she filled in the silence with a question that was almost a cry.

"How do you know it will last?"

"I don't know it at all," he replied with amazing frankness. "Every lover lies, of course, or is deceived, which amounts to the same thing. Affection usually does not last. The evidence of the world is before us; why not face it? How can I guarantee the future? I cannot. I know only my consuming faith that what has begun here so honestly and so free from taint is bound to have eternal meaning. Perhaps that is nature's clever illusion; but I cannot believe¯ it. It may not last, but what of that? Events are in the hands of the gods; yet what greater joy than staking all on the risks of life? Faith is the thing. And God knows I have faith—the faith that passeth understanding."

She would have more specific reasons. He gave them to her. First, he talked!

"You say I never sulk with you," he argued. "It isn't really sulking at all. Of course, I know you were only joking; but it is worse than boorish petulance, it is an absolute dumbness, an inability to speak. In these past weeks I seem to have broken from my bonds, and I believe it is you who have set me free. They say that Lewis Carroll had the same sort of infirmity except in the presence of his beloved children, and I can well understand how he must have suffered and how he had to get used to faring it alone. For my shyness I have paid a great penalty; I have had no playfellows as a child—I never got really acquainted with my own mother. Governesses and tutors used to shirk their job and let me alone. If I hadn't early learned to read and to like books, I suppose I should have grown up an ignoramus to boot! And you—why, look how I am talking!

"Now for reason number two. For the first time in my life I want to take my father's money and use it. You've made me want to do that. You have filled me with strange worldly ambitions. I want to take my place with other men and bear my share of the burden; and I want to buy you all sorts of things. I have a savage desire to clothe you and feed you and fix up your nest. And I have the wildest visions of a lot of kiddies— —"

She almost shot ahead of him.

"Don't run away," he called, and caught up with her. "You're a grown-up woman, and I'm so old that it frightens me. Why in the name of all the holy mysteries at once should we scare off at the thought of children? Woman, it is the most glorious thought in all creation! And they must be clothed," he went on, "and sent to school and to college and taken to Europe and 'brought out' and given a bang-up start in life. And all that takes money, heaps of it. We've just *got* to have money, woman; don't you see that?"

She saw that—better than he did, perhaps—but she could not trust herself to take up that point in the debate. Fortunately at this moment she caught through the trees a clear light shining far below in Phœbe Norris's cottage.

"I wonder what Phœbe is doing up at this hour?" she turned the subject. "She usually goes to bed with her Orpingtons."

"Suppose we find out?" he challenged her.

The returning trolley was grinding up the hill from Branchport and would soon expose them in the road. If the conductors, "Port" or "Champagne," ever caught a good glimpse of her, the news would spread quickly over Yates county.

"All right," she agreed, and they struck down the steep road just as the headlight from the car flashed up over the hill.

He talked eloquently all the way down, but while she listened she used the time to summon her scattered forces and get her mental house in order.

It had been a wild delight to let him fight down her will, but she was the daughter of her mother and no weakling.

One thing she was sure of, and it made her glad beyond words to express: his offer of marriage had not been prompted by charity. He was in earnest, terribly in earnest; but also he was, as usual, selfish. She was hearing his point of view, but he showed with every word that he had no conception of hers.

The world would say, when its scandal-loving ear had taken in all the facts, that Geraldine Wells, bankrupt, who had been brazenly living for several years on the savings of negro servants, had deliberately forced herself upon a rich young man—a notoriously rich young man, at that—had inveigled him into her home and had trapped him into making an offer of marriage. A Wells would never permit a situation like that!

Proud Miss Piddiwit!

And how the newspapers would seize the theme! Their searchlight would flare into every nook; nothing would prevent their discovery of the incognito and the "romance"; the latter, she knew, would be a particularly tempting morsel. They make no distinction between the great and the notorious, but play each impartially to the tune of their scareheads. Reporters would come by special train; even George Alexander would be interviewed! Just because a father had had a genius for accumulation an innocent second generation must suffer publicity. If Richard Richard had only been a nobody! But he was not; he was by very birth notorious.

She conjured up headlines that even a hardened city editor would not have sanctioned. The cable would carry the "news" to Europe. Their engagement would be one long nightmare of publicity; the marriage would be a vulgarian's holiday. And then she remembered the columnist and the cartoonist. The thought was revolting.

But she drifted, nevertheless, with the compelling events of the night. To-morrow with its harsh necessities would come in due time, and to-morrow and to-morrow.

She would do well to linger as long as possible in the exhilarating illusion of the moment. Even if it were all to be eventually cancelled and forgotten, it was delightfully thrilling to have this strong man by her side making most complimentary speeches. His earnestness was very soothing to her pride; one might as well steep as long as possible in the experience.

Meanwhile, out on the Lake, Walter had been struggling with his remnant of a soul, and had found some touch of that peace which comes to the Lake people, to all people who look out daily on vast stretches of water. It was peace, but it was tinged with tragic sorrow, and thereby, and only thereby, it was worthy and beyond price.

While Jerry and Richard were still strolling along the Penn Yan road, Walter was again at Phœbe's door. She had prepared herself for bed when his knock came; so she slipped on a kimono and came to the door wondering. When she saw his stern face, she stepped back quickly, and called on her Saint Francis, as a child in great fear might cry to the mother.

"You needn't be afraid of me any more, Phœbe," he spoke huskily but firmly. "I've been thinkin' things out.... You're right.... It wouldn't do.... It wouldn't do—for you.... I guess ... I guess," he faltered; "I guess this is where I get up or fall back again——"

"But you won't, boy!" she exulted. "You won't! You will stand up and fight for yourself, and you will fight for me, and be the man I'll be proud of all my life. All my life, boy.... For me, boy."

"Yes," he choked, but stood even a shade more erect. "For you, Phœbe."

And then he strode away in the moonlight.

And Phœbe watched him from the doorway, and cried little chirping words to herself; and a sweeping happiness seized her, touched with a vague regret; and some of it was for the victory she had won; and some of it was for the pity of it all; and some of it was for the long, empty years of her own life.

As Jerry and Richard neared the cottage they quieted their step and moved stealthily to the window at the side. Phœbe was stretched at length in a commodious leather chair. She was in a great blue kimono and her hands were clasped behind her neck, her bared arms extending languorously on either side. Her glorious red hair was smoothed back and it dropped in two long loose braids in front. Her big blue eyes were wide, and they focussed on some vast distance. She looked for all the world like some splendid fearless child.

As they gazed upon the picture the two eavesdroppers felt suddenly like culprits; so they walked noisily around the porch to the front and tapped on the door.

"Come in!" Phœbe called, but moved not an inch.

"Ah!" she chuckled wisely, and scrutinized them from her deep chair. "Gallivantin', as usual, eh?" On her face was not the slightest trace of the experience of the night; and her voice suggested never a sorrow. To the end of her days Phœbe Norris, and all her kind, would practise concealment of their suffering and of their virtues, reserving full confession to one only, and that one must be a mate proved by fire!

Only Richard and Phœbe knew the full significance of the accusation of "gallivanting." He remembered her etymology, "From 'galli,' 'a woman,' and 'vantin','' 'wantin' 'em bad.'" So he nodded his head and confessed.

"Absolutely guilty in the highest degree," he said.

"Oh, *ho!*" she exclaimed, and looked first at one and then at the other. "Oh, *ho!*" she repeated very sagely. "Is that the way the wind's a-blowin'!"

She acted as if the idea had never struck her before, but she so charged the atmosphere with accusation that Richard grew crimson and Jerry stiffened into angry opposition.

"There's no wind at all, Phœbe," Jerry blurted. "Don't be silly!"

"I'm not accusin' myself of bein' silly," she remarked quietly. "Oh, well!" she saw that she was making them both self-conscious; "perhaps the breeze has died down temporarily. It does in these parts, Richard," she turned to him learnedly. "The Keuka winds are that tricky, now! One minute they're roarin' as if the seven chained devils were loose an' after 'em—as you might have noticed this afternoon—first blowin' one way and then the other; an' before you can pull your cap over your ears and button up the top button of your coat, they're gone, and the Lake is as smooth as you see it to-night. But look out!" she cautioned, with a mischievous smile twinkling about her eyes, "look out! There's apt to be an ugly squall any minute. You never can be sure. Just look at that Lake now!" she pointed out of the long windows. The moon had lighted up its glassy surface; there was not a wrinkle on it. "Don't it look innocent and child-like, now? An' who would think that it could ever rise up and roil with passion?"

Her elaborate figure of speech—a very obvious parable—did not help matters. It was just clever enough to give Jerry a vivid picture of reality and to cause her to strengthen her obstinate resolution. But except for an extra look of firmness she disclosed nothing as she turned the subject.

"We peeked in the window as we passed by, Phœbe," Jerry confessed. "You looked adorably contented. A penny for your thoughts."

"H'm!" Phœbe gave a satisfied purr. "An' why shouldn't I be contented? It isn't every lone widow that has two suitors in one day."

"Two!"

They both spoke together.

"It isn't very complimentary to show such astonishment," remarked Phœbe. "I've me charms yet, I fancy. Yes, two. One comes along, a sea-farin' man, and says, 'Choose!' says he; 'choose between me and a quart of bad whisky,' says he. It was a hard problem, savin' your presence, Jerry; an' I couldn't decide as quickly as the sea-farin' gentleman wished. Besides, I was confused by the attentions of the other gentleman, a movie actor, who had come along in the mornin'."

"A movie actor!"

"An' why not?" she demanded. "It's gettin' to be one of the hazardous callin's, demandin' courage and daring. He plagued me so with verses — —"

"It was Jawn!" cried Richard.

"Jawn it was," agreed Phœbe. "He told me outright to my face—I like a man to speak the truth—that he had been disappointed in love some seventy or eighty times, but that now he had discovered that all his excitin' past was just preliminary training to get him ready and fit for me. But he took me best of all by his main argument. He said that he had just finished a fine weddin' hymn, an' that it was a shame to waste it. To be sure, he admitted that he had writ it for a lady who had gone off with another fellow; but with a slight change here and there, which would not spoil the rhyme and metre at all, he found it would just do for me. An' then he read it to me…. It was *very* seducin' verse, *very* seducin'!"

Phœbe was a natural actress. She had the one quality essential to all great players, the subtle voice tones which compel an audience to take the contagion of her mood. In one deft speech she had removed the awkwardness from the atmosphere and had substituted ease and friendliness. Jerry and Richard chatted and chaffed in total forgetfulness of their strained relationship. It was a wonderful dramatic achievement.

"Phœbe, you cannot mean to marry Walter?" Jerry asked abruptly. "The thing fills me with horror. Why, he is six years younger! We cannot let you sacrifice yourself like that. You are not really going to do it, are you?"

"No," said Phœbe quietly. "I am not. I thought at first that I could do it. It's no worse than nursing or school-teaching, and a woman must have some sort of occupation nowadays." As she spoke she felt a momentary shame for her flippancy; but she went on, true to her instinct to hide the good in her, and even to deny it if too closely prodded. "The job was too much for Saint Phœbe."

"But have you told Walter? Aren't you afraid he'll— —"

"He's all right. We've talked things out. There's a man in charge of that boy— —"

"What man?" Jerry looked toward Richard.

"A man named Walter, whom few of you seem to know much about. It's himself I mean. He thinks he's doing it for me; and I let him think so; but he's really out of my hands now. And one of these days, when he gets a good, sure grip on himself, I'll match-make him off so secretly that neither he nor she will ever know that I planned it all myself."

"She? Why, who— —"

"Well," she mused, "I'm not sure. If he keeps on the way he's goin' it'll be one of the Fernzie girls, the younger one, maybe. But if he improves a lot, I may pick out an Armstrong or a Sheppard!"

"Oh!" gasped Jerry. Only a native could understand the prodigiousness of that colossal joke.

The talk drifted here and there, always subject to Phœbe's clever will; and when she made some joking remark about the use of her cottage as a public bathing pavilion, and in the same breath announced that whatever those two "gallivanters" intended to do the rest of the night, she was going to her bed, the moment was right for Richard to raise two fingers mutely, "Let's go swimmin'," and for Jerry to fling up the answer, "All right."

It was an outlandish thing to do, but what water lover could resist? The night was warm, the Lake was waveless, and the lump of a moon lighted up the scene.

Richard was waiting on the dock for her. A light in Phœbe's room went out, and still he waited. For a moment he feared that Jerry had changed her mind, or perhaps had played a trick on him and had gone out the rear door and had fled home. Then the light downstairs went out suddenly; he heard the front door close with a click, and out of the shadow of the house he discerned the lithe brown figure moving towards him.

Somehow they did not plunge off instantly, as had been their habit. Instead, they stood on the edge of the dock and talked. He spoke of the new life opening before him; and he told her of his father, of his life of pathetic isolation. The pity of it struck her, and she showed it in her voice and in her eyes. Her hand touched his arm in sympathy.

Then Richard, who was a man first and a swimmer after, succumbed to the enchantment of the brown being before him and began again the vehement avowals which had never been quite completed to his satisfaction in the summer-house.

"Say you will marry me, Jerry," he persisted. "I want you and I will have you! I won't let you go! Will you marry me, Jerry? Will you? Will you?" with much unoriginal repetition of the same sort.

"No!" she said. He persisted in asking; but she said, "No!" Nothing daunted, he began all over again and grew even a shade more insistent.

The world and its ugly sneer began to fade away, but she fought against her growing irresolution. It was folly, but it was her best instinct, too. Every right marriage has in its history somewhere the struggle that precedes surrender. And years of Virginia tradition had put the seal of necessity on this final struggle. A Wells would force the tribute of conquest and capture!

"No!" she said vehemently. "No!" He would not be answered and took a step nearer, but she put out a hand as if to ward him off. "No!" she cried, almost hysterically, plunged into the water and struck off into the Lake.

He followed quickly. She was aiming straight towards the farther shore, and going forward at a dangerous pace. Fear seized him. With terrific strokes he caught up to her and begged her to come back, but she shook her head wildly and went desperately on. He promised that he would never pester her again, but she was blind to persuasion. So he kept at her side, although it tested his powers, swimming in silence, and watching every stroke with the keenest anguish.

Shortly she slowed up, and later turned on her back and floated. He waited until he thought the rest had brought back her strength and then coaxed her to return. For answer she began swimming onward again, this time with her long easy sweep; and he followed without a word.

She was in no condition for a distance swim. The day had worn her down, and the night's excitement had not helped; but she summoned her will and swung steadily on. On, on, on, they went while shore faded off and the great white moon filled the night.

Within a hundred yards of the shore she faltered. He reached quickly for her, but she cried out incoherently and struck at him. The last few yards was an agonizing attempt to reach the shallow water. She was threshing wildly, and calling on him blindly to "keep away!"—although he had not offered again to touch her—when her foot reached bottom; she tried to stand but could not, and fell upon her face. He picked her up, but she pushed him aside and stumbled on to the shore, where she dropped prone upon the grass, thoroughly spent.

He did not know what to say, fearing that his words might do further damage, so he sat mutely beside her and listened to her hysteric weeping, and suffered torments.

While he was waiting, a light flared up in Phœbe's cottage, and later he heard the clear rhythm of rowlocks. The distance straight across the Lake at this point was probably three-quarters of a mile, and, no doubt, in the stillness of the night the sound of every exclamation had floated over the flat water and had reverberated in Phœbe's room. The old Indian tradition that each year Keuka will take her toll of five had been all too often verified; so the Lake dwellers were trained to listen keenly when unusual cries came over the water.

In the white moonlight every object was clear, clearer, it seemed, even than day. So Richard rose quietly, went to a knoll a few feet away, and stood and waved his arm. After a time he saw the boat change its course and knew that Phœbe had marked him. Then he went back and sat on guard over the prostrate swimmer.

She was quieter now and, save for occasional swift shudders, her breathing had become almost normal. Suddenly she started to her feet, and made for the Lake.

"You are not going to swim back?" he protested.

She made no answer, and stepped into the shallow water; but he stood before her and seized her boldly in his arms.

"I will not let you go!" he spoke firmly, and tightened his grasp. She struggled and cried out upon him and told him that he was hurting her, but he drew her to him and was thankful for his strength. And all the while he talked to her, telling her things that he had told her many times before, matters which he had given his solemn word would never be broached again; acting, indeed, like the most and the least intelligent of swains. He used phrases that have been iterated since the world began to swim in space; there was not a spark of originality in him!

For a minute or two she tried her little powers against him; then suddenly she gave in, sobbing like a very contented child. She reached her arms slowly up and put them about him, and clung to him and confessed her complete surrender.

Proud Miss Piddiwit had melted quite away.

And thus they stood when the boat grated on the shelving shore and Phœbe drew in the oars, and turned about and faced them. She was again in her blue kimono and her wonderful hair fell in its broad braids.

"The saints in heaven!" she ejaculated. "An' have I got up out o' me bed an' rowed clear across the Lake only to spoil a pretty picnic party! An' with the yellin' and the splashin' it's drowned I thought ye were! What do you mean by disappointin' me like that!"

Out of the boat leaped Phœbe, not caring at all for six inches of water, and swooped down upon Jerry.

"Angel-child!" she cried as she reached to draw the wet brown form to her. "Don't let that big piggy have *all* the huggin'!" Jerry tottered into her wide-opened arms. "Dear-a-dear! Dear-a-dear!" Phœbe soothed as she rocked her precious burden to and fro. "An' it's cryin' ye are!... An' well ye may! An' well ye may!... An', by the cross of Saint Michael, it's cryin' myself I am!"